Child-Parent Research Reimagined

Child-Parent Research Reimagined

Edited by

Sandra Schamroth Abrams, Mary Beth Schaefer
and Daniel Ness

Foreword by Mary Kalantzis and Bill Cope

and

Afterword by Anthony J. Onwuegbuzie

BRILL

SENSE

LEIDEN | BOSTON

Cover illustration: Artwork by Charlotte Abrams

All chapters in this book have undergone peer review.

The Library of Congress Cataloging-in-Publication Data is available online at http://catalog.loc.gov

Typeface for the Latin, Greek, and Cyrillic scripts: "Brill". See and download: brill.com/brill-typeface.

ISBN 978-90-04-42171-4 (paperback)
ISBN 978-90-04-39602-9 (hardback)
ISBN 978-90-04-42172-1 (e-book)

To Charlotte, my teacher—what an honor to be on this journey with you
—SANDRA

•••

To Molly, my learning and travel companion
—MARY BETH

•••

To Eric, my son, my inspiration, and everlasting light
—DANIEL

••
•

Contents

Foreword: The Problem of Empathy

Mary Kalantzis and Bill Cope

This is a book of stories about parents and their children, and in one chapter, about a grandparent and his grandson. These have to be stories, because in the kind of research you are about to read, "n" is mostly one, and never more than three. In any event, even when the subject of research is more than one, persons can never quite add up.

Guy Merchant takes us through the story of his un-named grandson, so with them we can experience the multimodal moves between an Iron Man soft toy, Spongebob videos, and the grandson's story writing. "For all its playfulness," he concludes, "this is sophisticated work."

Sarah Prestridge tells the story of her son Cooper who from ages eight to twelve, spoke with his mother about the online game he played with his schoolfriends out of school time. *Fortnite* is a shooter-survival game where players collaborate in "victory-informed strategic game play" to fight off zombie-like creatures. She also spoke with him about connecting with his friends through SnapChat. Present in these spaces is something largely absent from school, Prestridge says, a sense of participation she calls "contribution."

Mother Kathleen M. Alley writes jointly with daughter Cassandra R. Skrobot about the anxiety disorder Cassandra experienced during College. "In narrating our experiences, we were able to represent the complexities of grappling with anxiety disorder as a subjective whole, as well as the parent-child relationship in our stories."

Alaina Roach O'Keefe writes about her son, simply named "E." Between the ages of two and five, she collected "80 discrete points of observational data...2160 hours of observation...1977 units of data (1184 photographs and 64 videos)..., 12 Shutterfly books, 29 pieces of artwork,...[and] 627 emails to/from the Early Learning Centre." This was to create a comprehensive picture of E's literacy practices, in order to disentangle a particular mix of digital and non-digital tools.

Lourdes M. Rivera, a career counselling educator, writes jointly with her daughters Nora Rivera-Larkin and Dahlia Rivera-Larkin about the systematic dialogue in which they engaged about their future careers. "With the example of my two daughters," concludes mother-researcher," I see two very different approaches to engaging them."

Joanne O'Mara and Linda Laidlaw's story is about how academic mothers talk with each other about their children. Joanne has a boy and a girl, and Linda has two girls. But we are not told their names or anything more than that "they represent a number of diverse positions in connection to health, heritage, and disability."

Then, in the last chapter, Bogum Yoon re-analyzes data she collected while her sons Junsuk and Junhyuck were in beginning ESL programs at school. The family migrated from Korea to the United States when the boys were in grades four and five. Her reanalysis from a "new literacies" perspective highlights identity dilemmas that the boys faced while learning English.

Parent-child research is by no means new. This book stands in the tradition of some famous parent researchers. Michael Halliday (1975) studied his Nigel's acquisition of language in the context of his wider semiotic universe. Gunther Kress studied his Michael's meaning in image (2003, pp. 42–43). In each case, the research depended on being close to the child for the ordinary interactions of everyday life—unusually close, in fact, as parents are, and this is the point.

This book explores the methodological implications of parent-child research. Its counterpoints are some conventional research expectations that become at least awkward, or perhaps impossible when studying human realities which are literally this close to home.

In the interests of "objectivity," academic practice tends to have us lose our subjects in one way or another, or at least lose their subjectivity and the intersubjectivity of researcher and subject in the research encounter. The most obvious way to lose personhood in research is counting by the criterial generalities of "n" students—n children, n girls, n ten-year olds, or n Hispanics—and so to homogenize by these or any other such social abstractions (Kalantzis & Cope, 2016a). Another research move is to "anonymize" identities, to strip away the grounded specificity of experience, as if other cases could ever possibly be quite the same.

∴

The virtue of the stories in this book is that they keep us grounded. We can see what is general in the context of what is richly particular. Even though we don't know all the names of the research subjects, they are identifiable in the singularities of their experiences. However, for this, the research is fraught in conventional research terms. Counting by category and reporting on distanced and anonymized experience starts to seem easy, by comparison.

In their overview chapter, Sandra Schamroth Abrams, Mary Beth Schaefer and Daniel Ness speak to the possibilities of less hierarchical structures of knowledge making, where "child-researcher and parent-researcher work together to co-construct knowledge...Striving for ethical symmetry in child-parent research means that the child and the parent must confront and negotiate new positions." However, the chapters that follow tell of practices that prove harder than this sounds.

Guy Merchant doesn't tell us the degree to which his grandson offered to collaborate in an activity that might in any sense be called research, from the child's point of view at least. And for his part, he says, "I can never quite be sure if I'm mortgaging my familial role to my professional interest—or just simply taking advantage of him, because he's there, a ready-made and biddable research participant."

Sarah Prestridge doesn't tell us whether her Cooper likes being involved in her mother's research. But we do hear from her that "he is pretty used to me asking 'weird' and wonderful questions." He must know that, weirdly, his mother is an academic.

Kathleen Alley's Cassandra is a co-author, however the voice of the anxious researcher is Katheen's. During recorded discussions, Kathleen says, "if I ever sensed any resistance, I quickly offered Cassandra an opportunity to talk with me at a later time or not at all."

In studying her two-to-five-year-old "E," Alaina Roach O'Keefe acknowledges that there was an unavoidable "power imbalance…by very virtue of my position as an adult with authority." Apparently, it was "E" himself who insisted on this anonymization of his name.

Lourdes Rivera describes her co-author daughters' reluctance at times to be involved. "She can be impatient and annoying at times," they said of her in the third person for the paper.

Joanne O'Mara, and Linda Laidlaw write about their own academic sharing, mother-to-mother. "[I]n response to their own desires not to have the details of their lives 'over-shared' we choose not to reveal that which could identify them individually, and we focus our shared gaze on our autoethnographic interpretations as researcher-educator-parents."

When Bogum Yoon asks her sons, now in their mid-twenties, to reflect on their experiences in their mother's research while they were at school, "they simply expressed that they were 'busy.'"

So, it's complicated. To the great credit of these authors, they honestly expose and analyze the complications.

∙∙
∙

The challenges addressed by the authors in this book are in essence methodological. However, we want to argue that these are not peculiarly challenges to parent-child research; they are challenges to the epistemologies and discourses of research writ large. From these methodological anxieties, we can learn some things that perhaps should make us anxious about research in general, or at least certain kinds of research.

Research in a conventional understanding is the process of communication of observable meaning. The researcher faithfully counts (quantitative research) or tells stories (qualitative research). Their records should be as "true" to the reality they are describing as possible, influenced as little as possible by the moral and theoretical predilections of the researcher.

From an "ethnographic" point of view, a researcher is a traveler into a strange land, making discoveries new to them, though of course these are ordinary to allegorical "tribes" in which their subjects live. Indeed, from the point of view of the research subject, it is the researcher who is strange for their making the subject strange.

Having arrived and set up camp in the ethnographic jungle, it is the responsibility of the researcher to be faithful to what they discover. They must reproduce what they hear rather than to impose their views. Somehow, Somehow, it is assumed that the researcher can bring their reporting into alignment with the meanings of their subjects.

Call this empiricism or positivism if you will. Whatever the name, its purported objectivity is always illusory at best, delusional at worst.

How could such objectivity possibly be the case with parent researchers and child subjects? Of course, it could never be, because the researcher is so obviously an interested party. In the nature of adult-child caring, age and role differences are structured into the relationship.

But all research faces the same problem, in the structuring of differences: expert versus subject; rapporteur versus reported; educators versus learners. Or, to reuse a distinction made by Edmund Husserl (1954/1970), the systematic getting-to-the-epistemic-essence that is science versus the casual, minimally reflective, everyday experience of the lifeworld.

The problem with research in general, which parent-child research brings to light with a particular poignancy, turns on a model of communication in which the researcher strives to meet the mind of the subject on terms which are true to the subject's reality.

This is a problem of definition where communication is conceived as shared meaning. In research, it is supposed, subjects share their meanings. Through the researcher's careful observational gaze, it is assumed that the researcher will be able to share with some degree of objectivity in the meanings they have encountered.

But meaning is not like this.

∴

Let's take Umberto Eco's model of semiosis. Here, there is a message sender, a message expression containing information, and an addressee who receives the message. Of course, Eco is not so naïve as to consider semiosis to be straightforwardly a process of transmission. His system is full of wise qualifications. There may be ambiguities in the message. The sender may have ideological biases that they do not acknowledge, dooming the message to failure even before it has been received.

But these are deviations from the ideal from the sender's perspective, failures to achieve congruence of meaning on the part of the addressee. Notwithstanding the complexities and the hazards, if the message sending proves successful, it must be because something remains of the message that is transmitted and shared.

Barring these aberrations, the "normal" state of communication remains sender => message => addressee (Eco, 1976, pp. 140–142). In this line of reasoning, normal research is meaning expressed by subjects => messages received by the addressee. So, researchers angst a great deal about the rigour and validity of their observations, and the truth of their reportage to the meanings they set out to discover.

Before we respond to Eco, a diversion. We've just finished a pair of books discussing this problem of communication (Cope & Kalantzis, 2020; Kalantzis & Cope, 2020). We have given these ideas the name "transpositional grammar," extending earlier versions of our thinking in the areas of "genre" (Cope & Kalantzis, 1993) and "multiliteracies" (Kalantzis et al., 2016).

So, dear reader, you will need to forgive us, this question of parent-child research has given us an alibi to work over these ideas again. By "transposition," we mean meanings that can be swapped out. This can happen across two vectors.

The first vector is meaning form. We can swap out meaning forms between text, image, space, object, body, sound and speech. Any and all of these forms can be used to mean the same things. Meanings can be expressed alternately in any of these forms, or any combination. But these meanings are never quite the same. Different forms have different affordances, which is why we use forms in combination to complement each other. Hence: multimodality. We see this vector of transposition happening richly, ubiquitously, in all the chapters in this book.

The second vector is meaning function, here we identify five cardinal functions, where "this" is any meaning you might wish to choose. Reference: What is this about? Agency: Who or what is doing this? Structure: What holds this together? Context: How does this fit with its surroundings? Interest: What is this for? Any and every meaning, no matter what the form of its representation, can be parsed for all of these functions. Here, we can swap out one orientation to meaning then another, as we change our attention to one of its meaning-functions, then another. Then, within each function, there is considerable movement.

An example of reference: something can be viewed in its complex, whole, singularity (an instance); or that same thing can be viewed as one of more than one (a concept). We can swap out one for the other. In traditional grammar, we would say this is making a singular into a plural. Or, in Vygotsky's (1934/1986) psychology, this is a move from complex to conceptual thinking.

An agency example: To you, I am a you. This is first and second person in traditional grammar. In our transpositional grammar, self and other are always being transposed. Your you is my me. When I hear you speak of me, I make a transposition. When I feel for you, I make a transposition.

And following on from this transposition, an example to the simultaneous presence of interest: if my purposes in relation to yours are good for both of us, they might be considered empathetic; if they are not, they might be considered antagonistic.

So, to this word "transposition" again. Against the categorical fixities of structuralism, every meaning is on the move. Indeed, more than that, it is expectantly impatient to be moved. Not fixed points, meanings are the range of things that they could in any moment become. But against the bewilderingly indefinite deferrals and the ineffable differences of post-structuralism, for a transpositional grammar there are distinct patterns in the movability. These, we want to trace.

∵

Now, apropos of family research, to speak of our grand-daughter Sophia. We tell the following story in our "Adding Sense" (Kalantzis & Cope, 2020) though at the time the story is set, we never thought the story would become research, let alone to recruit Sophia as a co-researcher. Perhaps, even now we have written it up, it is still hardly research.

A picture first, then the story that goes with the picture.

Sophia, aged two and a half, wanted to make a present for her Papou (Greek for grandfather). Her teacher helped her make an artwork, there in My Little Village, Sophia's preschool on Avenue A, "Alphabet City," in New York's East Village. ("A" is for assault. "B" is for battery. "C" is for crime. "D" for death, they used to say for each of these Avenues, before the East Village became fashionable.) Sophia said what the picture meant and her teacher wrote for her. It was for Papou's birthday.

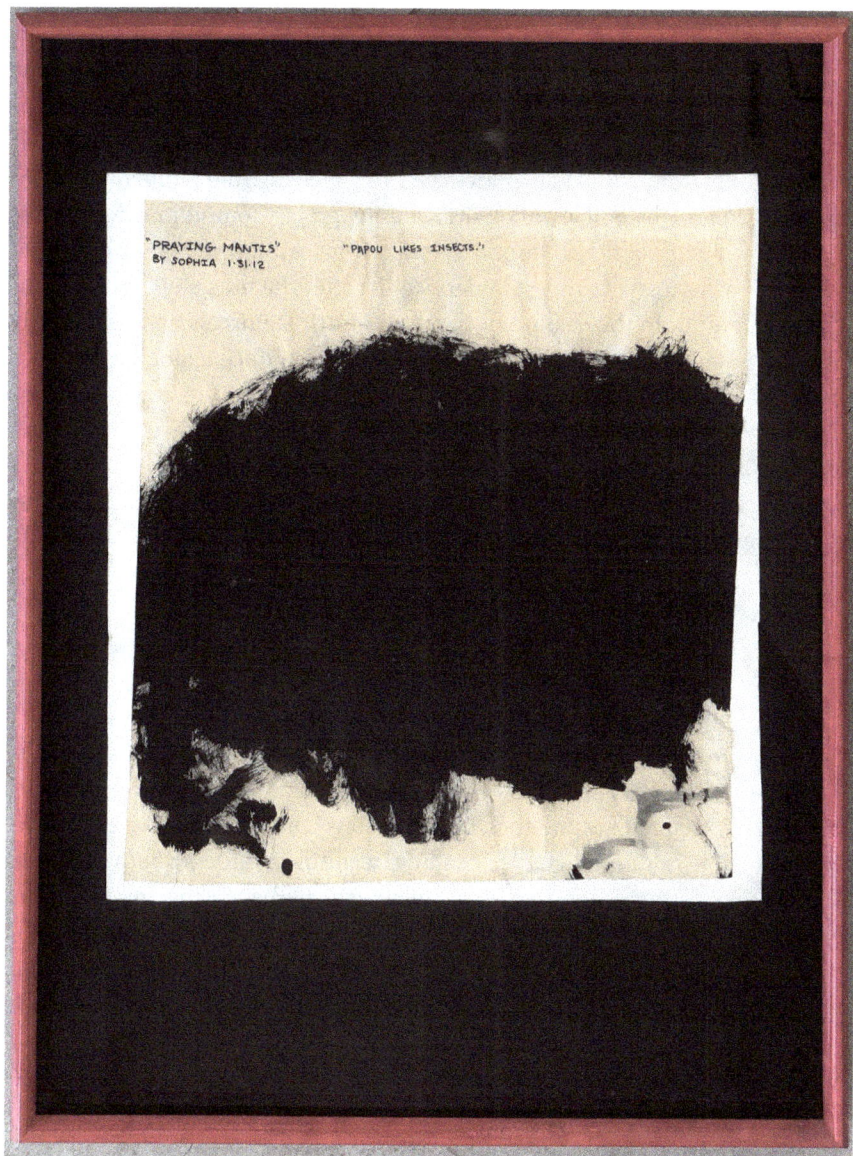

FIGURE F.1   "Praying Mantis," by Sophia

Later her Papou had the picture framed, in pink because he knew it was at the time her favorite color. (By five, she was in partial gender revolt; blue had become her favorite color, and she couldn't understand why Papou had framed it because by then, she had learned to do "better" pictures.)

What is this picture? Sophia is representing something she and Papou have seen together, though not in New York City, but at Papou's place in the country. Papou's gender game is not to be scared of these beautiful, delicate things—

you can take one gently without hurting it, and it will walk up your arm, funny feeling, but be brave! Look at these creatures with love and care. Be a scientist!

From representation to communication, there is a transposition: from the embodied meaning in the feeling of a praying mantis on the skin of your arm, to a painting; from Sophia's experience to her speech; from Sophia's speaking to her teacher's listening and writing; from art as communication to the interpretative aids of title, date and descriptive gloss following the conventions of art and galleries, with an explanatory gloss after the title, all pointing to the artist's intent; from the gesture of the gift to birthday rituals and "papous" of Greek, a language whose presence in New York is at once exotic for the polis and normal for the cosmopolis. Sophia must have told the teacher what a "Papou" was, and the teacher must have liked that, not to have translated it into English.

These are just a few vectors of interest in a polyphony of multimodal transpositions.

• •
•

Now, we want to come back to Eco, and the problem we see in his definition of communication. His definition of communication as meaning—he concedes this much—demands some sage qualifications. On the receiving end of the message, there is "unpredictable decoding" resulting in "interpretative failures" on the part of the addressee, some of which, perhaps, "the sender would never have foreseen." These may result in "aberrations" that are a "betrayal of the sender's intentions." And even though we are participants in "vast... probabilistic matrix" of meaning, the messages are not indeterminate (Eco, 1976, pp. 140–142).

But there are no such failures in Sophia's painting. Sophia's and Papou's meanings are nevertheless profoundly different—and this is how and why they work. They are a series of person-to-person, self-to-other meaning transpositions.

In our transpositional grammar, we develop a rhetorical view of communication. Now, these disjunctions in meaning are no longer failures, betrayals, or unfortunate circumstances of unpredictability. They are the rhetorical norm. We want to reverse these fundamental presuppositions about the intersection of interests in meaning.

The crux of the matter is not about what can be the same; it is about the differences. The ground of meaning is a not a place of architected, in-common sameness. It is a common ground where differences meet—innocently or benevolently at some times, not so innocently or maliciously at others.

Messaging purports, impossibly, to be transmission and communion. Rhetoric, in contrast, is an appeal based, for better and sometimes for worse, in differential interest.

Kinds of rhetoric might be found in evidence in information that one person has but another doesn't; an explanation that a person seeks; or an arguable orientation to some matter. In each case, the reason for participation is the difference. We don't have communion; we have common ground premised on the negotiation of difference.

$$\begin{matrix} \bullet & \bullet \\ & \bullet \end{matrix}$$

Returning to the Sophia story, we find the meaning, but not in the false hope of isomorphism that accompanies the word "communication." Communication in this sense cannot be more or less effective by virtue of its faithful transmission of meaning, because there can be no such thing. But the meanings-in-difference can be articulated and understood.

The practice of meaning in Sophia's experience of praying mantises is multimodal, and the meaning happens in the work of transposition. Any account of meaning must extend way beyond the making and the seeing of the picture and the reading of its text. Then, on a functional vector, this is not just an act of communication because the meanings integrally depend upon and anticipate acts of representation and interpretation.

On the common ground of meaning, we find teachers negotiating meanings with students, parents with children, artists with audiences, writers with readers, drivers with passengers, doctors with patients, builders with inhabitants, priests with congregations, sellers with buyers, men with women, bosses with workers, rulers with ruled. We also find researchers negotiating meanings with their subjects.

In every case, the meaning of participation in meaning is the difference. In every case, rhetoric takes form in multimodal transposition, moving across most or all of text, image, space, body, sound and speech. And functional transpositions: I, by empathy, can place myself in my meaning in the position of you. Some rhetorics may be solidary in this way, others antagonistic, and at any moment, any of these expressions of interest can lapse into any other.

Some of the differences that rhetoric brings together may prove to be unconscionable, when for instance the forms of rhetoric reflect and reproduce inequalities, authoritarianism or prejudice. Other rhetorics may be conscionable, representing necessary or transitory inequalities—parents and children, teachers and learners, experts and lay people, for instance. But even these momentarily conscionable rhetorics of inequality are fraught in a world where all-too-often they align with or refract unconscionable rhetorics designed to perpetuate inequality.

The result is that, in their rhetorical play, some differences of interest may be complementary and generative—we will call this "productive diversity" (Kalantzis & Cope, 2016b). But equally, the result may be in other moments of rhetorical interaction what Habermas calls "distorted communication" (1970/1985, pp. 310, 316). This may be deliberately so, an appeal to interests that is deceptive to the extent that its consequence is to serve one interest at the expense of the other, while purporting to share.

Whether more or less obvious, rhetoric has the capacity to wish away differential interests, as much as to put them to productive use. One such rhetoric is objectivist empiricism.

∴

We do pedagogical things with Sophia, too. And again, this was not because we ever thought we might some day turn them into "research." We do them out of curiosity, to see what kinds of new tools are being designed to support learning. We have been prompted to reflect on these in a researchy way now just because we have been asked to write a foreword for this book.

First, there was Mel Chemistry. We were interested in this subscription chemistry set for its multimodality and digital media supports. Every month for a year and a bit, a mysterious box from Russia turned up in our mailbox. (We did wonder how it was possible to get such a strange chemical cocktail through the mail from the United States' erstwhile Cold War enemy.)

In each box were two sets of gloves, one for the child and one for the parent—only to be done with adult supervision, said the instructions sternly. Two experiments per month, little bottles of chemicals with scannable labels, with the paraphernalia needed to do the experiments: petri dishes, vials, and candles if heating was needed. The interesting part for us was the multimodality. The instructions came in words with diagrams as well as YouTube videos, and in 3D visualizations of the molecules in using a VR viewer for the Mel Chemistry app that we had download onto one of our phones.

"How old are you, Sophia?" we asked her each time we started work on our "lab" (the laundry in our house). Twelve, she said, though she was only nine at the time, a standing joke about the parental advisory on the packets. We were being bad quasi-parents.

As for the chemistry, the magic and the drama of colors and fizzes was fun, but the chemical formulae given to us to explain the reactions were inscrutable. The YouTube videos of how-to-do the experiment were nicely made but proved slow and boring (interestingly so, we thought), and the quickest route to understanding how to do the experiment was the step-by-step diagram. Sophia wanted to look at this, not the videos.

And, showing single molecules in their (marvelous!) three-dimensional movement gave no clues about their transformation in chemical reactions. But perhaps that is just too hard, the gap between molecular representation and reaction too great? The representations of the molecules, we thought, were more like structuralism, and reactions more like what we call "transposition," the imminent changeability of everything, and these patterns of possibility. You can see, we could never have been on the same metaphorical research page as Sophia.

Then in painful academic mode, we had Sophia write up the experiments (she protested!), and sent them to her other academic YiaYia in Australia (Yelland, 2006). The result was more a description of what we did, with photographs, than anything deserving the name, science.

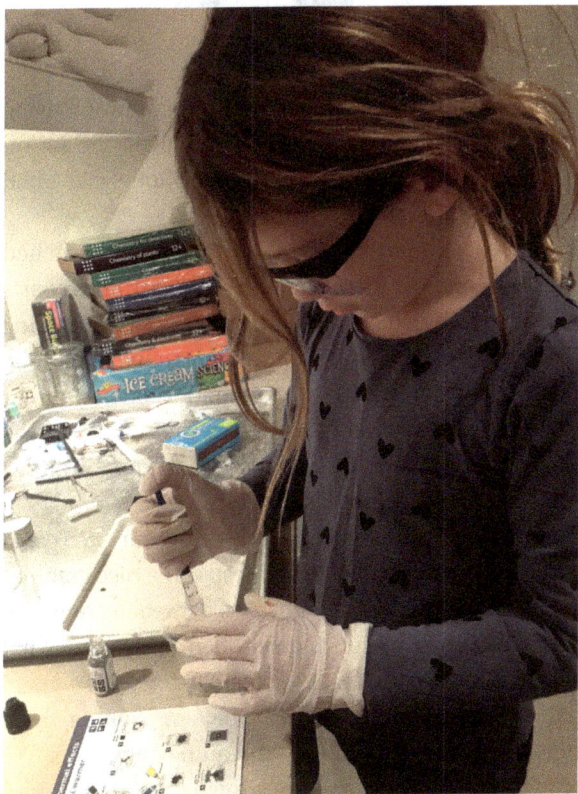

FIGURE F.2
In the "lab" with Sophia

Then there were three forays into computing, fascinating also for us as educators, but in ways they never could be for Sophia at her age. What was interesting to us was how eccentrically different these three were.

The Piper Computer kit had Sophia assembling a beautiful, improbably wooden Raspberry Pi computer using anachronistic "blueprints," walking her through various electronic components and switches with a Minecraft story about the end of the universe—but there was not much coding in the conventional sense.

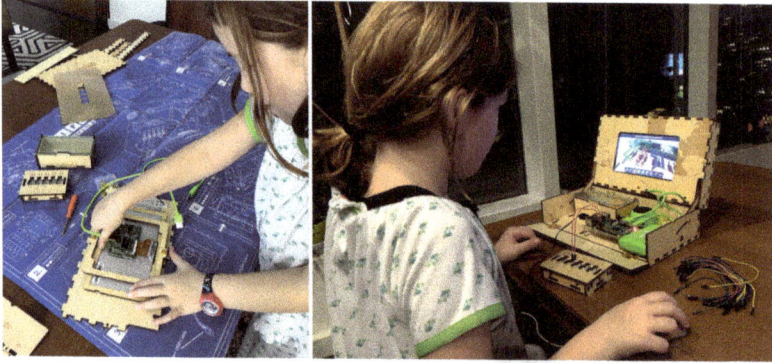

FIGURE F.3   Sophia making her Piper Computer

With littleBits Sophia also assembled a computer, then programmed using Scratch, a visual coding software designed for children. She loved the sound synthesis part of this, and even managed to program a piece of music she had been learning in her violin classes.

Then, we subscribed to BitsBox, counter-intuitively a box of hole-punched cards that came in the mail every month for a year. One of the funnest parts was putting the colorful cards in old-fashioned ring binders. The fascinating thing (again, for us) about this was that unlike Piper and littleBits, the code was "real," a version of JavaScript. Rather than try to explain the code—neither Sophia nor we every got to the bottom of what every part of the code meant— the idea was to copy it into a code editing app on a Chromebook, run it, and see what changed when you mucked around with the variables.

Then you could send a link to friends and family, and smart little animated game "apps" popped up on people's phones. Magic, but only because the nice graphics had already been coded by an expert. This, we thought, was a revealing return to didactic pedagogy, a reversion to learning-by-copying. But then again, that's what coders do—copy, adapt and combine already-available snatches of code.

Along the way through these various forays into learning with Sophia, there was no question of isomorphism between Sophia's meanings and ours. We chose the pedagogical things to do. She couldn't have known they even existed for the choosing. She couldn't have seen into these things the ways we did, and we wouldn't expect her to.

Sophia did these things with us, not because she had decided with us to do them. We gave these to her as Christmas and birthday gifts. (Was that overly serious?) They were fun for her to do and she liked doing them with us . But also at times they were boring and a chore because we had asked her to. Willingly doing them was her gift to us. Thank you Sophia, you are a lovely girl. We can't be objective about that, but it's the truth.

It's too late now, but here is our declaration of interest, not a conflict of interest, but wishfully a matching of complementary interests: we are educators. Now that we are writing about these interests in a book about "research," we suppose our interest has become research of sorts.

$$\because$$

We've called our chapter "the problem of empathy" in honor of Edith Stein. But to know her theory, we think you need to know something of her. Too often, the lives of scholarly authorities are lost in the abstract generalities that they generate, though the abstract generalities can only make sense in the context of the lives of their makers. (We tell this story at greater length in *Adding Sense* (Kalantzis & Cope, 2020).)

Between 1915 and his death, Edmund Husserl worked on successive drafts of a second volume of his masterwork of phenomenological theory, *Ideas*. It was not published until after his death. Initially, the manuscript was assembled and revised by Edith Stein, his doctoral student and research assistant. Stein's dissertation was published in 1917, *On the Problem of Empathy*. Husserl's work and Stein's became closely intertwined.

Stein: "A friend tells me that he has lost his brother...I become aware of his pain...[because] his face is pale and disturbed, his voice toneless and strained. Perhaps he also expresses the pain in words." This is not my pain, but I become pained, for him. Stein asks, "What kind of awareness is this?" Her answer: "the act of empathy" (Stein, 1917/1989, p. 6). Or, to rephrase, empathy is a solidary meaning, a transposition between other and self, expressed multimodally.

Husserl: "Such an intersubjective experienceability...is thinkable only through 'empathy,' which for its part presupposes an intersubjectively experienceable Body." In this way, "reciprocal empathy" is "unified into a nexus which constitutes intersubjective objectivities," the objectivities of society and history, "when we live with one another, talk to one another, shake hands with one another in greeting, or are related to one another in love and aversion, in disposition and action, in discourse and discussion" (Husserl, 1952/1989, pp. 101, 118, 192).

The problem now is to wonder is how much of the second volume of *Ideas* is Husserl's, and how much is the work of his empathetic research assistant. No matter how great the assistance, because she was a woman, Husserl didn't support examination of her habilitation thesis which would have allowed her appointment to the university as a professor.

A Jew by birth and an atheist while working with Husserl, she converted to Catholicism in 1921, taught in several religious colleges, then joined the Carmelite Order in 1933, assuming the monastic name of Teresa Benedicta of the Cross (Stein 1987/1993). When the Nazis came to power, for safety's sake the Carmelites transferred her to a monastery in the Netherlands. After the invasion of the Netherlands she was arrested by the SS and sent to Auschwitz. She died in the gas chambers in August 1942.

Edith Stein was made a saint by the Catholic Church in 1998, controversially for some Catholics, because they said she had not been martyred as a co-religionist. Rather, she had been murdered for her Jewish "race" (Cargas, 1994). Stein's entry to sainthood was on the basis of a miracle where the father of Benedicta, a little girl in New York who had swallowed enough Tylenol to kill her sixteen times over, prayed to her namesake, and the child miraculously recovered—a transposition by empathy, it might seem, of which only saints are capable.

∵

We like this word "empathy." It captures something that is charming about the writing in this book. Its writers are invested in their subjects. The stories told are about the co-construction of meanings. They are about the transposition of self and other. This involves co-construction of meanings, for sure, though not where the terms of participation in meaning are the sameness of equals. Rather, the meanings are in the irreducible differences. The meanings are also in the movement, the transpositions.

The truth of this book is the truth of intersubjectivity of researcher and subject. The challenge we face is how to make these exchanges of meaning productive rather than antagonistic. As the editors and co-authors of this book say, the process of meaning making is "critical-dialectical."

But surely, this is the challenge of all research, to create productively empathetic relationships. Here we have to make a contrast between the solidary interests of empathetic mutuality on the one hand, and on the other, the antagonistic meeting of differential interests.

The pundits of "research ethics" harp with painful frequency about what can go wrong in the unequal relations of researcher and research subject, as if we were all just about to become guilty parties. But they don't tell us about research empathy, or the sociable exchange of meanings where the differences are themselves the meaning.

Now we are talking about all research, and all human meaning. These are
the deeper and wider lessons to be learned from this book.

References

Cargas, H. J. (Ed.). (1994). *The unnecessary problem of Edith Stein.* Lanham, MD:
University Press of America.

Cope, B., & Kalantzis, M. (Eds.). (1993). *The powers of literacy: Genre approaches to
teaching writing.* London & Pittsburgh, PA: Falmer Press (UK edition) and University
of Pennsylvania Press (US edition).

Cope, B., & Kalantzis, M. (2020). *Making sense: Reference, agency and structure in a
grammar of multimodal meaning.* Cambridge: Cambridge University Press.

Eco, U. (1976). *A theory of semiotics.* Bloomington, IN: Indiana University Press.

Habermas, J. (1985). On hermeneutics' claim to universality. In K. Mueller-Vollmer
(Ed.), *The hermeneutics reader: Texts of the German tradition from the enlightenment
to the present* (pp. 293–319). New York NY: Continuum. (Original published 1970)

Halliday, M. A. K. (1975). *Learning how to mean: Explorations in the development of
language.* London: Edward Arnold.

Husserl, E. (1989). *Ideas pertaining to a pure phenomenology and a phenomenological
philosophy, second book: Studies in the phenomenology of constitution* (R. Rojcewicz
& A. Schuwer, Trans.). Dordrecht: Kluwer. (Original published 1952)

Husserl, E. (1970). *The crisis of European sciences and transcendental phenomenology.*
Evanston, IL: Northwestern University Press. (Original published 1954)

Kalantzis, M., & Cope, B. (2016a). Learner differences in theory and practice. *Open
Review of Educational Research, 3*(1), 85–132.

Kalantzis, M., & Cope, B. (2016b). New media and productive diversity in learning. In
S. Barsch and N. Glutsch (Eds.), *Diversity in der lehrerinnenbildung* (pp. 310–325).
Münster, DE: Waxmann.

Kalantzis, M., & Cope, B. (2020). *Adding sense: Context and interest in a grammar of
multimodal meaning.* Cambridge: Cambridge University Press.

Kalantzis, M., Cope, B., Chan, E., & Dalley-Trim, L. (2016). *Literacies* (2nd ed.).
Cambridge: Cambridge University Press.

Kress, G. (2003). *Literacy in the new media age.* London: Routledge.

Stein, E. (1989). *On the problem of empathy* (W. Stein, Trans.). Washington, DC: ICS
Publications. (Original published 1917)

Stein, E. (1993). *Self portrait in letters, 1916–1942* (J. Koeppel, Trans.). Washington. DC:
ICS Publications. (Original published 1987)

Vygotsky, L. S. (1986). *Thought and language.* Cambridge, MA: MIT Press. (Original
published 1934)

Yelland, N. (2006). *Shift to the future: Rethinking learning with new technologies in
education.* New York, NY: Routledge.

Preface

Several years ago, we three were standing in the hallway near our offices at St. John's University, conversing about our lives as academics *and* parents. As we delved into the challenges of balancing household responsibilities, carpooling, grading, and coding data, we continued to loop back to what we noticed about our middle school children and what they were doing. What circulated was a genuine interest in our children's literacies and we soon realized that we were speaking *about* and *for* our children, and that did not seem authentic. We wondered what our middle schoolers would say about their own practices. It was then that the idea of child-parent research emerged.

We each went home and spoke openly with our teen about what transpired at work that day. Our adolescent children—Charlotte Abrams, Molly Kurpis, and Eric Ness[1]—were intrigued and seemed excited to speak about their digital and nondigital activities. Some might wonder if our children were capitulating to appease a parent, but adolescence is complex and often includes push back and dissent. Rather than simply going along with an idea that their parents had, the teens noted that co-researching with us, their parents, was a way to have their voices heard. What they did not realize—and they acknowledge in the final chapter—is that, at the time, they held preconceived notions of school-based research, and they did not know what to expect from a co-researcher partnership. However, they were well aware that they were investigating themselves as part of a research team-based experience (e.g., they would be sharing their ideas and co-creating with others around their age and their parents' age). Charlotte, Molly, and Eric have provided their own thoughts—unfiltered, authentic, and un-"adult"erated (e.g., their words in this book are without parental influence or editing)—regarding the process and explain how it is that research unfolded for them and, as a result, the increased awareness of self and others they developed.

Although we could write a monograph about our experiences—and perhaps we will in the future—our objective was to bring attention back to child-parent research. What once was the provenance of education research vis-à-vis Dewey (Dyehouse & Manke, 2017) and Piaget (1936/1952), studying one's child or grandchild has since surfaced sporadically (Bissex, 1980; Dezuanni, 2018; Goodman, 2014; Goodman & Goodman, 2013; Halliday, 1975; Kabuto, 2008; Kabuto & Martens, 2014; Long, 2004; Martens, 1996, 2014; McCarty, 2012; O'Mara & Laidlaw, 2011; Wolf, 1992; Yoon, 2012) with only limited examples of co-research stances (Long & Long, 2014). In general, however, parent-researcher investigations have not gained momentum among education researchers likely due to the important question of ethics; we address this in Chapter 1. In our work with our children over the years, we continued to consider two points of concern also noted anecdotally by other researchers: How can one remain unbiased while working with one's own child? How might there be unintentional coercion and possible harm (e.g., what are the consequences if the child does not comply?) These are valid questions, but they build upon two problematic claims. First, in research, we know that there is no such thing as a full removal of bias. We can go to great lengths to recognize and mitigate biases, but to have a completely impartial study is impossible because people (e.g., humans who have experiences and belief systems) are examining the behavior, practices, and beliefs of other people. This tension would exist even when one is not familiar with the participant or, in our case, co-researcher. Second, we honor the tenets of ethical research, one of which is beneficence, or do no harm. This is true with participants who are unknown or known people in our lives. Plus, what parent would ever look to hurt his/her child? We certainly are not in the business of hurting others, let alone our own children. What is more, our children are at an age and stage where, if they do not like something or they are uncomfortable, they are open and ready to let us know.

When we work with youth in other studies, we remind them that they can discontinue their involvement at any time and that they do not have to answer any questions if they don't want to. We upheld this same stance with our teens, and we respected the distance from and proximity to the study *they* dictated with their words, their body language, and their schedules. Although we develop this point in our introductory chapter, we reiterate salient aspects here because we recognize that the field, while ready to embrace this form of participatory co-research, might have its concerns. We hope that our edited collection offers an opening for (a) education researchers to discuss openly the child-parent research they either want to engage in or are thinking of engaging in, (b) child-researchers to initiate their own lines of inquiry and develop their space in the discussion of education, which, after all, is *about them*, and (c) the field writ large to envision and re-envision ontological, epistemological, and methodological stances when child-parent research is figured into how we conceptualize meaning making.

Note

1   In alphabetical order.

References

Bissex, G. L. (1980). *Gnys at wrk: A child learns to read and write.* Cambridge, MA: Harvard University Press.

Dezuanni, M. (2018). Minecraft and children's digital making: Implications for media literacy education. *Learning, Media and Technology, 43*(3), 236–249.

Dyehouse, J., & Manke, K. (2017). The philosopher as parent: John Dewey's observations of his children's language development and the development of his thinking about communication. *Education and Culture, 33*(1), 3–22.

Goodman, Y. M. (2014). Foreword: Learning lessons from our children and grandchildren. In B. Kabuto & P. Martens (Eds.), *Linking families, learning, and schooling: Parent-research perspectives* (pp. xi–xvi). New York, NY: Routledge.

Goodman, Y., & Goodman, K. (2013). Shoshana learns to write: A longitudinal study. In R. Meyer & K. Whitmore (Eds.), *Reclaiming writing: Composing spaces for identities, relationships, and actions.* New York, NY: Routledge.

Halliday, M. A. K. (1975). *Learning how to mean: Explorations in the development of language.* New York, NY: Elsevier.

Kabuto, B. (2008). Parent-research as a process of inquiry: An ethnographic perspective. *Ethnography and Education, 3*(2), 177–194.

Kabuto, B., & Martens, P. (Eds.). (2014). *Linking families, learning, and schooling: Parent-research perspectives.* New York, NY: Routledge.

Long, S. (2004). Passionless text and phonics first: Through a child's eyes. *Language Arts, 81*(5), 417–426.

Long, S., & Long, K. (2014). They don't really know me: Mother-daughter insights for researchers and teachers. In B. Kabuto & P. Martens (Eds.), *Linking families, learning, and schooling: Parent-research perspectives* (pp. 123–137). New York, NY: Routledge.

Martens, P. (1996). *I already know how to read: A child's view of literacy.* Portsmouth, NH: Heinemann.

Martens, P. (2014). "I already know how to read!" Home and school perceptions of literacy. In B. Kabuto & P. Martens (Eds.), *Linking families, learning, and schooling: Parent-research perspectives* (pp. 92–106). New York, NY: Routledge.

McCarty, G. M. (2012). *Family science: An ethnographic case study of the ordinary science and literacy experiences of one family* (Doctoral dissertation). Retrieved from https://irl.umsl.edu/dissertation/332

O'Mara, J., & Laidlaw, L. (2011). Living in the iworld: Two literacy researchers reflect on the changing texts and literacy practices of childhood. *English Teaching: Practice and Critique, 10*(4), 149–159.

Piaget, J. (1952). *The origins of intelligence in children* (2nd ed.). New York, NY: International Universities Press. (Originally published 1936)

Wolf, M. (1992). *A thrice-told tale: Feminism, postmodernism and ethnographic responsibility.* Stanford. CA: Stanford University Press.

Yoon, B. (2012). Junsuk and Junhyuck: Adolescent immigrants' educational journey to success and identity negotiation. *American Educational Research Journal, 49*(5), 971–1002.

Acknowledgements

This edited collection is intended to inspire discussions about child-parent research and the emergence of children's voices in educational studies and policies. We are grateful to our contributing authors, as well as our reviewers who conducted a double-blind review of the manuscripts and whose feedback helped to add another layer of strength and integrity to the collection. We feel honored to feature a foreword by Mary Kalantzis and Bill Cope and an afterword by Anthony J. Onwuegbuzie—thank you for helping to frame the volume and offer another lens through which we can perceive child-parent research. And to our resident artist, Charlotte Abrams, we thank you for crafting the cover of this book.

We also appreciate the Brill | Sense team (Evelien van der Veer, Marti Huetink, Jolanda Karada), who have guided us throughout the publication process. Additionally, we thank the support of the St. John's University faculty and administration. Finally, no acknowledgment would be complete without recognizing our families—thank you for your steadfast support as we explored this exciting line of research. A special thanks goes to Charlotte Abrams, Molly Kurpis, and Eric Ness (in alphabetical order) for your inspiration, dedication, and willingness to let us join you on this journey.

Figures and Tables

Figures

Tables

Notes on Contributors

Charlotte Abrams

began this research in sixth grade as an eleven-year-old soon to be twelve. Now she is fourteen going on fifteen and is in ninth grade. Her interests include art, reading, and sports such as basketball, soccer, and tennis.

Sandra Schamroth Abrams

is a Professor of Adolescent Education in the Department of Curriculum and Instruction at St. John's University. Her research focuses on the intersection of digital and nondigital literacies and practices, and the powerful meaning making that exists in and across the blurred boundaries of these spaces. Abrams's publications can be found in *Teachers College Record, Journal of Media Literacy Education,* and *Journal of Adolescent & Adult Literacy.* Abrams also is author of *Integrating Virtual and Traditional Learning in 6–12 Classrooms: A Layered Literacies Approach to Multimodal Meaning Making* (Routledge, 2015), *Conducting Qualitative Research of Learning in Online Spaces* (co-authored, Sage, 2017), *Managing Educational Technology: School Partnerships & Technology Integration* (co-authored, Routledge, 2018), *Bridging Literacies with Videogames* (co-edited, Sense, 2014), and *Writing in Education: The Art of Writing for Educators* (co-authored, Brill | Sense, forthcoming). She is the recipient of the 2019 USDLA Distance Learning Quality Paper Award for the article "Gamification and Accessibility." Abrams is a co-editor of the *Gaming and Ecologies Series* and an Associate Editor of the *International Journal of Multiple Research Approaches.*

Kathleen M. Alley

is an Associate Professor of Middle Level Literacy in the Curriculum, Instruction and Special Education Department at Mississippi State University. Dr. Alley's research explores youth's literate and social practices, and the environments that sustain literacy and motivation growth within school and informal, out-of-school contexts. Her interests include writing pedagogy, children's and adolescent literature, technology integration, multiliteracies, rural education, and teacher preparation.

Bill Cope

is a Professor in the Department of Education Policy, Organization & Leadership, University of Illinois, Urbana-Champaign. His research interests include theories and practices of pedagogy, cultural and linguistic diversity, and new technologies of representation and communication. His and Mary

Kalantzis' recent research has focused on the development of digital writing and assessment technologies, with the support of a number of major grants from the US Department of Education, the Bill and Melinda Gates Foundation and the National Science Foundation. The result has been the CGScholar multimodal writing and assessment environment.

Mary Kalantzis

was from 2006 to 2016 Dean of the College of Education at the University of Illinois, Urbana-Champaign. Before this, she was Dean of the Faculty of Education, Language and Community Services at RMIT University, Melbourne, Australia, and President of the Australian Council of Deans of Education. With Bill Cope, she has co-authored or co-edited: *New Learning: Elements of a Science of Education* (Cambridge University Press, 2008; 2nd edition, 2012); *Ubiquitous Learning* (University of Illinois Press, 2009); *Towards a Semantic Web: Connecting Knowledge in Academic Research* (Elsevier, 2009); *Literacies* (Cambridge University Press, 2012; 2nd edition, 2016); *A Pedagogy of Multiliteracies* (Palgrave, 2016); *e-Learning Ecologies* (Routledge, 2017); and a two-volume grammar of multimodal meaning, *Making Sense* and *Adding Sense* (Cambridge University Press, 2020).

Molly Kurpis

started working on her adolescent research in seventh grade at the prime age of 13. She is now in the 11th grade at an international baccalaureate public high school in New York City. The 16 year old loves dancing and the arts, including drama and writing. She has been in many shows with her local drama group, such as *Newsies* and *42nd Street*. Molly has been a dancer for 10 years and competed with her competition team for 5. Whenever she gets the chance, Molly loves to work on her original novels. Her passions are what drive her through the rigorous IB programme.

Linda Laidlaw

is a Professor in Language and Literacy Education at the University of Alberta. Her research focuses on digital and mobile technologies in primary education, and she is particularly interested in the relationship between children's digital practices at home and their experiences at school. Her latest projects, funded by the Social Sciences and Humanities Research Council of Canada, aim to develop new frames and strategies for literacy education in a changing world.

Guy Merchant

is Professor of Literacy in Education at Sheffield Hallam University. He specialises in research on children's literacy with new technologies. He is widely published in international journals and is a founding editor of Early Child-hood Literacy. He has co-edited a number of books including *Literacy, Media, Technology* (Bloomsbury, 2017) and *The Case of the iPad* (Springer, 2017). His latest book, written with Cathy Burnett, *New Media in the Classroom* was pub-lished in 2018 by Sage.

Daniel Ness

is a Professor of STEAM education in the Department of Curriculum and In-struction at St. John's University. He specializes in spatial development and cognition from birth through the lifespan. His book, *Spatial Intelligence: Why It Matters from Birth through the Lifespan,* (Routledge, 2017) demonstrates the parallel nature of children's spatial propensities in constructive play activities and skills possessed by professional engineers, architects, and scientists. His co-edited book, *Alternatives to Privatizing Public Education and Curriculum,* (Routledge, 2017) has been awarded the 2018 Society of Professors of Educa-tion Outstanding Book Award.

Eric Ness

began his child-parent research in seventh grade as a 13-year-old. Much of his research is based on his interest in music. He began playing piano when he was three years old and cello when he was seven. In addition to cello and piano performance, Eric loves to fence, to read and to explore new subjects.

"E" O'Keefe

is an eight-year-old boy who is in grade three and loves to play hockey. He is determined and tenacious, with high social acumen, a very social child—outgoing, loving, and affectionate. He participated in this study for three in his early childhood (from age two until five). His research interests have evolved from investigating loose materials, blocks, and Lego, to now researching hock-ey history, from player and team profiles to statistical analysis.

Joanne O'Mara

is an Associate Professor in Language and Literature Education at Deakin Uni-versity, Melbourne, Australia. An experienced secondary English and Drama teacher, she has continued to work with young people and schools through her university research. Her research and scholarship focuses on young peoples' emergent literacies and new textual practices; digital games; drama pedagogy; and the spatial, social and temporal dimensions of teachers' work.

Anthony J. Onwuegbuzie

is a Senior Research Associate at the University of Cambridge. In addition, he is Distinguished Visiting Professor at the University of Johannesburg; Honorary

Professor at the University of South Africa; Visiting Senior Scholar, St. John's University, New York; and an Honorary Recognised Supervisor (Online), University of Liverpool. His research areas primarily involve social and behavioral science topics, including disadvantaged and under-served populations. Additionally, he writes extensively on qualitative, quantitative, and mixed methodological topics applicable to multiple disciplines within the field of the social and behavioral sciences. With an *h-index* of 95, representing more than 60,000 citations, Dr. Onwuegbuzie has secured the publication of more than 500 works, including more than 350 journal articles, 50 book chapters, and 5 books, with 5 more books in the pipeline. Further, Dr. Onwuegbuzie has received more than 20 outstanding paper awards. Dr. Onwuegbuzie is former editor of *Educational Researcher*. Currently, he is editor-in-chief of the *International Journal of Multiple Research Approaches* and editor of *Research in the Schools*. He is past President of the Mixed Methods International Research Association.

Sarah Prestridge

has been a researcher, university teacher educator and classroom teacher in the field of Educational Technologies for over 25 years. Her journey began with a rather large computer in her classroom where she tinkered with her grade 6 class on the use of simulation software in the early 90s. She ran an Edu-Tech Lighthouse project that examined ICT and mathematics, studied her Masters in Educational Technologies and worked as a Curriculum Adviser. Her PhD examined models of effective professional development to enable teachers to use technologies effectively in their classrooms. Her passion for leading others along the pathway of technology integration has been fueled by the excitement both teachers and students generate while playing to learn. Sarah currently lectures in Educational Technologies at Griffith University, Australia.

Lourdes M. Rivera

is an Associate Professor in the Counselor Education Program at Queens, CUNY. She teaches courses in career counseling and assessment, college and career readiness, multicultural counseling, and counseling techniques. Prior to becoming a counselor educator, she was a counselor in a college setting providing career, academic and personal counseling to a diverse student population. She enjoys reading fiction, watching movies, and spending time with her family.

Dahlia Rivera-Larkin

is in the eighth grade and preparing herself for high school. Starting next school year, her education will focus in engineering. Her interests consist of engineering, biology, chemistry, American history, and music. She enjoys hanging out with her friends in her free time as well as practicing martial arts and playing the electric and acoustic guitars, trumpet, and bass. She also likes to read and watch fantasy books and movies.

Nora Rivera-Larkin

is in the twelfth grade and will be going to Stony Brook University in the fall. She will be following her passion for storytelling and will be focusing in English and creative writing.

Alaina Roach O'Keefe

lectures with the Faculties of Education and Arts at UPEI and is employed full-time as Corporate Human Resources Planner at PEI's Public Service Commission. Alaina's experiences as an educator and researcher over a decade range from Early Childhood and K-12 systems to post-secondary education and innovative adult learning. Alaina's research interests include quantitative and qualitative projects in early learning and/or play, planning and evaluation, leadership, and professional learning communities. She has published in the *Journal of Childhood Studies*, the *Canadian Journal of Education – Special Capsule Issue on Children's Play, Canadian Children, Teaching Innovations Projects*, and the *Canadian Journal of Native Education*.

Mary Beth Schaefer

is an Associate Professor of Adolescent Education and Interim Associate Dean of Graduate Studies at St. John's University. Much of her research focuses on middle grades students' literacy activities as well as issues of college and career readiness for underserved populations. Her most recent publication outlets include *Middle School Journal, Journal of Adult & Adolescent Literacy*, and *Urban Education*. She is co-editor of the book (Information Age Publishing, 2015) *Research on Teaching and Learning with the Literacies of Young Adolescents* and recently received the Association for Middle Level Education (AMLE)'s Outstanding Article Award for a co-authored paper titled, "An Historical Overview of the Middle School Movement." Her new line of inquiry focuses on martial arts and college readiness.

Cassandra R. Skrobot

is an aspiring artist and writer. Mrs. Skrobot graduated from Mississippi State University in 2017 with a B.S. in Interdisciplinary Studies, specializing in Fine Arts/Photography and Communications. She is a graduate student at Kennesaw State University pursuing a Masters in Professional Writing, in addition to devoting her time to her young son and husband.

Bogum Yoon

is Associate Professor of Literacy Education at the State University of New York at Binghamton. Yoon has extensive teaching and research experiences both in South Korea and the United States. Her research interest is in the areas of critical global literacies, cultural pluralism, and positional identities. Yoon's publications including books (e.g., *Critical Literacies: Global and Multicultural Perspectives*, Springer, 2016) reflect her commitment to high quality teacher education for all students including English language learners.

About the Book

This edited volume[1] offers the field a range of studies, methods, and perspectives regarding child-parent research. The international authorship, representing four different countries on three different continents, provides multiple perspectives about meaning making while addressing important ethical and methodological tensions inherent in child-(grand)parent co-research. Across the volume, there is particular attention to the ethics of child-parent research, and each chapter ends with a section devoted to future research and ethical considerations. This section is particularly important in helping this line of inquiry gain traction. Furthermore, throughout this book, readers will hear the voices of children ranging in age from early childhood through early adulthood. At times, readers will hear the child's words directly from him/her[2]; at other times, the parent researcher will convey the child's words; and in other instances, the child has co-written with the parent.

Mary Kalantzis and Bill Cope acknowledge in their foreword, *The Problem of Empathy*, that the methodological challenges noted across this collection plague the overall field: "The problem with research in general, which parent-child research brings to light with a particular poignancy, turns on a model of communication in which the researcher strives to meet the mind of the subject on terms which are true to the subject's reality." Kalantzis and Cope call attention to the quick reprobation that often obfuscate and sometimes belie epistemological questions and expressions of meaning. The authors also weave in stories of their granddaughter's literacy practices and address the co-construction of meaning not only evident in their foreword, but also apparent throughout the volume.

In our introductory chapter, "Reimagining Child-Parent Research," we contend that child-parent research appears on a continuum of participation and involvement; using the metaphor of a wheel, we explain that, with child-parent research the "research process and level of involvement and partnership can move forwards and backwards, can spin or turn in different ways, and can rotate with various momenta." In other words, research is fluid and the role of the child and the parent can evolve over time in light of critical reflection, participation, dialogue, and, of course, the inherent tensions and ethics that accompany such research. Throughout this collection, there are various instances of involvement and partnership, and, even though the chapters align in various thematic ways, we have arranged the chapters according to the participatory stances they represent.

Chapters 2 and 3 feature studies that include a grandparent or parent examining his/her grandchild or child while learning, and the children offer clarifications. These children are involved in the co-construction of the research narrative. For instance, in his chapter, "Media Transformations: Working with Iron Man," Guy Merchant comes to the research with the complex hybrid identity of an "off-duty researcher and off-duty grandparent" exploring his "immersion" in a context that his seven-year-old grandson explains to him. Sarah Prestridge, in "Re-Designing Teaching for Tweens in Times of Streaks, Likes, and Gamers," draws upon her collaboration and communication with her adolescent son to learn about his social media and videogame practices, and, taking the stance as a mom, educator, and researcher, she offers ideas for curricula to draw upon students-as-producers and contributors.

Moving from involvement to participation, the children in the studies featured in Chapters 4, 5, and 6 also are co-authors of the manuscript. For instance, in "High Anxiety: A Collaborative Autoethnographic Inquiry," twenty-something-year-old Cassandra Skrobot and her mother, Kathleen Alley, engage in a retrospective examination of the anxiety Cassandra experienced during her college years. Here, Cassandra's full partnership in the collaborative autoethnography is essential, especially with regard to ethics and medical history. Readers also hear from an elementary schooler in "Remixing Digital Play in the Early Years: A Child-Parent Collaboration," a chapter eight-year-old "E" co-created with his mother, Alaina Roach O'Keefe. The study, which took place over three years, when "E" was two-years-old through five-years-old, offers another approach to child-parent research wherein there is a shift from involvement to partnership over time. Finally, in "Career Development? What's That: Engaging My Daughters in an Examination of their Learning Process and How it Can Inform their Future—Or Not," teens Nora and Dahlia join their mother, Lourdes Rivera, to explore their own meaning making in relation to their future. Like Cassandra and "E," the teens engaged in co-research and also co-authored the chapter *with* their mother, who also is an education researcher.

Chapters 7 and 8 offer another perspective of child-parent research, as the authors reanalyze their examinations of their children's' experiences. Joanne O'Mara and Linda Laidlaw previously examined each other's child in a study about youths' digital literacies. Their chapter, "Researching and Parenting in the iWorld: The Dialogism of Family Life," provides a methodological retrospective for engaging in child-parent research. Likewise, Bogum Yoon revisits previous research of her then-teen sons in "A Parent-Researcher's Reanalysis of Adolescent Immigrants' Literacy Experiences: Methodological and Theoretical Insight on Parent-Child Research." Through a literacy lens, Yoon considers her immigrant children's learning experiences.

The final chapter, "The Last Word: Teen Reflections," is written by three adolescents, who co-researched with us, their parents. The voices[3] of Charlotte Abrams, Molly Kurpis, and Eric Ness offer readers insight into the child-parent research paradigm through the eyes of the adolescent researcher. This addition to the text showcases an authenticity and empowerment that accompanies the child-as-co-researcher role. Literally, the teens get the last word in the last chapter.

In his afterword, Anthony J. Onwuegbuzie extends the conversation of child-parent research by contending that "all *parental* figures should be included in the definition of child-parent research, including step-parents, grandparents, and uncles and aunts." We couldn't agree more, and we envision this collection revitalizing the line of research and, more importantly, the voices of youth. Finally, Onwuegbuzie's thematic overview of practices for conducting child-parent research underscores the features of the research presented throughout the edited volume.

This collection is intended to be provocative so that readers contemplate the methods, the discussions, and the questions explored and generated by the children- and parent-researchers. Perhaps this text will inspire other iterations of child-parent research and lead to refined methodological and conceptual practices. Perhaps this book will contribute to another arm of participatory research that omits the adult researcher's filter. Perhaps the chapters will bring to light multiple perspectives of meaning making. Or perhaps the discussion of ethics will impress upon readers how child-parent research demands continuous reflection and layers of care not only to address inherent tensions, but also to uphold beneficence while considering the future of youth research and empowerment.

Notes

1   All contributions have undergone two double-blind peer reviews.
2   All identify as male or female.
3   Author and vignette arrangement appear in alphabetical order.

CHAPTER 1

Reimagining Child-Parent Research

Sandra Schamroth Abrams, Mary Beth Schaefer and Daniel Ness

Abstract

How can child-parent research be reimagined? This introductory chapter offers a historical context of children doing research and develops a conceptual framework for understanding facets of child-parent research. The premise of this line of inquiry includes authenticity, empowerment, and insight. The authors contemplate the range of involvement and partnership and provide a wheel metaphor to capture the dynamic and nuanced interplay of dialogue, critical reflection, ethics, tension, and participation. There are ethical concerns addressed through a critical discussion about hierarchies, power, and voice in child-parent research, which hinges on a shared purpose and requires an approach that is carefully cultivated to be egalitarian, inclusive, dialogic, and reciprocal.

1 Introduction

In an era when education research underscores the need to connect family and school (Edwards et al., 2019), there is a distinct interest in, and attention to, what happens in the home and the relationship among child,[1] parent, and meaning making. Couple this extant interest with a relatively new social norm—the advent of "sharenting" (Blum-Ross & Livingstone, 2017) that has included parents/caregivers sharing information about their children (e.g., accomplishments, milestones, frustrations, images) on social media—and the boundaries of home or family literacies and practices also expand and, often, become blurred. There is a third factor that also plays an important role, and that is the researcher, who also is a parent interested in learning *with* his/her child and, likewise, the child who is interested in co-researching with his/her parent.

Sometimes researchers, who also are parents, informally express an interest in understanding their children's meaning making, asking questions similar to, "I wonder why my child prefers to draw on the iPad instead of paper?" or "Isn't it interesting that my teen plays one type of videogame with one friend and reserves other games for other friends?" or "Today, I was looking up information on my

© KONINKLIJKE BRILL NV, LEIDEN, 2020 | DOI: 10.1163/9789004421721_001

phone, and my child asked me, 'Why do that if you can just ask Siri instead?'" These types of questions have surfaced in "watercooler" conversations wherein colleagues, when discussing their home lives, apply their researcher lens and begin pondering "why" or "how" instead of only stating what transpired.

Other times, the researcher-parent will post similar wonderings on Twitter, Facebook, Instagram, or another social media platform, but these posts often are accompanied by images of the child, what the child was doing, and/or artifacts of the child's meaning making. These posts often initiate a documented conversation among social media followers (who may or may not be researchers) regarding the activity. Although posts can be "liked" or re-posted, sometimes, the discussion of the child's meaning making and the parent's role—as observer, participant, or participant observer—has surfaced. These and other examples highlight the growing interest in parent-researchers addressing what and how they learn from their children (cf. Kabuto & Martens, 2014) and suggest that the field is ready to re-investigate what Piaget (1936/1952) and even Dewey (Dyehouse & Manke, 2017) started years ago—explorations of and insights into child meaning making by parent-researchers. We contend that the field also is ready to explore the child-as-co-researcher *with* his/her parent.

This edited collection offers the field a range of research that involves the child and parent in the investigation. In line with the call to shift away from objectifying the researched (be it a teacher or student, adult or child) toward embracing the participant-as-researcher (Cochran-Smith & Lytle, 1993; Onwuegbuzie & Frels, 2013), we recognize youth as researchers, thereby supporting an empowerment of young people and research as their mouthpiece, and adding another layer of authenticity to the research process. Thus, through this edited collection—which features a variety of ways youth are an integral part of the research process—we re-initiate the discussion of child-parent research, with a focus on the learning experiences that come to the fore, as well as the methodological and ethical implications of engaging in such research.

2 Why Child-Parent Research

The premise of this line of inquiry includes authenticity, empowerment, and insight. After all, if we remove the filter of the adult researcher and the child is partaking in every step of the research process—from ideation to data collection to analysis to presentation—then the field can hear what the youth *actually* have to say.

In their seminal text *Inside/Outside*: *Teacher Research and Knowledge*, Marilyn Cochran-Smith and Susan Lytle (1993) introduced the then radical notion that knowledge built by classroom teachers through thoughtful work on their own practice was not only "real" research, but research worth knowing and sharing. The objective of their edited book was to argue for teacher research as "a form of social change...[with] potential to redefine the notion of a knowledge base for teaching and to challenge the university's hegemony in the generation of expert knowledge for the field" (p. xiv). We took inspiration and heart from this text that challenged traditional notions of epistemology. Our explicit goals for this book derive from a similar critical and democratic ethos: we, too, argue for an upending of beliefs in what counts as research and knowledge. New knowledge and understanding can come from researchers examining meaning making in their own homes with their children or grandchildren (cf. Kabuto & Martens, 2014). Likewise, it can occur with children-as-researchers examining their own learning with their parents or grandparents, who also are researchers. By blurring the lines of traditional research relationships in and out of home contexts while underscoring ethical awareness, purpose, intent, and mindfulness, we aim to legitimize and promote research conducted and accomplished with and by children in formal and informal spaces.

This book is meant to be provocative. Indeed, not all members of academia will embrace the notion that children can and will do research. We hope this edited collection will prompt scholars to rethink ways in which children are researchers and to value careful, ethical child-parent scholarship.[2] We are not asking readers to cast cautionary thoughts aside. Rather, we recognize that *all* research has limitations and ethical considerations, and we advocate for lines of child-parent explorations that help to inform the field methodologically, conceptually, and practically.

Our objectives, then, are to: (1) stake a claim for the legitimacy and power of child-parent research; (2) build a conceptual framework for engaging in child-parent research; (3) create an epistemological framework built on understanding how researching *with* children is radically different from research *on* children; and (4) open spaces for new ways to think about how we go about creating and valuing knowledge. In what follows, we address each of these objectives and offer the field a working language to support and further child-parent inquiries.

3 Legitimizing Child-Parent Research

In this chapter, we address the historical context of the "taboo" nature of research with and on one's own children, we focus on ethical considerations, and we flesh out the concept of participatory research with children. We continue to

struggle with language that denotes power and, thus, purposefully have chosen the placement of "child" before "parent" in this volume's title, *Child-Parent
Research Reimagined*, and throughout this chapter, so as to not privilege the
dominant adult narrative. We also recognize that struggling with language is
important because it can raise a sensitivity and openness to social change.

Fitzgerald, Graham, Smith, and Taylor (2010) discussed children's participation in research as a *struggle over recognition* (p. 293, emphasis in original), which accentuates "participation as a negotiated space that is dialogical
rather than monological in nature, which, in turn, more adequately captures
the mutual and interconnected layering of children's participation" (p. 293).
The authors explained that there needs to be mutual recognition to achieve
equality, and they cautioned that misrecognition can lead to subordination
and injustice. Legitimizing child-parent research cannot be tokenistic; to do
so would defy the very authenticity that is at the heart of such research. To
achieve equal recognition, and for children to "participate meaningfully," there
needs to be a familiarity between the child and the adult:

> Adults' awareness of children's understanding and experience in their
> daily lives is a prerequisite for meaningful engagement with children.
> Close relationships between adult and child are necessary to establish
> intersubjectivity (a shared focus of understanding and purpose), which is
> essential for a dialogic approach to participation. (Fitzgerald et al., 2010,
> p. 300)

Such insights into child participation also reinforce the value of *knowing* the
child and building—or building upon—close relationships to engage together
in research that is authentic and mutual in nature.

As we stake a claim for child-parent research, we underscore the affordances of collaborative research wherein (a) the child is the agent of study, (b)
the child's voice is valued, not objectified, and (c) there is deep introspection
and self-awareness. We do this while understanding well that positionality and
power are inherent tensions in such research. Whereas we cannot undo the
child-parent relationship or connection (nor are we suggesting otherwise), we
emphasize the importance of remaining acutely aware of the social, political,
and authoritative tensions that exist when children and adults, who otherwise co-exist in some form of hierarchical structure, engage in research that
attempts to flatten hierarchies. It is through such sensitivity that all involved
can have their voices heard and valued.

Legitimizing any type of new approach or practice typically involves a paradigmatic shift that unveils new ways of perceiving the word and the world. We

provide examples of important practices and revelations that have challenged and advanced the field as a means to make a case for research that needs to be a widely accepted practice.

3.1   *Paradigm Shifts: From Taboo to Accepted Practice*

In almost all instances, novel discoveries yield criticisms at best and downright mockery and even humiliation at worst. When the latter happens, a latent discovery is initially considered to be bizarre, irrelevant, or taboo among a particular field's community of scholars. Given that there are occasional instances of parent-researchers studying their children (cf. Bissex, 1980; Dezuanni, 2018; Hackett, 2017; Halliday, 1975; Kabuto & Martens, 2014; Piaget 1936/1952) or, in even rarer instances, with their adult children (Long & Long, 2014), we see this collection as part of a latent movement in educational research that, we hope, gains greater traction, legitimacy, and growth.

In what follows, we offer a wide-angle view of historical shifts in normative practices across various disciplines. Doing so calls attention to discoveries and practices that have defied convention and underscores how these shifts helped to situate new ways of making meaning. The field of child-parent research is much like these exemplars in that it challenges or extends what is known and introduces a new paradigm and, with it, offers new epistemological understandings. Historical examples abound. Here are a few:

In 1842, Augusta Ada King, Countess of Lovelace, invented what we now know to be the first algorithm for an analytical engine, which is, in contemporary parlance, the first computer program. Unfortunately, her work was overshadowed by that of her male colleagues, particularly Charles Babbage. It is important to note, however, that the research community at the time was unaware that Ada King documented her synthesis and development of the first algorithm for an analytical engine in a series of notes from 1842 to 1843. With few exceptions among her mathematician peers, her work was considered irrelevant in her day because the utility of her algorithm was unclear. Fortunately, these notes were resurrected and republished by Bertram Bowden in 1953 as an appendix.

That is but one of many examples in mathematics and computer science. Moving to linguistics, in 1879, Ferdinand de Saussure posited the existence of a Proto-Indo-European (PIE) language, the original language that developed into what we know today as a system of 448 languages, which can be hypothesized through the study of laryngeal phonemic reconstructions. In his own day, Saussure was derided for even suggesting the existence of PIE—let alone the use of laryngeal theory to support the notion of a PIE language. It wasn't until the 1930s, through the findings of mid-twentieth-century linguists, most

notably Jerzy Kuryłowicz (1935), that Saussure was recognized for this significant discovery.

Moving from linguistics to physics, Albert Einstein is a novel case in that the
world-renowned physicist's theory of relativity, particularly general relativity,
gained little, if any, recognition until about 50 years later in the 1960s when
astrophysics blossomed as a field in the natural sciences. Mostly known during
the early twentieth century for the law of the photoelectric effect, Einstein is
most celebrated today for the theory of relativity, one that was challenged in
his day for two major reasons: (1) a putative lack of usefulness in both academic and lay circles; and (2) an overall lack of acceptance among most European physicists prior to World War II (Wazeck, 2014).

Like King, Saussure, and Einstein, Alfred Wegener, a German meteorologist,
was met with skepticism from the community of geologists who argued that
his notion of continental drift, first posited in the early 1900s, did not conform
to the findings of leading researchers in geology of the day. But, fortunately,
Wegener's reputation as an "outsider" in geology was short-lived; by the early
1950s, his contributions served as the primary foundation of the theory of plate
tectonics (Frankel, 1987).

In addition to researchers whose ideas have been met with derision, momen-
tous discoveries have at least another thing in common: As soon as they are
discovered, they seem self-evident. An example of this is problem-solving
methodology that was developed by the famous twentieth-century mathematician, George Pólya. Prior to the publication of Pólya's *How to Solve It* (1957),
the notion of a stepwise progression of solving problems, particularly in mathematics, was inconceivable and not often seen as obvious (Alexanderson,
2000). This is also true with novel ways to think about *who can do* research.

In his foreword to *Inside/outside: Teacher research and knowledge*, Freder-
ick Erickson (1993) acknowledged the newness of Marilyn Cochran-Smith and
Susan Lytle's conception of teacher research. Erickson stated thus: "Cochran-
Smith and Lytle have not only provided here a fresh and incisive review of a
developing field, they have been active in helping that field to develop" (p. vii).
Cochran-Smith and Lytle's (1993) sentiment about an unfolding field—
especially one in its nascency—is, at once, inspirational for researchers in
the fields of education and human development, as well as the subfields of
research methods and measurement, and, at the same time, apt from the perspective of the need to ensure the dynamism of methodological approaches.
Cochran-Smith and Lytle stated the problem succinctly in the opening chapter
of their book:

> Although current educational research has placed considerable empha-
> sis on developing a systematic and rigorous body of knowledge about

> teaching, little attention has been given to the roles that teachers might play in generating a knowledge base. Lack of significant teacher participation in codifying what we know about teaching, identifying research agendas, and creating new knowledge is problematic. Those who have daily access, extensive expertise, and a clear stake in improving classroom practice have no formal ways for their knowledge of classroom teaching and learning to become part of the literature on teaching. (p. 5)

Those who live the experience, therefore, should have a voice in the research. Cochran-Smith and Lytle noted the subjugation of the teacher's expertise to that of the university researcher when the authors argued that "efforts to construct and codify a knowledge base for teaching have relied primarily on university-based research and have ignored the significant contributions that teacher knowledge can make to both the academic research community and the community of school-based teachers." Like children in traditional research, teachers who are "most directly responsible for the education of children have been disenfranchised" (p. 5).

Research, regardless of field of inquiry, is in flux. From an ontological perspective, it has to be; that is the nature of research—the *élan vital* of the scientific method. But the extent to which research in a particular field changes seems to be greatly influenced by how the academic community accepts, or rejects, that change. Therefore, our experiences as contributors to a burgeoning concept in terms of both who does research and how it is conducted might face opposition, and we remain confident that child-parent research will gain normativity. We believe a paradigm shift is needed both methodologically and structurally in terms of who can engage in the process of researching. For too long, research was conceived of, almost exclusively, as a white lab-coat, mostly male endeavor, especially from the mid-nineteenth century through most of the twentieth century. Only since the last third of the twentieth century to the present has it included a wider scope of adult participation—namely, those who made it their goal to engage in research (Ceci, Williams, & Barnett, 2009). Rarely, if at all, has it included young people in its pool.

And we call attention to an inherent (and possibly unintentional) elitism that exists in the boundary-making between those who are deemed "researchers" and those who are not. It seems ironic that, in a field that looks to empower the otherwise voiceless, there is the relative absence of youth-as-researchers in the literature and at presentations; for the latter, even if raw data are presented and recordings of youth voices or images are played or shown, the adult researcher remains the filter when presenting the study. Long and Long (2014) pointed out, "Rarely is the question asked: What does it mean *to the child* when researchers interpret his or her words and actions to the broader educational community through articles, books, and conference presentations" (p. 124, emphasis in original). Budd Hall (2005) noted that, despite movements to create participatory practices in research that would counter "the monopoly over knowledge production by universities" (p. 22), there are still deeply rooted power structures that support the status quo: "While the university world explodes with new discourses on power in all its forms, the faces in the universities in my part of the world, the resumes of scholars we hire, the forms of sharing knowledge we use, and the structures of learning and knowledge production have changed but little" (p. 22). When it comes to including children, the traditional forms of research do not include them as researchers, but, instead, "they [children] tend to be excluded from educational policy-making and the 'rarefied world' of the academic: a hegemonic 'score-keeping' world where professional adult researchers separate themselves from others" (Murray, 2016, p. 705).

Although the idea of children and teens as co-researchers may seem novel in academia, the general undercurrent of child study, whether children have participated as equals or not, has been an important area of inquiry for over a century. *To be sure, then, child-parent research is neither taboo nor new to education research.* Although Dewey's formal writing did not identify his own children specifically, Dyehouse and Manke (2017) explained how Dewey's children were a source of inspiration: "Dewey's parenting experiences affected his thinking about language and communication...[and] helped him see language activity as primarily concerned with agreement in action" (p. 22). Dewey, however, is not known for his role as a parent-researcher, and only recently has his engagement in child-parent research received attention.

When researchers were overt about their work with their children, they faced scrutiny. As Kabuto (2008) noted, the linguist Leopold (1939) who examined his daughter's bilingualism, "felt his work went unappreciated" (p. 179). Likewise, when Piaget (1936/1952) developed theories of cognition based on his own observation of his infant children and his one-on-one clinical interviews with children and teens, his work was challenged by some of his peers (Braine, 1962; Graue, Walsh, & Ceglowski, 1998). Nonetheless, Piaget's investigation of the ontological and epistemological underpinnings of intellectual development[3] by creating and engaging in the Piagetian clinical interview— that is, *with the participation of children*—has helped to pave the way for future research. Piaget's novelty was not so much his newness of method as it was the nature by which children and teens exhibited their intellectual and cognitive abilities. In their research on everyday mathematical knowledge of preschool children, Ginsburg, Pappas, and Seo (2001) emphasized the idea of "asking young children what is developmentally appropriate" (p. 181), a Piagetian concept that we are incorporating and fostering in our research.

As we develop a conceptual framework and work towards a new epistemology, we do so acknowledging that just as "parent-research has held an ambiguous place in research designs, paradigms, and frameworks…[and] has often been marginalized" (Kabuto, 2008, p. 177), so, too, is child-parent research a nascent field that has yet to develop the exposure and development of established lines of inquiry. In the last forty-five years, there have been occasional parent-researcher investigations of (or inspirations from) their own child(ren)'s or grandchild's meaning making (Baghban, 1984, 2014; Bissex, 1980; Dezuanni, 2018; Gee, 2003; Goodman, 2014; Goodman & Goodman, 2013; Hackett, 2017; Halliday, 1975; Kabuto, 2008, 2014; Kress, 1982; Long, 2004; Maderazo, 2014; Martens, 1996, 2014; McCarty, 2012; Miller, 2014; O'Mara & Laidlaw, 2011; Shannon & Shannon, 2014; Wolf, 1992; Yoon, 2012) or of their own role as parent-researchers and advocates of their child(ren) (Haddix, 2014; Lopez-Robertson, 2014). There also have been limited examples of the child or, in the case of Long and Long (2014) the adult child, in a co-research or co-authorship role, privileging the child's voice and challenging traditional paradigms.

Even though parent-researcher investigations challenge the norm, the language of convention perpetuates hierarchies. Perhaps without realizing it, parent or grandparent-researchers have discussed "research on them [the children]" and learning from "studying" their children or grandchildren in some instances "by carefully examining specific features of [the child's] writing over time" (Goodman & Goodman, 2013, p. 518; Kabuto, 2014; Shannon & Shannon, 2014). As Kelli Long retrospectively considered her mother's role as a parent-researcher, she explained that her mother "studied my experiences learning Icelandic culture, my acquisition of the language in particular" (Long & Long, 2014, p. 123). We wonder how this research might have looked had the childhood or adolescent Kelli been studying her own practices and writing *with* her mother about her experiences.

Just as parent-researchers have offered important discoveries of child learning by situating the child as the object of study, they also have showcased the continued struggle to situate the child in parent research. Such a challenge is critical to explore in the child-parent research dynamic and is part of the methodological transparency needed to substantiate the line of inquiry (Kabuto, 2008). Likewise, these examinations are important to the genesis of this field of study, which has had sporadic pockets of research production, but no cohesive and steady growth. We hope this book will serve as fodder for the field to develop and refine child-parent research.

4   Creating a Conceptual Framework

Engaging in child-parent research involves conceptually understanding *how* or
in what ways the collaborative and participatory scholarship transpires. Yet it is
no easy feat to develop a conceptual framework that aptly captures the nuances
and rigor of research. First, we have found ourselves confronted with and by
traditional notions of research that are laden with hierarchical structures. Take,
for instance, the metaphor of the umbrella (Figure 1.1). We began with the overall concept of researching and envisioned (and still envision) co-researching
subsumed into that larger construct. Qualitative research, by its very traditional
notion, involves people with a particular skillset or expertise examining others'
behavior; thus, there is an inherent researcher versus participant dichotomy. To
mitigate this bifurcation of roles, we focus on co-researching and the collaborative and participatory aspects of it. However, much to our chagrin, the umbrella
concept of traditional research continued to preserve the adult researcher as
the one with authority. We also had difficulty identifying the degrees of participation or collaboration and the role of the child in the research. Thus, we
turned to ways the field has begun to resist traditional hierarchies and account
for participatory roles in research. In what follows is a discussion of participatory research and engaging youth as researchers. Thereafter, we present a
re-imagined conceptual framework for children-as-researchers.

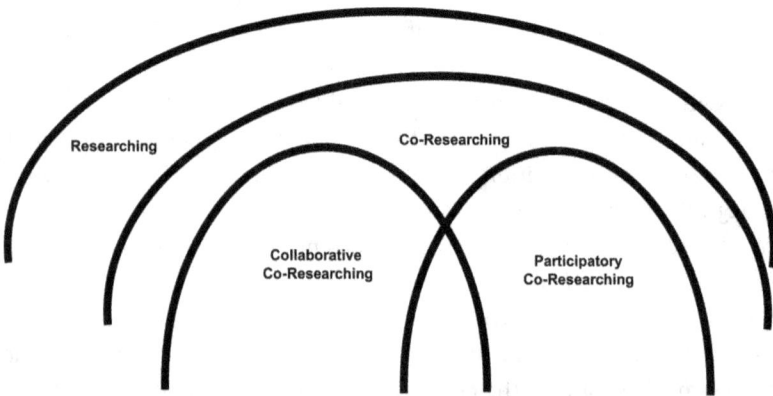

FIGURE 1.1   An initial perception of child-parent co-research that unintentionally preserves
             traditional constructs

4.1   *Participatory Research*
Over the course of time, the field has pushed against the hierarchies of research
to make room for participants *in* the research in varying degrees. Speaking
for oneself has tremendous power and authenticity, and research has proven

discrepancies between adult reporting and child self-reporting. For instance, Theunissen and colleagues (1998) found inconsistencies between the way parents and their children reported the "children's health-related quality of life" (p. 387). In the study of 1,105 Dutch children between the ages of 8–11 years old, Theunissen and colleagues found that there was a difference in agreement between child and parent reporting, suggesting "that parent reports cannot be substituted for child reports" (p. 395). If this is the case, why then are children's voices often presented through the adult mouthpiece? Counters to these concerns are addressed in participatory research, which is rooted in the understanding that knowledge can be created and presented in multiple ways and it is most authentic when the meaning maker is the researcher of his/her/their practices.

Participatory research stemmed from an international effort and was "first articulated in Tanzania in the early 1970s to describe a variety of community-based approaches to the creation of knowledge" (Hall, 1981, 2005, p. 5). Essentially, participatory research began as a concerted effort to mitigate the privilege and possible myopia of traditional research and moved towards empowering the otherwise silenced or less heard. Hall (2005) identified seven key components of participatory research: (1) it involves "powerless groups of people"; (2) it "involves the full and active participation of the community in the entire research process"; (3) the community—not the outside researcher—identifies the problem to be researched and then actively engages in analyzing and solving the problem; (4) the community directly benefits from the "ultimate goal" of the research, which is "radical transformation of social reality and the improvement of the lives of the people themselves"; (5) there is an increase in self-awareness: "the process of participatory research can create a greater awareness in the people of their own resources and mobilize them for self-reliant development"; (6) the approach yields an "authentic analysis of social reality"; and (7) there is a direct, not peripheral, involvement of the researcher (p. 12). These seven tenets of participatory research underscore the inherent involvement, personal investment, self-reflection, and overall empowerment of the learners involved in such research.

Similar to participatory research, but having roots in social psychology and management theory, action research typically focuses on "individual, interpersonal, and group levels of analysis" in an effort to support effective social systems (Khanlou & Peter, 2005, p. 2335). In an offshoot of action research, Participatory Action Research (PAR), wherein "Participants are enabled to contribute their physical and/or intellectual resources to the research," (Khanlou & Peter, 2005, p. 2336), there is a combination of action research and participatory research features:

the action research component provides an ongoing, spiral framework where the participants themselves evaluate the validity and the relevance of the research process. The participatory research component incorporates equity and resistance to societal oppression. (Khanlou & Peter, 2005, p. 2335)

Although PAR combines two empowering frameworks (participatory research and action research), and the "process itself can facilitate learning among community members regarding resources for self-determination and research methods" (Khanlou & Peter, 2005, p. 2336), there are ethical issues that can arise. If researchers are not sensitive to social, cultural, and political implications, those involved might be vulnerable to related consequences and unanticipated exposure. Additionally, given that the "knowledge gained from PAR is focused upon action, not understanding alone" (p. 2335), "researchers and ethical reviewers must consider whether a protocol truly has such emancipatory potential" (Khanlou & Peter, 2005, p. 2336).

Furthermore, because forms of participatory research involve co-researchers creating agreements pertaining to each step of the research process—from the design, to each researcher's responsibilities, to data analysis, dissemination, and ownership—there are concerns about equity in the partnership. Community-Based Participatory Research (CBPR), which supports "collaboration and equal partnership between researchers and participants," might have ethical and methodological issues if positioning and power structures are not acknowledged: "there is the potential of tokenistic partnerships and 'false equalitarianism' that can emerge, and as such can cause further harm to participants and the community" (Kwan & Walsh, 2018, p. 374).

Another arm of participatory research is one that includes a critical dialectical pluralist approach. Put simply, critical dialectical pluralism (Onwuegbuzie & Frels, 2013) underscores the integral involvement of the participant-as-co-researcher and helps to flatten conventional hierarchies associated with researcher-driven decisions related to a study's design, data collection and analysis, and dissemination of findings. Critical dialectical pluralism, therefore, specifically works toward

empowering the participants to make research-based decisions at the various stages of the research process (i.e., research conceptualization, research planning, research implementation, research utilization)... [and] either perform or present the findings themselves (e.g., using Web 2.0 applications such as YouTube) or...with the research-facilitator(s). (Onwuegbuzie & Frels, 2013, p. 15)

This methodological and conceptual frame helps to mitigate "token" partnerships and confront existing hierarchical structures. In the case of child-parent research, two are inherently present—the authority of the adults as parents *and* as education researchers.

4.2   *Youth Engaged as Researchers*

The concept of participation becomes a bit muddled when youth are part of the equation, especially because there is a "distinct risk that activities are only labelled 'participation' when they fit comfortably into the agendas of the organising adults" (Tisdall, 2008, p. 422). Therefore, the question of *who* may participate in research as researchers becomes important to address. According to the British Educational Research Association's (2018) *Ethical Guidelines for Educational Research*, "children who are capable of forming their own views should be granted the right to express those views freely in all matters affecting them, commensurate with their age and maturity" (p. 15). Although research suggests that the focus should be on developmental appropriateness instead of age (Chabot et al., 2012; Murray, 2016), there is an important distinction here, namely that children should be able to participate freely as long as, when appropriate, there is consent from a parent or guardian.

Research also suggests that participation, often defined as "taking part in," varies according to country, region, and culture (Mason & Bolzon, 2010, p. 128). For instance, in Asian countries, youth participation typically was associated with obligation, especially given the cultural emphasis on family and community instead of individual right (Mason & Bolzon, 2010). This perspective of participation contrasts with Western, individualistic understandings of "taking part in" activities often designed and orchestrated by adults; ironically, according to Mason and Bolzon, the children in Australia (i.e. Western-based culture) perceived a sense of obligation to participate. What is more, the Western "understanding of participation as investment in the future contrasts with majority-world conceptions of participation as making an active contribution in the present" (Mason & Bolzon, 2010, p. 128). In other words, simply noting that youth are participating in research does not automatically mean that there is equity in the research. If there is a sense of obligation to participate, then hierarchies persist.

Such threads of authority, however, can be mitigated if participation is viewed as decision making, which involves the transference of power between adults and children that can be "potentially transformative of adult-child relations" (Mason & Bolzon, 2010, p. 129). Decision-making based participation does not remove the tensions of authority. Rather, it involves "a commitment to the self understanding and reflexivity of children" in a dialogic, negotiated space of "reciprocal interaction" (Mason & Bolzon, 2010, p. 302). We suggest this inherently involves trusting in the child's forms of contribution regardless of age. As Landsdown (2010) explained, children form and express their views at an early age, and participation should not be limited to age or to the "expression of views in 'adult' language" (p. 12). Furthermore, children are capable of self-reflection and making evidence-based decisions. In Murray's (2016) study of 138 children aged four to eight, children made evidenced-based decisions as a "rational underpinning for forming epistemology—philosophies concerning what they counted as truth and knowledge" (p. 706). In other words, child participation is feasible, relevant, and noteworthy.

More specifically, for Murray's (2016) Young Children As Researchers (YCAR) project, three principles supported the research, which also involved reflexivity: (1) an emancipatory principal rooted in "collectivity, reciprocity, and respect"; (2) a participatory principle based on shared responsibilities and action; and (3) an inductive principle that supported the collaborative construction and interpretation of data (p. 708). Murray discovered that, as the youth partook in co-research with adult researchers, the youth engaged in four overarching research behaviors—"exploration, finding solutions, conceptualisation and basing decisions on evidence" (p. 711). These findings suggest that being a researcher need not be relegated only to those over 18 years of age or with an advanced degree.

Unfortunately, research that reveals children thinking like a researcher from a psychosocial perspective is relatively scant, and investigations that either directly or tangentially consider this area often fall within the realm of creativity studies. Nonetheless, one such line of research considers the young child as scientist and mathematician by exploring the architectural implications in young children's Lego™ and block constructions (Ness & Farenga, 2007). An expert's close analysis of children's constructions demonstrated that when children are engaged in spatially related constructions, they test their ideas, estimate lengths, consider options and alternatives, and even base their actions on previous constructions that might (not) have succeeded. In sum, young children's everyday mathematical and scientific thinking is inextricably linked to that of professional mathematicians and scientists. In a parallel manner, children have the potential to research topics in which they are motivated or inclined to investigate. These results strongly suggest, then, that young people's motivation to engage in research is not only common, but also potentially accessible. This accessibility advances the point that children are key constituents—equal to parents and other adults—within the concept of researcher.

5   Refining the Conceptual Framework for Child-Parent Research

Given the literature supporting youth research behavior (cf. Chabot et al., 2012; Christensen & Prout, 2002; Landsdown, 2010; Mason & Bolzon, 2010; Murray, 2016), coupled with our own research (Abrams, Schaefer, & Ness, 2019; Ness, Schaefer, & Abrams, 2018; Schaefer, Abrams, & Ness, 2018), we continued to flesh out how we conceptualized child-parent research wherein the parent also is a researcher. We soon realized that the role of the child-as-researcher is a continuum (Figure 1.2). On the one end, the child is involved in the research as one who offers or clarifies information, and the adult is the one primarily in charge of designing and conducting the research. Although this may be reminiscent of the research that children are "taking part in" rather than serving as a co-researcher, the child remains central to the study without becoming objectified because the child is, in some way, instrumental in data collection and/or offers insights into the analyses. Thus, the child is a co-constructor of knowledge. Qualitative research that includes the child's words *and* analyses, yet is told through the adult mouthpiece or with an adult filter, would be an example of the child-as-researcher "involved" in the study.

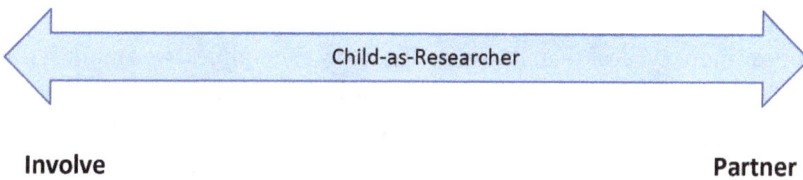

Child-as-Researcher

Involve   **Partner**

FIGURE 1.2   The role of child-as-researcher understood as a continuum

On the other end of the spectrum is the child-as-researcher who "partners" with another researcher (adult or child) and, like any valuable member of a research team, is part of the research process from the study's design through data analysis and forms of presentation. The child-as-researcher is a co-constructor of knowledge *and* of research. A methodology, such as critical dialectical pluralism, in which youth are "intricately and inherently central to conducting and analyzing the data at all phases of inquiry (Onwuegbuzie & Frels, 2013)" (Abrams, Schaefer, & Ness, 2019, p. 82), would fall in this range because the ethos of partnering is embedded in the methodological approach. In terms of child-parent research—unlike other forms of critical dialectical pluralistic research—there is a distinct familiarity among the researchers, and such a familiarity and "close relationship" between the child and parent is key to fostering and sustaining dialogue and working towards a shared purpose (Fitzgerald et al., 2010).

By envisioning the child-as-researcher continuum, we also suggest that there are variations and gradations of involvement and partnership. There is no dichotomy of the verbs, *involve* versus *partner*. Rather, depending on the situation and the child's developmental abilities, the degree of partnership might vary. Also, it is possible that a child might begin as a partner—as part of the team designing the research and collecting and analyzing data, but, due to one or more constraints, including, but not limited to, waning interest or scheduling conflicts, the child remains involved in the study but not as a partner researcher. Likewise, a study might begin with adults structuring the examination and the children involved in the data collection. As time passes and the children become more familiar with the research, their degree of partnership increases, and they might begin to lead the next steps of the investigation or presentation of data (Abrams, Schaefer, & Ness, 2019). The continuum acknowledges the dynamic nature of research and the shifts in involvement and partnership that can occur at any point during the study.

The child-as-researcher continuum also calls attention to the elements we see as inherent in such investigations and discoveries: dialogue, critical reflection, ethics, tension, and participation. Thus, we also envision the continuum to appear more cyclical than linear. As Figure 1.3 exemplifies, we embrace the metaphor of a wheel because the spokes—or the five elements (e.g., dialogue, critical reflection, ethics, tension, and participation)—provide structural integrity for research in which the child is involved or partners with the adult. Without any one of these elements, the participatory nature of the research would begin to falter and give way to traditional, hierarchical research structures.

Furthermore, the metaphor of the wheel serves two purposes: (1) It represents how this research is dynamic and that the child-researcher's role need not be static or relegated to one end of the spectrum. Like a wheel, the research process and level of involvement and partnership can move forward and backward, can spin or turn in different ways, and can rotate with various momenta. The interplay of the five elements can present options for the youth to partner in some ways and be involved in others. (2) It reinforces the importance of each of the five elements. In line with participatory research, the degree of participation is key to the child's role as a researcher. If there is only partial dialogue, then the child may only be involved in that part of the research. However, if there is an ongoing, dialogic relationship among the researchers regardless of their age, then the child becomes a partner in the research. Similarly, when there is deep, critical reflection, the child partners in the research rather than simply responding to prompts. Furthermore, identifying and accounting for tension will be important for any research in which the

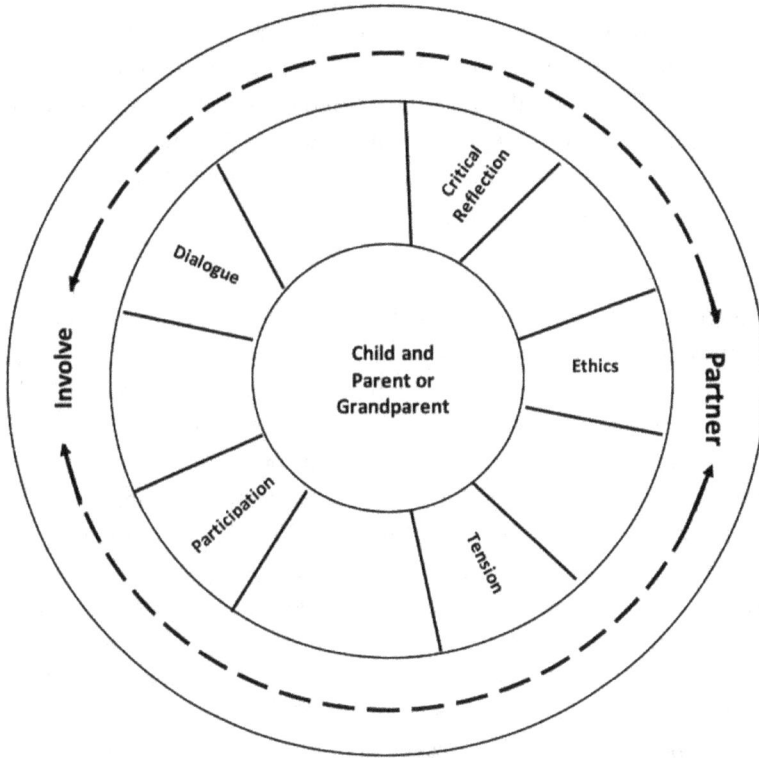

FIGURE 1.3   A conceptual framework for understanding the child as researcher

child is a researcher. An important part of the partnership is when the child-researcher addresses the tension (as opposed to the adult identifying whatever tension is perceived). Finally, as with any study, ethics are essential. However, for child-parent research, the ethical dimensions *must be addressed overtly*. Not only will doing so address concerns about beneficence (i.e., do no harm), but also it will help the field understand how individual studies have ethically and soundly engaged the child-as-researcher.

Because ethics are critical to any research and especially child-parent research, we have developed an ethical framework for research relationships with children-as-researchers. This next section specifically pertains to such a framework.

6   An Ethical Framework for Child-Parent Research

"Children's participation has been one of the most debated and examined aspects of the Convention on the Rights of the Child since it was adopted by the UN in 1989" (Landsdown, 2010, p. 11), and the ethical tensions that surface in research with children might arise because of "a lack of understanding that children have the capacities to contribute to decision making" (Landsdown, 2010, p. 15). In an effort to clarify and build upon the understandings that children can develop and contribute, we offer important definitions of terms and trace discussions of ethics and child participation. We also present an ethical framework for child-parent research.

In accordance with the United Nations' Convention on the Rights of the Child (CRC), an internationally ratified set of standards that explicate children's rights (United Nations, 1989), we define a child as a person under the age of 18. However, in certain contexts, we also use the word "youth" to indicate an older child. We, three education researchers from the United States, should also mention that, while we refer to the CRC throughout this chapter, specifically to Articles 12 and 13, the document itself was ratified by all members of the United Nations with the exception of the United States (Bartholet, 2011). It is our hope that the United States will join the international effort to support youths' rights to seek information and speak freely.

To help communicate the role of children engaged in child-parent research, we take up Christensen and Prout's (2002) definitions of ways children might be positioned in research: They argued that in research with and on children, the child has been perceived in four ways: as an object; as a subject; as a social actor; and "as participants and co-researchers" (Christensen & Prout, 2002, p. 480). The first two positions are common and traditional whereby the child is understood as an object or subject—a being to be acted upon or understood. The third positioning—the child as social actor—understands children as active, social beings who both change and are changed by their social/cultural world. Extant research of parent-researcher examinations of their children or of their own roles as parents acknowledge this standpoint (cf. Kabuto & Martens, 2014). Following work by Alderson (2000) and Woodhead and Faulkner (2000), which recognizes the child as agentive, the fourth perspective "constitutes children as active participants in the research process" with the idea that "children should increasingly become involved as co-researchers" (Christensen & Prout, 2002, p. 481). The third and fourth perspectives reflect a growing body of research that recognizes children's rights and abilities to actively engage in research as knowledgeable and contributing participants (Bell, 2008; Christensen & Prout, 2002; Dockett, Einarsdottir, & Perry, 2009; Lundy & McEvoy, 2011). As the field of child-parent research moves forward, we recognize the rights of the child as inhering in the latter two positions; in this chapter, indeed in this book, children are recognized as social actors, active citizens, and sentient beings who help bring and create knowledge when participating as researchers and co-researchers. The implications of this stance, specifically the ethical implications, will be taken up next.

6.1   *Engaging in Ethical Activity*

Understanding children's position in research as participants and co-researchers necessitates that we identify and contextualize ways that children authentically might be involved in knowledge building and creating. For this discussion, we draw on the literature from the wider field of researchers who conduct research "with" children. To date, there is a dearth of literature on child-parent research, so we look to research that positions children as participants and co-researchers (Christensen & Prout, 2002) to help build a theoretical and ethical space for parents engaging in research with their children in formal and informal spaces. The more traditional approaches that position children as research objects and subjects do not reflect the vision of research that we are presenting here: First, a parent who sees his or her child as a research object or subject potentially squanders rich opportunities that may present themselves when the child is an involved participant or partner in the research context. Additionally, like Murray (2016), we recognize that "when adults deny children opportunities to make decisions in matters affecting them, they subjugate them" (p. 708), and we take issue with that point on an ethical level as well. Hence, we take up Christensen and Prout's definitions of non-traditional research with children as most helpful and relevant to child-parent research. Children are: (1) social actors who "take part in, change and become changed by the social and cultural world that they live in," where children are given "autonomous conceptual status" (p. 481); and (2) "active participants in the research process [promoting] the idea that children be involved, informed, consulted and heard" (p. 481). In this second conception, the child partners with the parent as a co-researcher—but in both conceptions, children's voices, interests, routines, values and desires are foregrounded in the research activity and become the key pieces of a framework for ethical practice.

Ethical research with children moves from a view of research that desires to avoid harm/damage[4] to one that "invites potential positive experiential possibilities" in ways that brings a "positive research experience" to children (Mortari & Harcourt, 2012, p. 236). Accordingly, it is helpful to examine some of the ways that researchers have ensured that the research activities they engage in with children do, indeed, manifest in such a positive experience. Generally, researchers try to promote what Christensen and Prout (2002) call "Ethical symmetry," an a priori assumption whereby "the researcher takes as his or her *starting* point the view that the ethical relationship between researcher and informant is the same whether he or she conducts research with adults or with children" (p. 482, emphasis in original). In practice, this means that the activities involved in research must be drawn from children's "experiences, interests, values and everyday routines" (p. 482). Ethical symmetry means that research activities not only are interesting to the child (Lundy & McEvoy, 2011), but also hinge on listening to children carefully and encouraging verbal interactions (Christensen & Prout, 2002; Dockett, Einarsdottir, & Perry, 2009; Dockett & Perry, 2011).

It also is ethically important, in involved and partner child-parent research, that children exercise choice in research directions and activities—this includes choice of expression (e.g. oral, written, digital representations) and voice in research concerns and agendas (Dockett, Einarsdottir, & Perry, 2009; Mortari & Harcourt, 2012; Pinter & Zandian, 2014). This responsibility is, of course, related to the idea that children are active, agentive cornerstones of the research. Striving for ethical symmetry means that the agency of the child is valued, respected and attended to as an ongoing and integral process of the research (Dockett, Einarsdottir, & Perry, 2009). Attentiveness to the process of consent and the willingness of children to continue in research activities is a critical researcher responsibility and ethical imperative (Bell, 2008; Docket & Perry, 2010). Engaging in quality research with children requires an ethical symmetry that is based on a working relationship built around trust, respect, and reflexivity. Nowhere in the world of research is that special, trusting, valued, respectful relationship more self-evident and important than in formal and informal contexts wherein child/ren and parent/s research together.

6.2   *Ethical Relationships and Responsibilities*
In Figure 1.4, we build on the idea that ethical research with one's own children has different levels and forms of collaboration. We denote positions on a continuum from "involved" to "partner" in order to reflect the idea that there can be degrees of children's participation in research. For example, there might

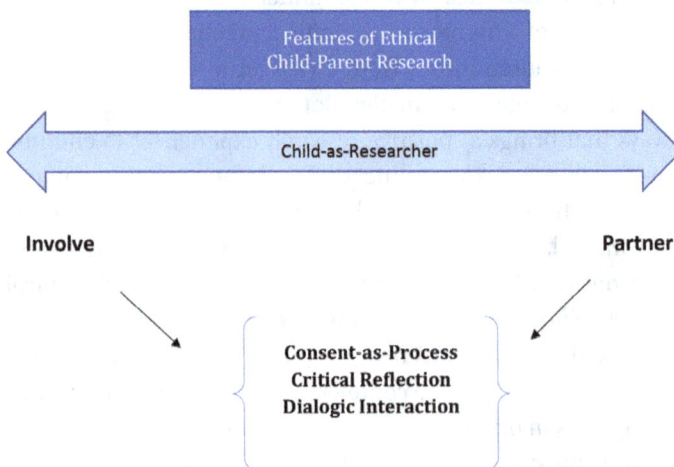

FIGURE 1.4   A conceptual framework for ethics of child-parent research

be developmental reasons to begin research with one's child with different, perhaps minimal levels of involvement, and then as the child becomes more developmentally ready, it can be a mutual decision to move towards a partnering position. In the context of child-parent research, both positions are ethical and imperative. In the involved stance, the "child-as-researcher" participates not as an object to be studied, but as a social actor with his or her own experiences and understandings that require research methods and activities that reflect his or her interests, values and everyday routines (Christensen & Prout, 2002). An ethical child-parent research position, then, commits to drawing research questions from the child's everyday world and adding a layer of communication to that world so that the social actions of children can be carefully understood. Sometimes that might mean just sitting with one's child and observing everyday play activities and interactions. Other times it might be a combination of observation and question—but the ethical position privileges the idea that the research draws from the child's world and his or her interests. On the partner end of the child-parent research continuum, the child desires to participate as a fully engaged co-researcher of his/her everyday activities or experiences. In this position, the child becomes a fully vested partner in the research relationship; this means, among other things, that the child-researcher creates and analyzes data, determines next steps for the research project, and participates in formalizing and reporting findings.

Striving for ethical symmetry in child-parent research means that the child and the parent must confront and negotiate new positions—new ways of looking at power and privilege, new ways of speaking and collaborating, and new ways and opportunities for the child to direct his or her degrees of participation. Engaging in child-parent research involves communicating, and hence listening, in (potentially) new ways. In turn, the nature of the child and parent relationship likely will evolve beyond the confines of an otherwise hierarchical structure. As some of the researchers in this volume can attest, issues of power, authority, boundaries, bias, balance and privacy come to the fore in sometimes disconcerting, discomforting ways. Those moments of disequilibrium can also present rich opportunities for further understanding and inquiry.

The three facets of ethical research that we present here—consent-as-process, critical reflection, and dialogic interaction—are drawn from ethical issues experienced by researchers in this book and designed to help child-parent researchers maintain an ethical stance while enhancing research methods and findings. As such, the ethical framework offers the field opportunities to envision child-parent research while understanding that there remains an openness to update and customize each of these facets as child-parent research evolves.

6.3 *Consent-as-Process*

In order to engage in research activity with children in the United States, the researcher must obtain "assent" from the child and "consent" from the adult. Differentiating "assent" from "consent" builds a negative connotation for the former word; because "consent" must be given by the adult guardian, "assent" implies a lack of full understanding of the research, with children needing an authority's "consent" to compensate for that lack of understanding. In this section, we prefer to draw upon the British Educational Research Association's (2018) *Ethical Guidelines for Educational Research* and use the word "consent" to describe the child's role in child-parent research.[5] Focusing on consent instead of assent helps to illustrate parent-researchers' ongoing commitment to leading their children in full knowledge of their rights and responsibilities. Consent implies knowledge. Consent implies power. Seeking *ongoing* consent from the child-researcher is a continuous process and ethical burden of the parent-researcher.

In her research on adults reflecting on childhood trauma, Etherington (2005) recommended obtaining "process consent," as a way of "ensuring at each stage that participants are still willing to be involved in the project and reminding them of their right to withdraw at any time" (p. 305). In child-parent research, making consent an ongoing part of the research process is essential (Dockett, Einarsdottir, & Perry, 2009; Kabuto, 2008), especially in light of some of the issues that can come to the fore, including bias, balance, power, and boundaries. Take, for instance, issues of ethical symmetry that might arise when a parent-researcher enters into new and perhaps secret spaces of their child's world—perhaps the inner world of thought, or the world of private play. Although the child has chosen to disclose this information, a veil has been lifted to some degree. Both the child- and parent-researcher need to consider the boundaries of ethical participation, asking questions, such as: What is kept private? What kind of surveillance is an inherent part of play (vis-à-vis video-game play)? How, if at all, is ongoing observation allowable? Even with a child's ongoing consent, is it okay to shift the context and adjust play in service of some research agenda? While we revisit these kinds of questions later when we talk about critical reflection, they are also germane to issues of consent.

One way to obtain and secure ongoing consent is to develop a strategy of asking children, before each planned or spontaneous research session, questions such as: Do you want to participate in this session? How do you want to participate? Here the parent is in a privileged position of familiarity: the parent-researcher might notice that her/his child's body language suggests the need for privacy. The parent-researcher might also know that her/his child did not sleep well that night or had an argument with a best friend. These contextual influences matter. It may be argued that parents are in the best position to "read" their child's willingness to consent. An awareness of power imbalances and a commitment to ongoing discussions of the research itself (Dockett & Perry, 2011) help support children in their decisions about consent. In ongoing and frank discussions about consent, it always should be made clear to children that any kind of participation—long term or short term—is their choice (Dockett & Perry, 2011). Additionally, over time, the child-researcher will develop the language and routine for discussing ongoing consent, and, although the parent-researcher will need to remain continuously vigilant of ethics, the child-researcher will become instrumental in creating and adjusting degrees of participation and offering boundary-setting and boundary-extending language and designs for research. Critical reflection is essential for achieving such agentive ethical work.

6.4   *Critical Reflection*

Although engaging in thoughtful reflection about one's own biases and assumptions is an important element of most research methods, when engaging in child-parent research, this element is crucial. Here both child and parent can foreground particular issues and tensions that arise during the course of their research together, including, but not limited to, relationships, boundaries, power, surveillance, control, privacy and trust. The fact that these components are not static adds another layer of complexity and underscores the importance of ongoing critical reflection. Each researcher has an ethical responsibility to consider and discuss the intended or unintended consequences of participating in research together (Dockett & Perry, 2011). In research that claims a level of ethical symmetry, both the child's and the parent's reflections inform the research processes and findings.

Critical reflection can appear in formal and informal capacities. For instance, child- and parent-researchers alike might keep research memos in which they record how they feel that day about the dynamic of the research team, the direction the research is taking, the role(s) each researcher is playing, and what, if any, assumptions the child is making about the parent or the parent is making about the child. For the latter, it is essential for the child- and parent-researcher to remain cognizant of how, when, and why they use their knowledge of the other to provide context. Take, for instance, a child discussing his/her favorite music. The parent might unintentionally insert his/her knowledge that the child has enjoyed listening to Ed Sheeran. Yet, the child might be thinking about a new artist or genre that the parent did not consider or is unaware of at that point in time. Moments like these—when thoughts run parallel—must be accounted for in any research, but especially in child-parent research because of the inherent hierarchy that accompanies conventional family structures. We are not saying that critical reflection will mitigate assumptions although that might be possible over time. Rather, we advocate for ongoing critical reflection that accounts for in-the-moment and retrospective constructs of how each of the researchers, regardless of age, has (a) presented oneself to the research team and to the data collection process—this can include a range of behaviors revealing levels of openness, trust, or (dis)interest; (b) inserted internal dialogue to make sense of the data; (c) interpreted and understood the data and developed analyses; and (d) built upon previous experiences. Hence, critical reflection is central to securing trustworthiness in (and of) the data, as well as advancing the inquiry's shared objectives.

Informally, the child and parent can speak aloud or jot in the margins of transcripts of meeting minutes their assumptions and surprises. When reviewing research meeting transcripts, for instance, the child and parent separately (or together) might write questions that arise, note what surprised him/her, and admit assumptions circulating as an inner dialogue. It is especially important to reflect critically upon the inner dialogue—that which one thinks but does not necessarily speak aloud—because the integrity of child-parent research is upheld by the ongoing, dialogic relationship between the child and the parent.

The child new to the field of research might not immediately critically reflect upon the experience. Instead, the child might need prompts to help spur such reflection, and these prompts—preferably designed by the child and parent together, but possibly designed by the parent-researcher—also should guide the parent-researcher's critical reflection. The child might reflect upon (a) what was confusing and not confusing; (b) ideas that were articulated; (c) ideas that arose but were not said aloud and explain why the ideas were not voiced; (d) feelings of confidence or lack thereof; (e) discoveries about the parent; (f) concerns about and hopes for the research trajectory.

Additionally, the research team needs to engage in ongoing critical reflections about methods and ethics, including, but not limited to, the research agenda, personal discoveries, and the child-parent relationship in and beyond the roles as research team members. Furthermore, each member of the research team needs to remain sensitive to the inner workings of the child-parent research relationship. A dialogic partnership needs to include a discussion about how, when, what, where, and why data collection and analysis can and will take place. This means establishing and re-establishing the boundaries of the research. Critical reflection is at the heart of such an iterative approach and further develops the trustworthiness of the data and the ethics and the integrity of the research process.

6.5 *Dialogic Interaction*

As mentioned previously, the United Nations Convention on the Rights of the Child (CRC) (United Nations, 1989) resulted in a series of articles related to the rights of children. Of particular interest to child-parent research are Articles 12 and 13. Article 12 stipulates the right of the child to form and express his or her views, and Article 13 claims, "The child shall have the right to freedom of expression; this right shall include freedom to seek, receive and impart information and ideas of all kinds...either orally, in writing or in print, in the form of art, or through any other media of the child's choice" (UNCRC, 1989). Both of these claims address the responsibility of the adult researcher to build a research culture that cultivates and privileges dialogic interaction.

How do child- and parent-researchers know when the conversations and interactions they have with each other are dialogic? Recognizing the call for a dialogic research relationship with children (Fitzgerald et al., 2010), we also use the term "dialogic," but through a Bakhtinian lens to signal conversations that are fluid, relational, and dynamic. Bakhtin (1984) talks about two speech concepts that are helpful to explore when thinking about discussions that represent an authentic co-construction of knowledge: dialogization and heteroglossia. Dialogization refers to interactions whereby language, culture, and discourse infuse in speech exchanges so that there is a negotiation of values and meaning. Its opposite, authoritative, monologic discourse, "permits no play with the context framing it" (p. 343). In authoritative, often adult-led discourse, there is only one meaning. Heteroglossia supports the dialogic approach because it embraces multiple meanings and the "centripetal forces of the life of language" (p. 271) that work against the norm—against the authoritative discourse, or what Bakhtin calls "official" language. Heteroglossia invites a multiplicity of ideas, voices and opinions. It challenges the authoritative discourse sometimes adopted by parents and many researchers. Infusing children's voices in dialogue in, on, and about research creates opportunities for deeper understanding. Bakhtin suggests that "understanding and response are dialectically merged and mutually condition each other; one is impossible without the other" (p. 282). Affordances related to these active speech acts are exciting to think about in the context of child-parent research. As Bakhtin explains, "every utterance is oriented toward this apperceptive background of understanding, which is not a linguistic background but rather one composed of specific objects and emotional expressions" (p. 281). In research where new knowledge and understandings are enabled by dialogized interactions, having a child-researcher and parent-researcher who are already familiar with each other's culture, values, and ideas can provide a context for dialogization that produces stunning insights, new knowledge, and perhaps even a new kind of research discourse.

In dialogic, heteroglossic conversations with children researchers, the child participant is a full partner in any discussion (Ely, 1991/2003). Referring to our metaphor of the wheel (Figure 1.3), we contend that such a dialogic, hetero-glossic relationship—and, thus, the level of involvement or partnership—is both discursive and recursive. Continued communication and re-evaluation help to build and sustain ethical strength and support the integrity of the research process.

Because the parent-researcher has the privilege of previous experience with scientific inquiry, the initial and ongoing onus is on the parent to ensure that the investigation is ethical and thoughtful. Furthermore, parent-researchers cannot expect their children to engage in research automatically. The child and the parent need to work in tandem as they begin and continue their inves-tigation. Relatedly, in their discussion of engaging in meaningful research with children, Lundy and McEvoy (2011) argued that, although the research litera-ture is "replete with efforts to ensure that practices are respectful and attend to a number of key children's rights issues in critical, reflexive ways" (p. 130), there remains an issue with helping children to understand their own views and formulate a way to express those views. While Lundy and McEvoy (2011) developed strategies to help children build capacities for participating in dis-cussions of research, in the child-parent relationship, those capacities can be understood and developed in very different ways given that parents and chil-dren can engage in research activities in a wide variety of contexts (i.e. cars, stores, home, playgroups) and a child's understanding of her/his parent (and vice versa) can help facilitate discussions of research findings. In many cases, the parent can support the child when research discussions or activities falter. Clarifying questions and queries can be built around the child's known inter-ests and abilities. Furthermore, an ethical, dialectical position helps to create a safe space wherein the child can make spontaneous, perhaps "off-topic" remarks, asking questions, and moving the discussion (and research) in ways that the child finds interesting or important (Pinter & Zandian, 2014). In this way, heteroglossia is invited, dialogic interactions are courted, and new under-standings are acquired.

7   Towards a New Epistemology

By staking a claim for child-parent research and offering a conceptual and ethical framework for such study, we work towards a new epistemology for research in which the child-researcher and parent-researcher work together to co-construct knowledge. This requires an understanding and belief that chil-dren, even at a young age, have the ability and desire to communicate, explore, and explain. It also requires that adults resist applying their own values and language to understand and express what the child-researcher is communi-cating (Landsdown, 2010; Murray, 2016). In short, in ethically symmetrical child-parent research, the child's voice permeates every aspect of knowledge construction—from research activities, processes and findings to conclusions and ideas for future study.

The field of child-parent research is nascent indeed and not without epistemological challenges. The authoritative voice of the researcher is nec-essarily challenged and changed. In ethically symmetrical research, the parent-researcher and his or her child together create a different kind of dis-course around research: It is dialogized, it is heteroglossic, and in some ways, it is rebellious. Child-parent research, as envisioned here, not only blurs the lines of traditional research and familial relationships, but also has the capacity to change those lines and shift boundaries. This blurring, bending, and shifting is enabled by an involved or partnering child whose voice is valued, discern-able, and authentic, and whose interests and abilities are embedded in the pro-cesses and products of the research itself.

In ethically symmetrical child-parent research, research trajectories and activities are decided with children, based on their routines and interests. Par-ents who research their children as subjects or objects risk privileging hierar-chical structures, invoking specious partnerships, and promoting undialogized findings. That is not what we are advocating here. Rather, the child-parent research we envision hinges on an ongoing, dialogic relationship between child-researcher and parent-researcher with the collaboration focused on a shared purpose (Fitzgerald et al., 2010) and requires a parent-child relationship that is carefully cultivated to be egalitarian, inclusive, dialogic, and reciprocal. The positioning of child as research partner becomes important to acknowl-edge and remain acutely aware of because child-parent research inherently confronts traditional, authoritative and hierarchical structures that typically privilege the adult researcher's values, voices, and viewpoints. As the wheel in Figure 1.3 suggests, power structures and ethical dimensions should be taken up overtly, with thoughtfulness, courage, and creativity. The continuum intro-duced in Figure 1.4 builds on these dimensions and offers ways to imagine, reimagine, and value degrees of child participation in research activities so that children are empowered not only as investigators of meaning making, but also as meaning makers themselves.

From the area at the far end of our continuum, where the child is a research partner, we expect that a new kind of academic discourse will be created. We understand that this new kind of discourse, born of child-parent research collaboration, likely will challenge the norms of the academy. As Bakhtin (1984) warned, "linguistic norms" work within "an officially recognized literary language" in order to defend "an already formed language from the pressure of growing heteroglossia" (p. 271). Much as Kuhn (1977) described normalizing forces that resist paradigmatic shifts, so too does language seek to coalesce, centralize, and preserve the status quo. Academic writing has a distinct cadence and tone. Traditionally, when academic language includes children's thoughts, words, and ideas, these child-focused pieces are put in their place—contextualized, as it were, within a larger framework—be it research findings, framework (i.e. narrative inquiry), methods, or conclusions. In child-parent research on the other hand, the child's own words, thoughts, values and interests can be flung from the margins and into the academic work itself. After all, like an adult member of a research team, the child-researcher analyzes the data and offers interpretations that shape the research trajectory.

The dialogization of academic writing is not without risk—infusing children's voices in knowledge building activities has the potential to disrupt norms while also challenging editors, review board members, and fellow researchers. The field should not cower from such a paradigmatic shift. Rather, with an openness to change and the excitement of developing new knowledge, the field needs to embrace the potentials of the child-researcher as partner and support inquiries led by child-parent research teams.

7.1   *Reimagining Research*

Over 25 years ago, Cochran-Smith and Lytle (1993) forged an important path by calling for teachers as researchers. In the same way, our edited collection intends to open methodological, epistemological, and ontological arms to the child's voice, especially at every facet of scientific inquiry. Although the contributing authors herein present a diversity of ways in which children engage in research—accounts that involve and partner with child-researchers, as well as feature retrospective methods—our goal is to elevate the roles that children play in the unfolding of research to one whereby children and other frequently alienated groups are demarginalized from the process. Indeed, child-parent research needs to be rigorous, methodical, ethical, and careful; we contend it needs to be all the more rigorous than conventional research in that children's participation—whether it be one of involvement or one of partnership—demands a meting out of appropriate ethical practices that protect historically marginalized populations and extend otherwise traditional boundaries that separate the researcher from the researched. Although skepticism is a healthy counterpart to novelty, it is our hope to overcome obstacles that are often set by critics who are steadfast on keeping the status quo in terms of who does the researching. We argue that, instead of hermetically sealing research and researcher boundaries and roles, scholars should engage in hermeneutical debates (Packer & Addison, 1989) to further consider the ethics and logistics of child-parent research.

To be sure, we anticipate the provocative disposition of this book. The overarching purpose, to call attention to the child-researcher working along with her/his parent-researcher—prompts the field to reimagine methods and approaches that challenge traditional, hierarchical constructs and embrace partnerships with ethical strength and integrity. This edited volume provides a robust account of what it means to do research within the broad continuum of child-parent investigations, with involvement on one side and partnership on the other. The community of scholars—in our context, the field of education research—already has witnessed metamorphoses with regard to who does research, with whom, when, and where. The field cannot be complacent and needs to consider the far-reaching implications of participatory research that reaches those otherwise silenced, be it because of race, ethnicity, or age (to name a few factors). The work in this volume pushes boundaries by offering a new epistemology for research with the child-as-researcher and the child-parent research team offering new dimensions for inquiries and understandings.

8   Opening Spaces for Future Directions

This edited volume is intended to be a vista for the *some of the ways* in which child-parent research can exist and what it can mean for research in general. Purposefully provocative and offering a variety of accounts of child-parent research, this collection also provides the field an entree to exploring and expanding what previous education researchers have started—learning from and, we contend, with their children. We use a continuum to represent a range of child-parent research, and a continuum is apt, for the arrows point in directions that may yet to be realized.

Consider, for example, the idea of dialogizing academic writing whereby children's conceptual, theoretical and/or methodological work is visibly partnered with that of their researcher parents. In dialogized writing we might see and hear children's voices working through problems of practice—and whether they write or have their thoughts transcribed, these voices might have a different tone from the parlance of senior researchers' published works. We contend that the field needs to hear youth voices raw, and no one should shy away from language or beliefs that push against established structures and ways of being. Critical participatory research with youth begins to break this barrier as well, opening even more possibilities to youth articulations and representations of meaning making.

Additionally, the youths' ideas, thoughts and musings are not just considered data. In partnered child-parent research, children's voices are authoritative, explanatory, and legitimate. One example of dialogized writing can be seen in the last chapter of this book, where the unadulterated thoughts and musings of our children, with whom we have partnered in research, give us inside knowledge of what it means to be adolescent researchers partnering with their parents. Given that this is an edited collection, we six as a child-parent research team agreed that honoring the child-researchers' unadulterated (and un-"adult"ed) voice would be essential. The child-researchers asked that no one "meddle with" their written work, and having their work featured separately is but one way to respect the partnership and offers another layer of integrity. Readers hear directly from the child-researchers. This is not to discredit a combined approach, which underscores a partnership across all facets of the research process (Abrams, Schaefer, & Ness, 2019). We challenge the field to contemplate a variety of permutations of partnership in writing, considering what these musings might look like in a research article where both child and parent muse, reflect, ruminate and investigate either in tandem or in a combined fashion.

We also call for a closer examination of two specific points of privilege. First, there are education researchers who might not have the "convenience" of co-researching with children or grandchildren. We contend that child-parent research is, in fact, inconvenient, because of the great lengths necessary to work against existing hierarchies. In fact, it is important for child- and parent-researchers to engage in the investigation at times separate from daily routines and household responsibilities. This is a difficult task given the child's school, social, and work activities coupled with the parent's work and home responsibilities. And, given the parent's research experience, at least initially, the task of carving out specific times for research is likely to fall on the parent, an action that risks undermining the flattening of hierarchies. Furthermore, there is the essential and difficult task to avoid assumptions that arise when there is familiarity among the research team. For example, the child might make a claim about limited screentime, and the parent, who has a different perception, must negotiate the boundaries of opinion and judgment. Child-parent research requires exquisite awareness of ways in which a research relationship influences and is influenced by the familial parent-child relationship. These kinds of reflections are a necessary responsibility and challenging component of child-parent research. Additionally, not all children of researchers will want to engage in co-research, and we encourage the field to recognize that child-parent research is neither easy nor quite accessible.

Second, there is the privilege of access to educational resources and research experiences. More specifically, the U.S. Department of Education National Center for Education Statistics (2018) identifies a racial disparity among full-time faculty, which, in turn could perpetuate a similar privilege among child-researchers:

> Of all full-time faculty in degree-granting postsecondary institutions in fall 2016, 41 percent were White males; 35 percent were White females; 6 percent were Asian/Pacific Islander males; 4 percent were Asian/Pacific Islander females; 3 percent each were Black males, Black females, and Hispanic males; and 2 percent were Hispanic females. Those who were American Indian/Alaska Native and those who were of two or more races each made up 1 percent or less of full-time faculty in these institutions.

We acknowledge this racial disparity as problematic and call for child-parent research to include more families of underrepresented communities. This means not only seeing more equity within academia—something that is long overdue—but also extending the boundaries of *who can do research*. We call for the inclusion of child-parent research beyond the walls of academia and the exploration of child-parent research as part of school curricula; such curricula likely will be structured, but they cannot be scripted because there needs to be a flexibility and an ongoing conversation that evolves and develops over time. This also will require children and parents learning together, and support of child-parent research communities will be essential. Furthermore, the increase in critical examinations of research could support child- and parent-researcher consciousness of privilege and racial disparities. Such a raised consciousness is but one step in making important changes to achieve greater equity.

Future directions require bold research with children's voices. This might surprise, displease, and even offend those in the educational community, especially when the research pushes at the ends of the child-as-researcher continuum (see Figure 1.2). What is clear, however, is that this line of research needs to be addressed at greater length. We envision a time when children engaging in educational research becomes a normative practice. Thus, we call for greater conversations about methods and greater openness to hear what children are saying about research, about themselves as researchers, and about the child-parent research team dynamic. As we look to expand future child-parent research, interested children and their parents might consider forming research communities where support and collaboration can help to push crucial conversations about research issues such as methods and ethics. We also call for academic journals to solicit child-parent research and consider special issues and collections. Working together, and especially with more longitudinal child-parent studies informing the field, we imagine ways that the aforementioned continuum might become clarified, challenged, or confirmed, and we support a line of research that promises to inform understandings of meaning making, to centralize the voice of the child, to underscore ethical research, and to strive for greater equity in educational research and practice.

Notes

1   In this volume, the terms, "child" or "youth," are used to indicate any person under the age of 18 years old. At times, distinctions are made among young child, young adolescent, and adolescent (or teen).
2   Grandchild-grandparent scholarship is subsumed into the child-parent scholarship paradigm.
3   We use the term "intellectual development" here in the same light as did Piaget and his predecessors, mainly Alfred Binet and Theodore Simon, whereby "intellectual" refers not to "intelligence" (as early twentieth-century American psychologists and the developers of the IQ would have it), but to the notion of the knowledge of an individual—what the individual knows within a particular topic.
4   We are not suggesting that anyone should inflict harm. Rather, we suggest that ethical research can be about possibilities, as well as protection.
5   The British Educational Research Association's (2018) *Ethical Guidelines for Educational Research* notes that there are instances when child assent and parental consent are necessary: "In the case of participants whose capacity, age or other vulnerable circumstance may limit the extent to which they can be expected to understand or agree voluntarily to participate, researchers should fully explore ways in which they can be supported to participate with assent in the research. In such circumstances, researchers should also seek the collaboration and approval of those responsible for such participants" (p. 15).

References

Abrams, S. S., Schaefer, M. B., & Ness, D. (2019). Adolescents' digital literacies in flux: Intersections of voice, empowerment, and practices. *Journal of Media Literacy Education, 11*(2), 79–94.
Alexanderson, G. L. (2000). *The random walks of George Pólya.* New York, NY: Cambridge University Press.

Baghban, M. (1984). *Our daughter learns to read and write: A case study from birth to three*. Newark, DE: International Reading Association.

Baghban, M. (2014). Looking backward in order to look forward. In B. Kabuto & P. Martens (Eds.), *Linking families, learning, and schooling: Parent-research perspectives* (pp. 138–151). New York, NY: Routledge.

Bakhtin, M. M. (1984). *The dialogic imagination: Four essays* (Vol. 1). Austin, TX: University of Texas Press.

Bartholet, E. (2011). Ratification by the United States of the convention on the rights of the child: Pros and cons from a child's rights perspective. *The ANNALS of the American Academy of Political and Social Science, 633*(1), 80–101.

Bell, N. (2008). Ethics in child research: Rights, reason and responsibilities. *Children's Geographies, 6*(1), 7–20.

Bissex, G. L. (1980). *Gnys at wrk: A child learns to read and write*. Cambridge, MA: Harvard University Press.

Blum-Ross, A., & Livingstone, S. (2017). Sharenting: Parent blogging and the boundaries of the digital self. *Popular Communication, 15*(2), 110–125.

Bowden, B. V. (1953). *Faster than thought: A symposium on digital computing machines*. New York, NY: Pitman.

Braine, M. D. S. (1962). Piaget on reasoning: A methodological critique and alternative proposals. In W. Kessen & C. Kuhlman (Eds.), *Thought in the young child. Monographs of the Society for Research in Child Development, 27*(2), 41–63.

British Educational Research Association (BERA). (2018). *Ethical guidelines for educational research* (4th ed.). London. Retrieved from https://www.bera.ac.uk/wp-content/uploads/2018/06/BERA-Ethical-Guidelines-for-Educational-Research_4thEdn_2018.pdf

Ceci, S. J., Williams, W. M., & Barnett, S. M. (2009). Women's underrepresentation in science: Sociocultural and biological considerations. *Psychological Bulletin, 135*, 218–261.

Chabot, C., Shoveller, J. A., Spencer, G., & Johnson, J. L. (2012). Ethical and epistemological insights: A case study of participatory action research with young people. *Journal of Empirical Research on Human Research Ethics: An International Journal, 7*(2), 20–33.

Christensen, P., & Prout, A. (2002). Working with ethical symmetry in social research with children. *Childhood, 9*(4), 477–497.

Cochran-Smith, M., & Lytle, S. L. (1993). *Inside/outside: Teacher research and knowledge*. New York, NY: Teachers College Press.

Dezuanni, M. (2018). Minecraft and children's digital making: Implications for media literacy education. *Learning, Media and Technology, 43*(3), 236–249.

Dockett, S., Einarsdottir, J., & Perry, B. (2009). Researching with children: Ethical tensions. *Journal of Early Childhood Research, 7*(3), 283–298.

Dockett, S., & Perry, B. (2011). Researching with young children: Seeking assent. *Child Indicators Research, 4*(2), 231–247.

Dyehouse, J., & Manke, K. (2017). The philosopher as parent: John Dewey's observations of his children's language development and the development of his thinking about communication. *Education and Culture, 33*(1), 3–22.

Edwards, P. A., Spiro, R. J., Domke, L. M., Castle, A. M., White, K. L., Peltier, M. R., & Donohue, T. H. (2019). *Partnering with families for student success: 24 scenarios for problem solving with parents.* New York, NY: Teachers College Press.

Ely, M. (1991/2003). *Doing qualitative research: Circles within circles.* New York, NY: Routledge.

Erickson, F. (1993). Foreword. In M. Cochran-Smith & S. L. Lytle (Eds.), *Inside/outside: Teacher research and knowledge* (pp. vii–ix). New York, NY: Teachers College Press.

Etherington, K. (2005). Researching trauma, the body and transformation: A situated account of creating safety in unsafe places. *British Journal of Guidance & Counselling, 33*(3), 299–313.

Fitzgerald, R., Graham, A., Smith, A., & Taylor, N. (2010). Children's participation as a struggle over recognition: Exploring the promise of dialogue. In B. Percy-Smith & N. Thomas (Eds.), *A handbook of children and young people's participation: Perspectives from theory and practice* (pp. 293–305). Abingdon: Routledge.

Frankel, H. (1987). The continental drift debate. In H. T. Engelhardt Jr. & A. L. Caplan (Eds.), *Scientific controversies: Case studies in the resolution and closure of disputes in science and technology* (pp. 203–248). Cambridge: Cambridge University Press.

Gee, J. P. (2003). *What video games have to teach us about learning and literacy.* New York, NY: Palgrave McMillian.

Ginsburg, H. P., Pappas, S., & Seo, K. H. (2001). Everyday mathematical knowledge: Asking young children what is developmentally appropriate. In S. L. Golbeck (Ed.), *Psychological perspectives on early childhood education: Reframing dilemmas in research and practice* (pp. 181–219). Mahwah, NJ: Lawrence Erlbaum Associates.

Goodman, Y. M. (2014). Foreword: Learning lessons from our children and grandchildren. In B. Kabuto & P. Martens (Eds.), *Linking families, learning, and schooling: Parent-research perspectives* (pp. xi–xvi). New York, NY: Routledge.

Goodman, Y., & Goodman, K. (2013). Shoshana learns to write: A longitudinal study. In R. Meyer & K. Whitmore (Eds.), *Reclaiming writing: Composing spaces for identities, relationships, and actions.* New York, NY: Routledge.

Graue, M. E., Walsh, D. J., & Ceglowski, D. (1998). *Studying children in context: Theories, methods, and ethics.* Thousand Oaks, CA: Sage.

Hackett, A. (2017). Parents as researchers: Collaborative ethnography with parents. *Qualitative Research, 17*(5), 481–497.

Haddix, M. M. (2014). Preparing teachers to teach other people's children while homeschooling your own: One Black woman scholar's story. In B. Kabuto & P. Martens

(Eds.), *Linking families, learning, and schooling: Parent-research perspectives* (pp. 66–79). New York, NY: Routledge.

Hall, B. L. (1981). Participatory research, popular knowledge and power: A personal reflection. *Convergence, 14*(3), 6–17.

Hall, B. L. (2005). In from the cold? Reflections on participatory research from 1970–2005. *Convergence, 38*(1), 5–24.

Halliday, M. A. K. (1975). *Learning how to mean: Explorations in the development of language.* New York, NY: Elsevier.

Kabuto, B. (2008). Parent-research as a process of inquiry: An ethnographic perspective. *Ethnography and Education, 3*(2), 177–194.

Kabuto, B. (2014). What do those marks really mean? A simiotic perspective to writing in a bilingual context. In B. Kabuto & P. Martens (Eds.), *Linking families, learning, and schooling: Parent-research perspectives* (pp. 19–33). New York, NY: Routledge.

Khanlou, N., & Peter, E. (2005). Participatory action research: Considerations for ethical review. *Social Science & Medicine, 60*, 2333–2340.

Kress, G. (1982). *Learning to write.* London: Routledge & Kegan Paul Ltd.

Kuhn, T. S. (1977). *The essential tension: Selected studies in scientific tradition and change.* Chicago, IL: University of Chicago Press.

Kuryłowicz, J. (1935). *Études indoeuropéenes.* Krakow, Poland: Polska Akademia Umiejetnosci.

Kwan, C., & Walsh, C.A. (2018). Ethical issues in conducting community-based participatory research: A narrative review of the literature. *The Qualitative Report, 23*(2), 269–386.

Landsdown, G. (2010). The realisation of children's participation rights: Critical reflections. In B. Percy-Smith & N. Thomas (Eds.), *A handbook of children and young people's participation: Perspectives from theory and practice* (pp. 11–23). Abingdon: Routledge.

Leopold, W. (1939). *Speech development of a bilingual child: A linguist's record.* Evaston, IL: Northwestern University.

Long, S. (2004). Passionless text and phonics first: Through a child's eyes. *Language Arts, 81*(5), 417–426.

Long, S., & Long, K. (2014). They don't really know me: Mother-daughter insights for researchers and teachers. In B. Kabuto & P. Martens (Eds.), *Linking families, learning, and schooling: Parent-research perspectives* (pp. 123–137). New York, NY: Routledge.

López-Robertson, J. (2014). My gift to you is my language: Spanish is the language of my heart. In B. Kabuto & P. Martens (Eds.), *Linking families, learning, and schooling: Parent-research perspectives* (pp. 80–91). New York, NY: Routledge.

Lundy, L., & McEvoy, L. (2011). Children's rights and research processes: Assisting children to (in) formed views. *Childhood, 19*(1), 129–144.

Maderazo, C. O. (2014). The struggle for literacy: Leo's story. In B. Kabuto & P. Martens (Eds.), *Linking families, learning, and schooling: Parent-research perspectives* (pp. 51–65). New York, NY: Routledge.

Martens, P. (1996). *I already know how to read: A child's view of literacy*. Portsmouth, NH: Heinemann.

Martens, P. (2014). "I already know how to read!" Home and school perceptions of literacy. In B. Kabuto & P. Martens (Eds.), *Linking families, learning, and schooling: Parent-research perspectives* (pp. 92–106). New York, NY: Routledge.

Mason, J., & Bolzan, N. (2010). Questioning understandings of children's participation: Applying a cross-cultural lens. In B. Percy-Smith & N. Thomas (Eds.), *A handbook of children and young people's participation: Perspectives from theory and practice* (pp. 125–132). Abingdon: Routledge.

McCarty, G. M. (2012). *Family science: An ethnographic case study of the ordinary science and literacy experiences of one family* (Doctoral dissertation). Retrieved from https://irl.umsl.edu/dissertation/332

Miller, E. T. (2014). Whiteness, discourse, and early childhood: An ethnographic study of three young children's construction of race in home and community settings. In B. Kabuto & P. Martens (Eds.), *Linking families, learning, and schooling: Parent-research perspectives* (pp. 34–48). New York, NY: Routledge.

Mortari, L., & Harcourt, D. (2012). 'Living' ethical dilemmas for researchers when researching with children. *International Journal of Early Years Education, 20*(3), 234–243.

Murray, J. (2016). Young children are researchers: Children aged four to eight years engage in important research behaviour when they base decisions on evidence. *European Early Childhood Education Research Journal, 24*(5), 705–720.

Ness, D., & Farenga, S. J. (2007). *Knowledge under construction: The importance of play in developing children's spatial and geometric thinking*. Lanham, MD: Rowman & Littlefield Publishers.

Ness, D., Schaefer, M. B., Abrams, S. S., Ness, E., Kurpis, M., & Abrams, C. (2018, May). *Rethinking Piaget and adolescent intellectual development through play: Adolescent co-researchers examine multimodal digital activities*. Jean Piaget Society Conference, Amsterdam, The Netherlands.

O'Mara, J., & Laidlaw, L. (2011). Living in the iworld: Two literacy researchers reflect on the changing texts and literacy practices of childhood. *English Teaching: Practice and Critique, 10*(4), 149–159.

Onwuegbuzie, A. J., & Frels, R. K. (2013). Introduction: Towards a new research philosophy for addressing social justice issues: Critical dialectical pluralism 1.0. *International Journal of Multiple Research Approaches, 7*, 9–26.

Packer, M. J., & Addison, R. B. (1989). Introduction. In M. J. Packer & R. B. Addison (Eds.), *Entering the circle: Hermeneutic investigation in psychology* (pp. 13–38). Albany, NY: State University of New York Press.

Piaget, J. (1952). *The origins of intelligence in children* (2nd ed.). New York, NY: International Universities Press. (Original published 1936)

Pinter, A., & Zandian, S. (2014). 'I don't ever want to leave this room': Benefits of researching 'with' children. *ELT Journal, 68*(1), 64–74.

Polya, G. (1957). *How to solve it: A new aspect of mathematical method.* Princeton, NJ: Princeton University Press.

Schaefer, M. B., Abrams, S. S., Ness, D., Kurpis, M., Abrams, C., & Ness, E. (2018, October). *What middle grades students discovered while researching with parents.* Annual Conference for Middle Level Education, Orlando, FL.

Shannon, K., & Shannon, P. (2014). At home at school: Following our children. In B. Kabuto & P. Martens (Eds.), *Linking families, Learning, and schooling: Parent-research perspectives* (pp. 107–120). New York, NY: Routledge.

Theunissen, N. C. M., Vogels, T. G. C., Koopman, H. M., Verrips, G. H. W., Zwinderman, K. A. H., Verloove-Vanhorick, S. P., & Wit, J. M. (1998). The proxy problem: Child report versus parent report in health-related quality of life research. *Quality of Life Research, 7,* 387–397.

Tisdall, E. K. M. (2008). Is the honeymoon over? Children and young people's participation in public decision-making. *International Journal of Children's Rights, 16,* 419–429.

United Nations. (1989). *Convention on the rights of the child.* Retrieved July 30, 2019, from https://www.ohchr.org/en/professionalinterest/pages/crc.aspx

U.S. Department of Education, National Center for Education Statistics. (2018). *The condition of education 2018* (NCES 2018-144). Characteristics of Postsecondary Faculty.

Wazeck, M. (2014). *Einstein's opponents: The public controversy about the theory of relativity in the 1920s.* New York, NY: Cambridge University Press.

Wolf, M. (1992). *A thrice-told tale: Feminism, postmodernism and ethnographic responsibility.* Stanford, CA: Stanford University Press.

Yoon, B. (2012). Junsuk and Junhyuck: Adolescent immigrants' educational journey to success and identity negotiation. *American Educational Research Journal, 49*(5), 971–1002.

CHAPTER 2

Media Transformations: Working with Iron Man

Guy Merchant

Abstract

This chapter explores some of the ethical dilemmas of being both a researcher and a family member. Intrigued by the media play of his 7 year-old grandson but without the structure of a formal research project, the author constructs a series of analytical reflections that are filtered through his grandson's plush toy, Iron Man. Iron Man is involved in a number of original media texts that re-work narratives from popular culture including episodes from Peppa Pig, Spongebob Squarepants, and Friends. The author shows how Iron Man (and his owner) are located in a complex media ecology. Being in the family offers unique opportunities for understanding the influences and experiences that give texture to this exploratory media play.

1   Press Record Grandad

There's a small red circle, a cluster of pixels, the size of a halfpenny at the bottom of the screen. I touch it with my forefinger and then filming begins. Sssh! Strict rules of silence must be observed. All the main characters are on set— Iron Man, M&M, Elmer, Shin, and Juice-Cuppy. Others, like Gazzie and Tigga, have walk-on parts. We have a theme tune, as usual, and filmic technique is everything. Continuity, camera angle, and movement—even reverse shots for dialogue, and it's all filmed in a continuous sequence with no post production editing or stop-motion style. It must be said that the plot is difficult to follow, and when the single take is done, the criteria by which this or that version might be said to "work" is baffling to say the least. If it passes muster, it may find its way on to his YouTube channel. It might have a title like "Hey car with the obstacle course badge yellow team wins everyone had cups" or "Tigga is sick she stay at home then the other chasers went to her house"—a form of words more like a plot summary than a title, all composed with the help of predictive text.

I have been trying to understand this world of video composition for a couple of years now, but I haven't been researching it—whatever that means. I've just been trying to understand it because it plays into my life in two ways. The first, and most important, is that I want to understand my seven-year-old grandson, the world he experiences, and the world as he sees it. I want to share that, enjoy it, and value it. That has everything to do with love and relationship—things that don't normally feature in research, unless of course, the research is about love and relationship. But secondly, unavoidably and perhaps recklessly entwined with this is my own professional interest in children's meaning making, particularly in the arena of digital literacy (see Burnett & Merchant, 2018, for example). Unavoidable because I just can't help myself, and reckless because I can never quite be sure if I'm mortgaging my familial role to my professional interest—or just simply taking advantage of him, because he's there, a ready-made and biddable research participant.

I refuse to write about him in such terms. And as a result, I am caught in the horns of an ethical dilemma. No research aims, no design or ethical consent—although in my defense I must say that we regularly talk about what writing about his media play might mean. He likes the idea of seeing Iron Man, M&M, and all the others in a book, and in fact he's recently started making books of his own with these characters in them. But a chapter in a book about how he makes videos? He doesn't quite get that, but then it's an ongoing conversation. Is that enough? I'm still not sure. Should I stop?

There are precedents, of course. For example, social semiotics would be nowhere without the pioneering work of Michael Halliday who studied the language development of his son, Nigel. In his ground-breaking study *Learning How to Mean*, you'll find a section entitled "Data from the present study" in which Halliday describes his method:

> I made notes of the child's utterances, using only the traditional equipment of the field worker, well suited to this stage, a notebook and pencil. I listened in, sometimes taking part in the situation and sometimes staying outside it, hiding behind doors and furniture; and I noted down any meaningful expression that I thought I was observing for the first time. (1975, p. 11)

It's perhaps difficult to see now why this was such a groundbreaking approach. But in a field then dominated by a psychological paradigm, looking at the development of language in the everyday, naturalistic context of the home was revolutionary. While we might be amused to read about this influential researcher, on his hands and knees, hiding from view, jotting down notes about his son, many of us owe much to him. His approach to fieldwork was innovative, and the functional approach to language study that emerged out of this paved the way for what we now call social semiotics. But it might also strike us as odd that his son is referred to as "the child," his everyday talk as "utterances" and his ordinary activity as "data." In hindsight, it is easy to see why Halliday did this. It bestowed the gravitas of scientism on what might otherwise have been easily dismissed, perhaps even ridiculed by a stuffy research community. And it constituted Nigel and his language as an object of study.

Evoking Halliday is not an attempt to legitimize my own work—this chapter, after all, is a far more modest affair, based as it is on small episodes and brief observations. But Halliday's work does serve to illustrate some of the potential dilemmas of researching in the family. When, for example, was he obliged to drop his notebook and pencil to comfort or confront Nigel, or when did his feelings of love and affection intrude, disrupt or derail his scholarly endeavor? What about fetching juice, a snack, tidying up after, and all the rest? All this is hidden from view. And then, what was life like for Nigel later on, when he realized that so much ink had been spilt discussing his speech, the emergence of his 'heuristic function'—'NL4 (13.5–15 months)'—or, for that matter, his obsession with the toy bird (Halliday, 1975, p. 40)? Perhaps it was nothing, and in an era in which photographic images were rarely used in scholarly work, maybe Nigel got off lightly.

Others have taken similar directions when researching language and literacy in their own families. For instance, Baghban (1984) tracked her daughter's early reading and writing whereas Campbell (1999) focused on his granddaughter's emerging print literacy. Bissex, in her introduction to *Gnys at Wrk*, deals directly with the sensitivities involved in studying her son's literacy development:

> At eight he was self-conscious enough to object to obvious observation and notetaking, which I then stopped. One day when I was making informal observations of his laterality, he looked at my notebook to see what I was jotting down and said, I don't like to be charted in everything I do (8:o). (1980, pp. vii)

Of course this sort of sensitivity, a resistance to being observed, a withdrawal, could come up in any context and indeed it often does in classroom research. But because the parent-adult-researcher is a hybrid identity it is all the more complex, there are different power dynamics, and consequently different ways of securing co-operation, and withdrawing from co-operation.

Given changing conditions it is hardly surprising that research in family contexts now includes studies of media engagement. For instance Robinson and Turnbull (2005) documented text production and consumption across media, Briggs (2006) looked at Teletubbies, whereas Giddings (2007) focused on his two sons playing videogames. Bazelgette (2018) gives a fuller account of the challenges of such research. In her reflections on studying the movie-watching of two of her grandchildren, she contrasts the work of the independent researcher with the inside view of the family member:

> However well integrated she [the researcher] is with the family, and however friendly and relaxed her relationship with the child, it will not be the same as a longstanding family relationship. (pp. 52–53)

In other words, she is explicit about the possibilities and potential gains of family research. But could it be that more can be gained—not just because of the strength of the relationship but because of an ongoing immersion in the context?

2   Working with Iron Man

In what follows, I struggle to get a closer understanding of my grandson's media play, but the approach I use is unconventional in that it does not follow the contours of a formal research project—in fact I remain uncomfortable about my positionality because it is an awkward mixture of off-duty researcher and off-duty grandparent. In order to compensate for this, the device I use is to bring a plush toy—Iron Man—to the fore, and to place him in a central position, giving him a voice and, towards the conclusion, entering into dialogue with him. Working from scribbled notes about media play (not field notes), drawing on informal discussions with my grandson (not interviews), and careful watching and re-watching of the finished projects I attempt to piece things together (not analysis). I also had to track down those texts from popular culture TV programmes, books and YouTube memes that acted as source material, and to trace how they were reflected in what I will call 'The Iron Man stories'.

    To be clear then, Iron Man, his plush toy, is a character in my grandson's stories, but he is also a very important part of my grandson's life, and to reflect this he is central to my re-storying device. Of course a toy can't give ethical consent, and I am pretty confident that there are no copyright issues at stake, but I do want to suggest that an object-oriented approach like this has rich potential as a research approach, both in more general terms as well as in the particular case of research in families. I explore this issue in more detail in the final section—but now, I want to introduce you to Iron Man.

Iron Man is multiple and mutable. He has many forms, but his appearance in this chapter is as a six-inch high plush toy from the Marvel Comics franchise. He is also my grandson's Iron Man and people in the family speak of him as his alter-ego. He lies passive, like a stuffed toy, on the pillow where he sleeps, but he's first up at daybreak jumping out of bed, springing into life. He watches TV, gets thrown about the room for catching practice, goes on slides at the park and waits patiently for him to come home from school. He's also OK about dogs. He is fearless, and what's more he features in most of the videos. *Yesh*— he speaks in sibilants, his voice pitched slightly lower than my grandson's, *yesh*. He growls, he replays things and then sometimes he hides, or rests, taking time out from the demanding work of being his Iron Man.

Hey Iron Man if you ever get to read this I'd like you to see it as a celebration. A celebration of how you taught me to see the world through your eyes. A celebration of your joie de vivre. A story of how I made some sense of your sense making. I'd like to feel that you understand my motives in writing a story that I think needs to be told—and that you won't feel embarrassed, exposed or misrepresented. But I know it's a risk. It's a risk I'm going to take and I imagine you'd understand that.

FIGURE 2.1
Iron Man

After all that's what you do, Iron Man, you take risks, like the superhero you are. You're a shapeshifter, too Iron Man—it's in your DNA.[1] *And now let your adventures begin!*

2.1   *Episode 1: Iron Man Meets Spongebob*

There are shrieks of excitement, I can hear the refrain 'din-din-din-din', then 'brrrr-brrrr… brrrr-brrrr', some rustling sounds and then 'No, this is Iron Man!' followed by a screeching sound (probably whistling). And it's all getting louder. I go in. On top of the superhero quilt there's a collection of characters sitting alongside the tablet: Lined up are M&M, Elmer and Gazzie and Juice Cuppy. They seem to be watching—the main action involves Iron Man and Shin and an old smartphone of mine. Again 'NO, THIS IS IRON MAN!' He looks cross, Iron Man, with his frowning eyebrows; or if not cross then determined. Could that determination be something that goes with annoyance, anger or even frustration? It certainly sounds like that. The refrain once more: 'NO, THIS IS IRON MAN!' (shouted). But maybe that shouting is seasoned with a touch of humour or irony—maybe?

    I haven't got a clue what's going on. I ask, but it doesn't get me anywhere at all. I think about how frustration or anger might get played out, and I've just about talked my way into believing it's OK when I'm shown another video on YouTube. It's a meme. The source is Spongebob Squarepants Season 2 Episode 23, first broadcast on November 16th, 2000 (Knowyourmeme, 2018). The formula: a sequence of turns. It's straightforward. Patrick is working at the Krusty Krab restaurant.

The phone rings.

Customer 1:	Is this the Krusty Krab?'
Patrick:	No this is Patrick!

Patrick hangs up and starts whistling.

Customer 2:	Is this the Krusty Krab?
Patrick:	NO THIS IS PATRICK!

Patrick slams down the phone and continues whistling.

Customer 3:	Is this the Krusty Krab?
Patrick:	**NO THIS IS PATRICK !**

Patrick slams down the phone even harder this time, so hard it rocks in its cradle. He folds his arms and mutters through his teeth,

Patrick: I'm not a Krusty Krab...

Enter Spongebob from the left, waggling his outstretched finger at Patrick.

Spongebob: Err, Patrick, that's the name of the restaurant.

There's an evening of meme watching ahead, but you get the gist. Much in the way of the old slot-and-filler language learning routines, you can substitute different names for Patrick ad infinitum, and the joke (if that's what it is) remains unchanged. Whatever the copyright holder Nickleodeon might think, the meme and the remixing is unstoppable; it's everywhere on YouTube. It's gone viral.

2.2   *Episode 2: Iron Man and the Missing Swimming Trunks*

Conversations stretching back over the last 18 months have repeatedly focused on my boots. The question 'What colour are your boots?' is often asked. 'Grandad, are your boots green?' I don't really know how to answer that, but pretty soon I realise that I keep on getting it wrong. My walking boots are brown but this isn't the answer. I have to say that they're green even though they're obviously not. I do have some running shoes that could pass as mossy green and beige—but apparently that's wrong too. Confusing. Occasionally I've been asked if I've got golden boots. I've tried lying but that doesn't meet with approval. In the end I just take to saying yes. I have got green boots. It's just the way it is.

Iron Man finally helps me out. He's found his way into a picture book now, 24 pages of A3 stapled together. It's called *Iron Man and his Swinning Trungs* (Figure 2.2)—the title contains a misspelling of 'swimming trunks'. It features all the usual suspects, M&M, Elmer, Shin, Gazzie and Tigga and they're all having a whale of a time jumping in puddles of water—maybe they've gone to a water park? All's well until you get to page five (Figure 2.3). Here Iron Man is standing apart from the group and he's crying. He's lost his swimming trunks! Turn the page and you see him chasing after a bird. The bird has stolen his swimming trunks, she's wearing them. The chase goes on over many pages and to very different places—the ocean, the forest, the moon and back until Iron Man is finally reunited with his swimming trunks. And then it's time for some celebratory jumping in water (Figure 2.4).

"The Golden Boots." Does that sound familiar? "Peppa Pig and the Golden Boots," a 15-minute special released on February 14th, 2015. Peppa and her

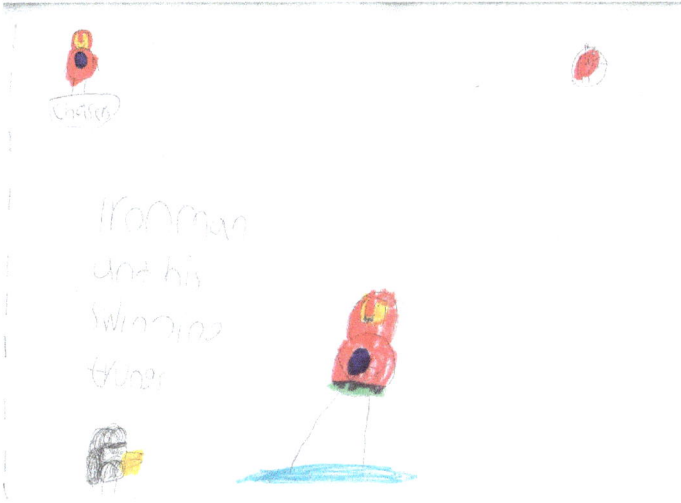

FIGURE 2.2   Iron Man and his Swinning Trungs (book cover)

FIGURE 2.3   Iron Man cries

family are joined by Suzy Sheep and others for a session of jumping in muddy puddles. Afterwards Mrs Duck goes off with Peppa Pig's golden boots. Peppa chases after Mrs Duck, across the ocean, to the moon and back, until she is finally reunited with her boots. And then it's time for some celebratory puddle jumping.

FIGURE 2.4   Jumping in puddles

3   Transformation/Representation

Representation is a quintessentially human endeavor. It involves bringing something to mind again by recalling its likeness, and re-presenting it to ourselves for ourselves, or for others—or, as Wikipedia would have it, it is: "the use of signs that stand in for and take the place of something else. It is through representation that people organize the world and reality through the act of naming its elements" (Wikipedia, 2018). These seem rather grand descriptions to bear in mind in reflecting on the ephemeral, playful, and idiosyncratic production of texts described in the two episodes above. But if we are to take childhood, media, and meaning making seriously these are connections that have to be made. They are, after all, how young children build bridges between their first-hand experience and the world out there. It is how, to return to Halliday (1975), they tap into the "meaning potential" (ibid.), the social semiotic resources to hand.

Take *Episode 1* as a starting point. Circulating around the lives of young children is a dense and complex web of images and narratives, reaching down from global media corporations, publishing houses and toy manufacturing franchises—the movies, books, toys, t-shirts and all the rest that populate their lives. Spongebob Squarepants—funny, trivial, entertaining, banal, or however you wish to describe it—is just one small manifestation of this. Spongebob, Iron Man and Peppa Pig all co-exist in what Appadurai describes as mediascapes.

Mediascapes, whether produced by private or state interests, tend to be image-centred, narrative-based accounts of strips of reality, and what

they offer to those who experience and transform them is a series of elements (such as characters, plots and textual forms) out of which scripts
can be formed of imagined lives, their own as well as those of others living in other places. (1996, p. 35)

Strong words indeed. And they present us with a paradox. Iron Man in the
global mediascape and Iron Man as a simple soft toy, a comfort to a small boy
who sometimes finds it hard to get to sleep at night. But things are never as
straightforward as that paradox suggests. The Iron Man of *Episode 1* is part of
a meme. He is involved in re-presenting or transforming a short segment from
Spongebob Squarepants. In doing this he is engaging with a popular media
practice which has attracted the attention of scholars working in the field of
new literacies. Digital remixes like this Spongebob meme are sometimes seen
as a new kind of writing (Lankshear & Knobel, 2011, p. 101), a new literacy in
its own right. Alternatively, memes can be seen as the hallmark of creative cultural production (Merchant, 2009) with a much longer history than the word
meme.[2] Either way Iron Man is involved in the enactment of a Spongebob
meme, and imbuing it with new meaning.

Episode 2 works in a similar way. This time Iron Man is drawn into a longer
narrative—Peppa Pig and the Golden Boots—and it's one that shares its episodic structure with many traditional children's stories—a chase. The narrative of Peppa Pig's golden boots is appropriated and re-purposed as Iron Man
losing his swimming trunks. You could see this as typical of the way in which
media play involves the appropriation of 'available signs' (Dyson, 1996, p. 474)
in order to make sense of the world. In her lucid writing about superhero play,
Dyson's version of the mediascape is poetically evoked as a constellation in
the nighttime sky, dotted with 'cultural stars'. Children 'organize themselves
with reference to those stars' (ibid., p.473). In Dyson's account, children are
depicted as agentive producers actively working with what is given—and that
would include media stories and characters as well as toys, tablets, pens and
paper—negotiating a place for themselves in the world.

Iron Man takes on the role of Patrick in *Episode 1* in an act of transformation—a re-enactment of the Spongebob phone call. From a social semiotic
perspective, this is an instance of transformation which Kress refers to as 'the
site of the new' (Kress, 2010, p. 42). *Iron Man and the missing swimming trunks*
is a more complex creation. The transformation is more far-reaching, the characters and settings are changed, leaving just the narrative structure and some
key events intact (for instance, Iron Man cries at the same point in the story as
Peppa Pig did in the original). But also the entire story has migrated from the
medium of moving image to a handwritten book, transferring across modes in

a process that Kress refers to as transduction (2010, p.124). For all its playfulness, this is sophisticated work.

3   The Media Ecology

With the diversification of media, their widespread availability and the expansion of global media corporations, children now have access to far more texts
than previous generations. Media scholars often use the metaphor of an ecology to describe this environment. Scolari (2012) provides a useful overview
of the different ways in which the metaphor has been applied touching on
related concepts like ecosystem and evolution, co-evolution and competition,
extinction and survival—all of which have been applied to the ways in which
media co-exist, dominate or decline and have begun to pattern our lives. The
ecology metaphor is a useful way of understanding this next episode because
it draws on a diversity of resources:
– The Warner Brothers TV show 'Friends' (2001)
– The ITV Quiz Show 'The Chase' (2009)
– The Iron Man plush toy from Marvel Comics
– M&M (Red) plush toy part of a marketing campaign for chocolates
– The YouTube platform

3.1   *Episode 3: Iron Man and the Chasers 'Why God, Why'?*
Iron Man, M&M, Shin and all the rest have become The Chasers, a tight knit
group of plush toys ready to tackle any media challenge. If you look carefully
at the cover of Iron Man and the Swinning Trungs (Figure 2.2) there, in the top
left hand corner, is their logo—a miniature image of Iron Man standing on a
label that says "Chasers." Let me trace the geneology of these chasers. It all goes
back to *The Chase*, a daytime TV show first broadcast in the UK. Now, thanks to
catch-up and a dedicated channel called "The Challenge," you can watch any
old episode any old time. *The Chase* is an ITV game show, released on 29th June
2009, in which contestants are pitted against professional quizzers whom they
'chase' on general knowledge questions for a cash prize. These quizzers have
come to be known as "The chasers." Mark Labbett, Shaun Wallace, Anne Hege-
rty, Paul Sinha and Jenny Ryan are these gameshow 'superheroes': the original
chasers. So why not call this fearless gang The Chasers, too?

My grandson's YouTube channel often shows them all together. For instance,
there's one called 'Chasers it was everyone birthday competition m&m was crying because he doesn't like growing up' (see Figure 2.5). But what is that all about?

FIGURE 2.5 The Chasers

Here's the soundtrack from that particular video.

M&M:	*Why* God *why*?
M&M:	*Why* are you doing this?
Whaaaaaaa!	(canned laughter)
The Chasers:	Happy birthday...(singing)
M&M:	It's not fair to be growing up.
Whaaaaaaa!	(canned laughter)
M&M:	It's not very fair...

I have to ask for help in making sense of this one, but it doesn't take me very long. I ask around and eventually I find out that it's a remix of his favourite episode of *Friends*—Season 7, Episode 14 'The One Where They All Turn Thirty' in which Joey reveals that he thought he'd made a pact with God not to let him age (IMDb, 2018). In the *Friends* episode they all stand round Joey—Rachel, Monica, Phoebe, Ross and Chandler as the 'Why God why' lines start up. In the remix, M&M's dialogue isn't a direct copy, but it captures the essence of it in the railing against the aging process. And in *The Chasers* remix they all stand

round M&M, too. But this time it's Little Rabbit, Gazzie, Shin and Tigga standing and M&M (not Joey) who are crying—*Why* God *why*?

4   Hang on a Minute!

*You shaid you weren't shure. You heshitated. And now look what you've done,
you've jusht carried on regardlesh. You, with your fine wordsh and your fanshy
ideash. Have you completely forgotten about what you shaid before?*

Well, not exactly. I am aware of what I'm doing, but well, actually I'm still not
sure if that's excusable.

Excushable?

I'm reducing your life, your engagement with media, and the transformations you enact in making the world your own—reducing them to short and
perhaps entertaining extracts which I can then read in a scholarly way.

Shscolarly?

In writing this piece I'm creating surplus value out of your humble digital
labour, just by making some sort of sense of what I can make sense of. But if
the truth be known, these are reductive fictions, thin strips of a world of things
soft and hard, such as toys and technologies, bodies and feelings—both yours
and mine—intermingling with a constellation of mediated meanings and discursive practices. What do they really mean? They are selected, curated and
enacted with all the inclusions and exclusions that those words evoke, ani-
mating everyday struggles and occurrences with another layer of meaning...
Iron Man.

Yes!

5   Future Research and Ethical Considerations

The video and story episodes I have presented are not easy to follow. A hermeneutic process is required in order to trace the media transformations
described. And it might just be the case that these insights into consumption and production can only be gained from a position deeply embedded
in the home context, in the way that Bazelgette (2018) suggests. However,
approaching the complex bricolage of practices and narrative representations
captured in the episodes would not have been possible without the work of
others, because their very specificity requires intimate knowledge. Family
researchers often hold such knowledge, and when they don't they may have
easy access to it (for instance, in my case through other family members).

This is not to deny the significance of work like Dyson's (for example Dyson, 1996, 2003)—certainly a source of inspiration, but it is also worth noting that her observations were based on extended ethnographies and supported by a team of talented research assistants—a resource that is in short supply these days.

The observations I make here though are further testimony to the nature of the media ecology that children participate in—and it's worth stressing that word *participation*, because in the examples explored above, one thing that stands out is the to and fro of media consumption and production. Iron Man and the other plush toys become The Chasers who then act out a transformed episode of *Friends* which is later uploaded to YouTube. This is a far cry from the passive consumption of media that still worries many. It is instead, a densely layered participation in media forms and production.

Play, storying, and re-storying have probably always been like this, at least in general terms (see Mackey, 2017). Certainly in my own childhood, I can remember acting and re-enacting TV shows and movie themes. I placed myself in those narratives, I adopted and adapted the characters, and when asked to write at school, that was the material I had to draw upon. But the material here, I think, shows greater complexity—or at least it shows more complex processes at work. There is a shift in the materiality of meaning making, too. My generation could only imagine how action might be framed on a screen, and when the first affordable movie cameras were available, you needed some serious apprenticeship, something like a college course, just to learn how to work with the Super-8 footage. On laptops and tablets it's all there, immediate and accessible, and the 'finger flowment' described by Potter and Bryer (2017) makes it even quicker and easier. Quicker than traditional writing.

How this media engagement develops over time, how it emerges in play, and how it develops through informal learning is receiving an increasing amount of attention, particularly from media scholars and theorists. Nevertheless, more empirical work is needed, and more work that focuses on young children in out of school contexts would help to develop our understanding. Family-based research could make an important contribution here although, as I have suggested, it is not without its challenges. Foremost of those challenges is how to negotiate the complex ethical terrain, of how to gain consent from children who may not be fully aware of what they are consenting to—to be part of a book that's about their videos and stories.

A small concession to this ethical challenge has been to avoid including any specific information, beyond saying 'my grandson'—that and a liberal scattering of pronouns throughout the text. I have experimented with using Iron Man as a vehicle for some of the re-telling and have referred to this as an object-oriented approach. Such an approach has considerable potential and could be developed into interviewing technologies-in-use in the sort of ways that Adams and Thompson (2011) suggest. And in fact, without Iron Man this chapter would be nothing at all.

Notes

1   The original Marvel Comics character of Iron Man is in fact a cyborg—an augmented human being. https://www.marvel.com/comics/discover/97/iron-man-must-reads
2   The term 'meme' was first coined by Dawkins (1976) to describe a contagious idea.

References

Adams, C., & Thompson, T. (2011). Interviewing objects: Including educational technologies as qualitative research participants. *International Journal of Qualitative Studies in Education, 24*(6), 733–750.

Appadurai, A. (1996). *Modernity at large: Cultural dimensions of globalization.* Minneapolis, MN: University of Minnesota Press.

Baghban, M. (1984). *Our daughter learns to read and write: A case study from birth to three.* Newark, DE: International Reading Association.

Bazelgette, C. (2018). *Some secret language: How toddlers learn to understand movies* (Unpublished PhD thesis). UCL Institute of Education, London.

Bissex, G. L. (1980). *Gnys at wrk: A child learns to write and read.* Cambridge, MA: Harvard University Press.

Briggs, M. (2006). Beyond the audience: Teletubbies, play and parenthood. *European Journal of Cultural Studies, 9,* 441–460.

Burnett, C., & Merchant, G. (2018). *New media in the classroom: Rethinking primary literacy.* London: Sage.

Campbell, R. (1999). *Literacy from home to school: Reading with Alice.* Stoke-on-Trent: Trentham Books.

Dawkins, R. (1976). *The selfish gene.* Oxford: Oxford University Press.

Dyson, A. H. (1996). Cultural constellations and childhood identities: On Greek gods, cartoon heroes, and the social lives of schoolchildren. *Harvard Educational Review, 66*(3), 471–496.

Dyson, A. H. (2003). *The brothers and sisters learn to write: Popular literacies in childhood and school culture.* New York, NY: Teachers College Press.

Giddings, S. (2007). "I'm the one who makes the Lego Racers Go": Studying virtual and actual play. In S. Weber & S. Dixon (Eds.), *Growing up online: Young people and digital technlologies* (pp. 37–50). New York, NY: Palgrave Macmillan.

Halliday, M. A. K. (1975). *Learning how to mean—Explorations in the development of language.* London: Arnold.

IMDb. (2018). *The one where they all turn thirty.* Retrieved from https://www.imdb.com/title/tt0583489/

Knowyourmeme. (2018). *No, this is Patrick.* Retrieved from https://knowyourmeme.com/memes/no-this-is-patrick

Kress, G. (2010). *Multimodality: A social semiotic approach to contemporary communication.* London: Routledge.

Lankshear, C., & Knobel, M. (2011). *New literacies: Everyday practices and social learning.* Maidenhead: McGraw Hill.

Mackey, M. (2017). Television as a new medium. In B. Parry, C. Burnett, & G. Merchant (Eds.), *Literacy, media, technology past, present and future* (pp. 25–40). London: Bloomsbury.

Merchant, G. (2009). Web 2.0, new literacies, and the idea of learning through participation. *English teaching: Practice and Critique, 8*(3), 8–20.

Potter, J., & Bryer, T. (2017). 'Finger flowment' and moving image language: Learning filmmaking with tablet devices. In B. Parry, C. Burnett, & G. Merchant (Eds.), *Literacy, media, technology: Past, present and future* (pp. 11–127). London: Bloomsbury.

Robinson, M., & Turnbull, B. (2005). Veronica: An asset model of becoming literate. In J. Marsh (Ed.), *Popular culture, new media and digital literacy in early childhood* (pp. 51–72). Abingdon: Routledge.

Scolari, C. (2012). Media ecology: Exploring the metaphor to expand the theory. *Communication Theory, 22*(2), 204–225.

Wikipedia. (2018). *Representation (arts).* Retrieved from https://en.wikipedia.org/wiki/Representation_(arts)

CHAPTER 3

Re-Designing Teaching for Tweens in Times of Streaks, Likes and Gamers

Sarah Prestridge

Abstract

Through an examination of how her tween son's socially mediated life affects his educational perspectives, the author considers how this understanding informs and reforms current thinking about contemporary teaching and learning. In the age of social media and digital games, tweens are more engaged in what could be considered learning at home than they are in schools. What matters to the tween frames a new way of thinking about teaching and learning for both what these students need now and for their future work and learning practices. Emerging from this research are learning principles grounded in collaboration and communication in which tweens are contributors in all facets of teaching and learning.

1 Introduction

Today, most people have access to digital technologies but, more importantly, digital media mediates their lives. For tweens, such mediation involves an unprecedented level of dependence on and engagement in social media. This is evident in Steinberg's (2011) conceptualization of Kinderculture where tweens are considered to be infantilized by corporations like, for example, "Kiss My Booty" jogger-pants. The Kinderculture's socio-theoretical conversation has been likened to the influence of social media on children (Steinberg, 2011). She claims that rethinking childhood is necessary in a media-saturated society where "playing effortlessly" is polarized to Vygotsky's (1978) Zone of Proximal Development (ZPD). A media-created electronic ZPD, with its apps, mobile phones, computers, iPads, Playstation, xBox, virtual realities, can be the space for sophisticated thought work. In these virtual content-generating spaces, tweens construct their identity, negotiate, redesign, and add value to each other's work, as well as become experts in subject matter (Horst, Herr-Stephenson, & Robinson, 2009). Working under the premise that complex learning

© KONINKLIJKE BRILL NV, LEIDEN, 2020 | DOI: 10.1163/9789004421721_003

changes one's identity, coupled with the fact that tweens are high-end users of social media, leads the field to question if these media savvy gamers' and SnapChatters' social-learning activities have any relationship to or impact on formal schooling. As a researcher, teacher, and parent of a 14-year-old boy, I am interested in understanding how my son's socially mediated life affects his educational perspectives, and how this understanding informs and reforms my perspectives on contemporary teaching and learning.

As a mom, I have seen three of my children move through the tween phase. I am a university prepared elementary school teacher and have taught in schools for over 10 years. I have been a teacher educator at the university level for over 16 years. My life has been dedicated to understanding the process of children's learning. I confess that I have scrutinized my children's assignments. I have battled with my children's teachers over valid demonstrations of their under-standings. I have encouraged my children to speak up and challenge ideas in the classroom. I have fought for the inclusion of technologies in learning as this has been my passion.

But I haven't taken heed of the child in the technology-pedagogy paradigm. Indeed, in validating the use of technology for teaching and learning, claims of relevance and authenticity rest with child-based learning interests. But much of what is discussed and presented in policy and curriculum comes from adult dialogue prescribed for the child. In contrast to this seemingly top-down approach, the focus of this chapter will be as much a polar opposite as it can be, taken from, and inclusive of, the views of my now 14-year-old SnapChatter, *Fortnite* gamer.

For clarity, the term "tweens" will be used in this chapter as an endearing term that represents the gap between childhood and an older teenager, refer-ring to those children aged 8–14 years old, who are becoming more socially aware of the world in which they live (Velding, 2017). Tweens in first-world countries are now living in a time and space where access to the Internet is near universal and a range of digital devices is considered a necessity. When walking into a restaurant or hotel, the first thing my tween looks for is the pass-word to free WiFi. As 92% of tweens go online daily (Lenhart, 2015), access to the Internet becomes a search for a social lifeline and data are considered a valuable commodity. Technology ownership and access have become more pervasive for tweens (Wang, Hsu, Campbell, Coster, & Longhurst, 2014), with most daily activities impacted by technology. Findings from nearly ten years ago, which are comparable today, identify the fact that tweens' out-of-school use of technology is more frequent through use of social networking (Face-book, YouTube), messaging and gaming, but this use of technology is not complex (Luckin et al., 2009; Wang et al., 2014). Tweens are digital technology users performing basic functions, such as socializing—posting, liking, and commenting, for entertainment—and googling web-based information outside school. Similarly, inside school, formal learning technologies tend to be for word-processing and web-searching, again supporting basic functions (Wang et al., 2014). Using technology for complex tasks to support creativity and productivity, such as blogging, web editing and game design, is still ad hoc and infrequent in schools.

Acknowledging that tweens are frequent social media users and gamers and that digital technology use in schools, in general, is limited to basic curation of information and images, I contend that it would be worthwhile to see a greater alignment between in- and out-of-school use of technologies that supports complex thinking so that our tweens develop the skills to be critical creative problem solvers who can function and be adaptive in a rapidly changing world. In exploring this phenomenon, I begin this chapter with a review of what is currently recognized to be contemporary teaching and learning. This will help frame an understanding of how tweens are positioned within the teaching and learning dynamic and where social media and gaming tools are thought to add value. In the subsequent section, my son, Cooper, explores with me his social media and gaming world and how he relates these experiences to his formal learning in school. I then consider implications of Cooper's social media experiences and suggest possibilities for educators working with tweens.

2   Contemporary Teaching and Learning

Two themes evident in the research literature and education policy documents will be discussed here. These two themes—personalized learning and rapid changes in technology—promote contemporary teaching and learning in 21st-century schools. Personalized learning and rapid changes in technology direct discourse to promote empowered students who can respond to challenges in our ever-changing world. Both themes have emerged from the evolution of pedagogy from an Industrial era of teaching, which focused on content delivery based on behaviorist notions of learning, to a knowledge economy, which shifted the pedagogical focus to the development of skills to deal with vast amounts of information based on constructivist notions of learning. This evolution identifies such transformation of pedagogy and enrichment of learning experiences to be student-centric, promoting higher-order thinking skills (Yang, 2012). Effective teaching is simply not delivering content through technology. Rather, the focus is on students' learning with technology to assimilate, transform, and build new knowledge (Poitras, Doleck, Huang, Li, & Lajoie, 2017).

Technology integration in schools is considered one of the key game changers of the 21st century (Scherer, Siddiq, & Teo, 2015). However, Fullan (2013a, 2013b) has been arguing for some time that the valuing of content over students thus positions our current education system as outdated and that deep integration of digital technologies in pedagogy, along with changes to the roles of teachers and students, are needed to realize personalization of learning.

During the mid-20th century, two different views of learning started to emerge that served as underpinnings of different approaches to teaching: behaviorism (based on the work of B. F. Skinner) and constructivism (based on the works of Jean Piaget and Lev Vygotsky). Behaviorism views learning as bounded in a stimulus-response mechanism in which a behavioral change occurs. Behaviorists believe that a learned behavior can be predicted, controlled, and measured (Harasim, 2012). Focusing on the stimulus (external condition) and the response representing the resulting overt behavior, classical conditioning is one form of behaviorism. The second form of behaviorism, called operant conditioning, concentrates on shifting to the consequence of the responses. Pedagogical approaches incorporate the following aspects of behaviorism: (a) organizing students' learning until they master learning requirements by repeating tasks and sequencing practice from simple to complex, known to unknown, and knowledge to application; (b) using various features (text, visual and audio) to reinforce students' responses; (c) responding to instructional stimuli through discussion in order to encourage students to become more active; and (d) discussion between students, peers and teachers resulting in operant conditioning (Harasim, 2012; Schunk, 2008). Thus, the key benefits of behaviorism in teaching and learning include reinforcement and organized or programmed learning.

Constructivism is based on the perspective that "students construct their meaning during learning based on their experiences and through a social negotiation of that meaning during the learning process" (Davidson-Shivers & Rasmussen, 2006, p. 45). This learner-centred approach focuses on encouraging ongoing interaction between students while actively engaging them in constructing their own learning. Drawing heavily on the work of Vygotsky, social constructivism positions social processes as fundamental to learning. This approach rejects the view that the construction of knowledge lies solely within the individual. Rather, the social constructivist emphasizes that social interaction shapes cognitive development and is an essential component of the learning process (Krause, Bochner, Duchesne, & McMaugh, 2010). Constructivism and social constructivism have generated a number of teaching approaches based on the following principles: (a) active learning encouraging students to participate in learning activities; (b) learning through opportunities to search for information and experiment; and (c) scaffolded and collaborative learning (Harasim, 2012).

The move to personalized learning through contemporary teaching lies in the application of both behaviorist and constructivist approaches. More dominantly, the social constructivist view of learning is embodied through collaborative learning and the positioning of the student as central and actively participating in the teaching and learning process. These tenets are evident in policy and literature illustrating contemporary teaching and learning from educational institutions. Worldwide, there has been a move to focus contemporary learning on the development of 21st-century capabilities that include general cross-cultural skills such as literacy; numeracy; civic literacy; global awareness; critical and inventive thinking; and communication, collaboration and information skills (see Table 3.1 for a comparison on Singapore's and Australia's general capabilities frameworks as exemplars). These 21st-century general capabilities are foregrounded in response to the need to help students engage in a rapidly changing world and for future employability. They are not a list of additional requirements that teachers need to help students develop; rather, the requirements sit within domain-specific knowledge and are taught with and through content knowledge; these capabilities provide opportunities to add depth and richness to student learning.

TABLE 3.1   Australia's and Singapore's 21st century general capabilities framework

Australia's general capabilities[a]	Singapore's general capabilities[b]
Numeracy	
Literacy	Civic literacy
Critical and creative thinking	Critical and inventive thinking
ICT capability	Communication, collaboration and information
Personal and social capability	skills
Ethic understanding	Global awareness and cross cultural skills
Intercultural understanding	

a https://www.australiancurriculum.edu.au/f-10-curriculum/general-capabilities
b https://www.moe.gov.sg/education/education-system/21st-century-competencies

Collaborative learning experiences become foregrounded when 21st century general competencies are brought together with constructivist learning theories and supported by the need to enhance teaching practices with the integration of technologies. In an example provided in current education

policy, collaborative learning experiences are being touted as an effective pedagogical strategy to "provide students and teachers with the opportunities to
explore, experiment and be challenged in their thinking. Through problem
solving, critical thinking and working creatively, learners build capacity, skills
and resilience" (Catholic Schools Office Lismore, Australia, 2016, p #).

   Collaborative learning has been defined as a small group of students working together to complete a task where there is shared meaning and shared
contribution resulting in combined understanding (Johnson & Johnson, 1996).
Underpinning this process is a disposition for mutual and respective action to
ensure positive learning outcomes for all members of the group (Deutsch, 1949).
There are various versions of collaborative learning, such as when students
work together on a shared task but take responsibility for an individual component. This later, less wholesome version of collaborative learning is more easily
adopted in schools that require independent student assessment because students do not collaborate on all components in the learning sequence. Looking
toward the development of general capabilities with subject specific content,
one might find that collaborative learning opportunities facilitate students'
deeper application of skills within tasks through shared problem-solving and
shared responsibility. The principles of collaborative learning align well with
projected future work-related skills needed for an internationalised economy
(see Table 3.2).

TABLE 3.2   Aligning collaborative learning skills with future work-related skills

Collaborative learning skills (Johnson & Johnson, 1996)	Future work-related skills (Autor & Price, 2013)
– Interdependences	– Abstract problem solving
– Individual and group accountability	– Organisational activities
– Interpersonal and group work skills	– Managerial activities
– Interaction through different modes (face/online)	– Physical adaptability
– Group processing	– Social interactions

So far, I have identified that general capabilities, the use of collaborative
learning experiences, and the integration of technologies are inter-related
components of contemporary teaching and learning. However, does this relationship among skills, pedagogies and technologies exist in today's schooling?
Considering for one moment what is currently evident in research around the
integration of technology, the answer would simply be "no" for the majority of

classrooms given that there is little evidence of actual integration of general capabilities, or constructivist learning principles through collaborative learning experiences with the integration of technologies (Australia, Department of Education, 2018). Teachers' current uses of technologies tend to replicate instructional or teacher-centric practices, with studies indicating that the pedagogies required for the effective integration of educational technologies are not yet in evidence amongst the majority of teachers (Ertmer & Otten-breit-Leftwich, 2013; Niederhauser, Howard, Voogt, Agyei, Laferriere, Tondeur, & Cox, 2018; Prestridge & de Aldama, 2016). On the whole, teachers are applying behaviorist principles by asking students to learn "from" computers through Googling information, practice and reinforcement exercises, and/or writing-up assignments. This has been confirmed in Hsu's (2016) study of K-6 year teachers who rely heavily on viewing websites for representation and information practices. The idea of "technologising" learning by adding on a tech component to established practices with no actual enhancement to learning or pedagogical reformation has long been occurring in schools (Lankshear & Bigum, 1998; Prestridge, 2012). This situation is concerning because we have had computers in schools for over 40 years and the "digital classroom" currently exists in most developed countries (Green & Bigum, 1993).

I see two clear underlying issues that maintain this limited application of technologies in schools. Firstly, we learn through experience, from behaviors that are modelled to us. Teachers appropriate technologies, in the first instance, in ways they were taught to use computers in their schooling. For instance, if as a child they practiced math algorithms through a computer game like a Maths Fact game or created Powerpoints on various topics, they tend to replicate these practices as teachers. The second issue is the fact that teachers place emphasis on the actual technology rather than shifting their focus towards pedagogy (Prestridge, 2017). This aligns with the long-held view of Jonassen (1995) that, when teachers think about technology integration, they should view technologies as tools to learn "with" rather than "about." With this said, we need to consider how teachers are using the technologies in classrooms, specifically, what pedagogical approaches are being used, which in current policy, as well as in research, suggests a greater focus on student-centric constructivist approaches. This supports the notion that technologies are pedagogical tools that teachers use for particular targeted learning purposes.

Ertmer, Ottenbreit-Leftwich, Sadik, Sendurur, and Sendurur's study (2012) identified three categories of technology use in schools that is helpful for identifying the breadth and depth of technology use as pedagogical tools: to (a) Supplement the required curriculum where teachers use technology to motivate, reinforce and practice subject skills such as math facts; (b) Enrich the existing curriculum where teachers use technology as an educational tool for teaching content and higher order thinking; and (c) Transform an emerging curriculum where teachers' use technology as a transparent tool for 21st century literacies that transform the way students learn. In other words, teachers "replace" new tools for old ones, like the whiteboard for the blackboard (category a); or they "add" technology to the task, such as when teachers add websites to research or transfer course work to online spaces that become information repositories (category b). Both replacing and adding technology means little pedagogical change that affords new ways of engaging with students. These ways of thinking about technology replicate existing practices. On the other hand, the third category works because technology can transform an emerging curriculum and support new ways of working with students. Therefore, when thinking about technologies, a transforming approach to both curriculum and pedagogy innovation and experimentation is needed. Later in this chapter, I will extrapolate contemporary teaching in light of Cooper's, my tween, out-of-school experiences to provide a more holistic framework for learning.

One further point to moving towards a redesigning of teaching for tweens, an Australian report chaired recently by David Gonski, *Through growth to achievement-Report of the review to achieve educational excellence in Australian Schools* (2018), identified the why, what, and how of future directions for ensuring contemporary curriculum, learning and pedagogy (see Figure 3.1). In Figure 3.1 I have highlighted this reasoning (why), the curriculum (what) and the pedagogy (how) to ensure that Australian students can be creative, connected, and engaged learners in a rapidly changing world (National Education Priority).

In this report, technological reasoning was identified as the impetus for change, that is, a shift in technologies and jobs, with a solution to focus on

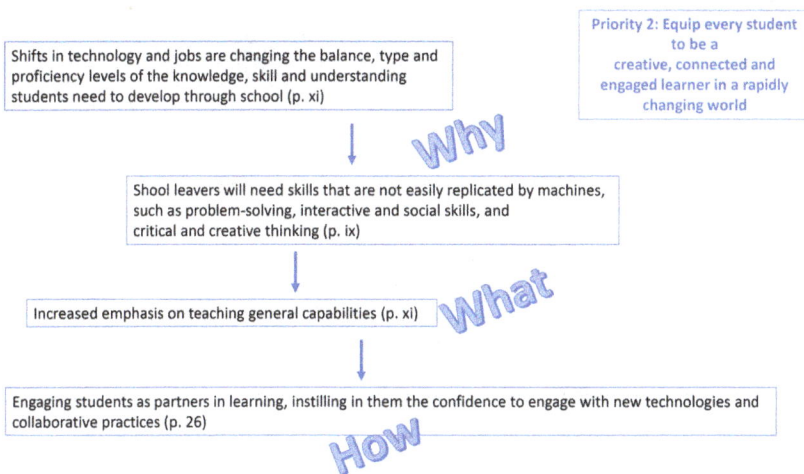

FIGURE 3.1   David Gonski's directions for ensuring contemporary curriculum, learning and pedagogy

the development of students' general capabilities for learning, such as problem-solving, interactive and social skills, and critical and creative thinking through the adoption of collaborative teaching practices. This report considers the what and how tweens should learn in schools, which is on target with Ertmer's et al.'s (2012) transformative approach (category c) to an emerging curriculum that changes how tweens learn, but Gonski's report does this from the top-down, using external requirements. In this chapter, I take a different approach and consider building this new paradigm from the outside-in, that is, from what the tapestry of real out-of-school learning experiences of students look like and how this reshapes our pedagogical processes to help tweens learn *with* technologies inside school.

3   Tech for Tweens in Schools

Before turning to a specific Tween's experience, I first consider actual use of technologies in school. The US report, *From Print to Pixel: The role of videos, games, animations and simulations within K-12 education*, states that there has been an increase in teachers' use of digital content in the classroom from 2012 to 2015 (Project Tomorrow, 2016a). An increase use does not indicate the effective application of teaching with technologies to learning processes, but it does mean an increase in evidence of the use of digital tools and content: videogames, online textbooks, animations, virtual field trips, self-created videos, and simulations. Interestingly, the report presented tween use of technologies with implications for formal learning summarised in Table 3.3 (Project Tomorrow, 2016b). Those relevant to social media use have been presented in the table. The report emphasises the need to increase visual based learning content because of tweens' saturation in their digital worlds but also because "engaging and interactive forms of information transmission in our society today cannot be underestimated" (p. 3).

TABLE 3.3   Summary of students' use and views of technologies in schools

Learning via YouTube: Students (38%) reported online videos help them with their homework; 27% regularly watch teacher created videos.
More games please: Almost two thirds want to use digital games for learning in school.
Teacher – I have a question: 15% Students are texting their teachers about school
Twitter: 47% of students in Grades 9–12 use Twitter
Watching online video: 74% of students in Grades 6–8 say they watch online videos for schoolwork, and they mostly do this for Science.

SOURCE: PROJECT TOMORROW (2016B)

Interestingly, the creation of videos by teachers for 'reinforcement' (12%) and YouTube videos for "illustrating concepts" within a lesson (68%) is more prevalent than student creation or use of video (20%). The following year (2017), this project shifted the focus to analysing teachers' digital practices with the finding that moving from students consuming digital content (emphasising teacher-centred practices focused on content delivery) to a student-centred approach to using technologies that enhanced student creativity, was the greatest challenge that teachers faced. The Report in 2017 stated that technology leaders (67%) indicated that the greatest challenge they faced in implementing digital learning or expanding technology use was motivating teachers to change their traditional instructional practices to use technology more meaningfully with students (p. 2). This reinforces what has been previously identified here: that students are increasingly becoming digitally active but their experiences to learn with technologies in schools remains teacher-centric.

4 Cooper's Digital Practices

There are certain ways and means of engaging in conversation with a 14-year-old. My most successful one has been during car trips to sporting commitments. I have, what one might consider a "window" of opportunity from the point when Cooper gets in the car to when he puts on Spotify. Once the music is on, there is no more talking. Given that I am a teacher-researcher-mum, he is pretty used to me asking "weird" and wonderful questions and he does try to answer me and is very honest. These conversations often begin with something I am curious about learning, and I turn to Cooper for his perspective and experiences.

My car inquiry took place over the last eighteen months, starting when Cooper was 12 and-a-half until now when he just turned 14. I usually record him on my phone. He usually controls the audio recorder because I am driving, but I have to keep reminding him to check that it's actually recording. We discussed the fact that these chats about his social media and gaming practices were going to be used as part of a research project. I asked him directly if he wanted his real name used if I were to publish our discussions. Cooper was agreeable and said, "sure." So, our car inquiry began. I don't ask him questions every time we drive; it's more every so often, about once a month for 5 minutes to 1 hour. His participation depends on his moods also and only takes place when Cooper agrees. Additionally, over dinner or in the kitchen, for instance, I'll ask Cooper a question or two about something he is doing on SnapChat or how his computer game is going. If Cooper is comfortable discussing his experiences, then he does, and I usually jot down Cooper's response noting the date and time. My interviewing techniques draw from years of qualitative research within a naturalistic inquiry paradigm. Importantly, I tend to act like I don't "understand," so that I do not make assumptions. I never present myself as understanding his world. Through a process of on-going thematic analysis that occurred *in situ* during this eighteen month period, the key theme of communication emerged with sub-themes that illustrated what was shaping Cooper's mediated social engagement. These sub-themes were gender-neutral space; informed strategic play; maintaining friends; social currency; and language patterns. These will now be discussed.

This account of Cooper's digital practice is meant to provide insight into ways of living with technology that a tween experiences. It is written as my reflection of these accounts with direct speak from Cooper to illustrate what shapes his communication practices. Cooper attends an all-boys school. He is currently in Grade 9, which is Middle Years, in Australia. He loves his school and is very proud of the brotherhood the school engenders.

I start with our discussion of his current, all consuming after school activity: playing *Fortnite*, a sandbox survival game that he plays with his mates on a PlayStation 4. I'll let him explain it to you:

> It's a battle type game 100 people get dropped into a map with different named locations you choose a location, get dropped in, grab weapons, if anyone is around you, you try to kill them I guess. About every 2 minutes the map closes in and a storm comes. You have to run from the storm as it can kill or damage you, last man standing wins.

Cooper plays this game way too much. I think that with a mother's hat on. With an educator's hat on, I see the value in his game play. It represents a form of social communication. He plays *Fortnite* for a couple of hours every afternoon, sometimes after dinner (foregoing his homework). I've heard a lot of parents say the same thing of their boy tweens. He organises to play the game at school or the boys text each other at night to see who is "getting on." When discussing game play with Cooper, I found a few interesting things come up. Firstly, he said that this game is gender neutral, and that more boys play because girls think that the game is stupid. Cooper would happily play *Fortnight* with a girl, but he would have to know this girl, if she was a friend so that he could communicate with her. Being able to communicate effectively "to win" seemed to be very important: "Like if I don't talk to her that much on another social media then I wouldn't play with her." There seems to be a strong link between game play and the need for effective communication (Abrams & Lammers, 2017). Cooper only wants to play with friends with whom he can talk, be it a girl or boy.

Exploring gender and game play further with Cooper, the topic of "skins" in the game arose. Skins are worn by each player's avatar in the game. Two highly valued skins in the game were female characters—an elite agent and a mission specialist. Cooper explained, "I used to play as a female character all the time because the skin looks nice. It's a cool skin." To get one of these skins Cooper had to do seven challenges a week to get 5 to 10 battle stars. You need 10 battle stars to go up a tier. He kept doing these challenges and leveraged off tiers to get cool skins. Playing in a "cool" skin, be it female or not, provided some social currency. Cooper explained that everyone wears skins so a player's gender is unknown and unimportant.

Fortnite game play is exciting and action packed. A game lasts for 15 to 20 minutes. There are times of heightened intensity but also wait times. Being aware of one's surroundings, remembering names and types of weapons, thinking about location, and watching for threats all at once ensures that the player is multi-tasking. Game strategy is evident per Cooper's account: "If that person doesn't know where you are, you can shoot them or wait or get to the higher ground you can get a better shot at them." Cooper usually plays with his mates in a team of four. He says that communication with his team is most important to winning:

> We just got a victory. Cause like we know one another and know how to work together so like we were all communicating together like we can push now because they just got out of their fight and they are going to be low.

The emphasis on communicating effectively was evident when Cooper talked about successful game play. Familiarity and comradery meant that he knew "the play," how his friends would act, the support he would get, the shared language they had, which all combined to become victory-informed strategic game play. Listening to him play was intense. The sharp, loud, directional language was bombastic mostly interspersed with laughing. As a self-admitted "lazy" child, he is intensely active in *Fortnite*. As a final comment, when not on *Fortnite*, Cooper is watching YouTube clips of other game players who stream *Fortnite* through Twitch, he says, to improve his game play but mainly "cause I just like watching it."

To my surprise, in having to choose between SnapChat and *Fortnite*, Cooper admits that SnapChat wins hands down:

> SnapChat is definitely my go to. Better than the game if I had to choose one. I can talk to a different variety of people. Like I can talk to everyone on SnapChat. I'm limited to people who have PlayStation 4. SnapChat is better for me than Instagram. SnapChat I communicate with my friends. Instagram I just like some photos.

Again, there is an emphasis on communication and being able to connect with his friends. I asked Cooper to describe to me a typical day, to get an insight into his use of social media and its impact on his daily routine. He said:

> I wake up in the morning and I'll have 10 Snap Chats. I'll do the streaks or the conversation from last night. When I get home I'll have 30 Snap Chats. Kids have their phones at school and use Snap Chats but I don't have data and I don't want my phone taken off me. So when I get home after I have some food I'll check my phone. I just keep it on all night and just hear it ding. I put my phone on silent when I go to bed otherwise it'd wake me up.

Between *Fortnite* and SnapChat, Cooper is constantly busy communicating with his friends:

> Sometimes if there is no topic you send photos of anything, the floor, the wall, but as a topic arises you'll talk about that. All my friends are on SnapChat. I know everyone on my SnapChat. I have lots of people who add me who I don't know or I don't like so I just leave them. I only have one account.

The emphasis seems to be that SnapChat is used to maintain his friendships. If Cooper, for example, doesn't know or like talking to a given person, then he doesn't add them to get more friends. He said Instagram is more about the number of friends but "SnapChat is about the friends you want to talk to. I used to try to talk to everyone multiple times but now I just talk to my friends." Instagram is about 'likes' and 'photos' whereas SnapChat is a more interactive fast paced communication device. The use of the SnapChat app serves a purpose and, for Cooper, he sees more purpose in communicating through SnapChat. However, over the last eighteen months his use of SnapChat has changed.

When he was 12, "streaks" were social currency. The more streaks one had, the more notoriety that person had at school. A streak is an interchange between two people that is maintained over consecutive days. This interchange is usually a photo of something. At one point, Cooper was maintaining five streaks.

One streak was with a friend called Lee (pseudonym for a girl) and they had 51 streaks. He told me that one of his friends went on holiday, on a cruise ship. This friend, Andrew (pseudonym), asked his mate to keep up his streaks while he was away. He gave his mate his SnapChat logon details. It was very important to maintain the streaks. Cooper explained it was like letting your friends down if you lost the streak. He even said that he was worried one time that his Dad took his phone off him and he had to sneak into the kitchen late at night where his phone was to keep the streak. Cooper noted, "My biggest Streak was 150 but others have had like 500. I'm lazy and so is Kody ([best friend]. I'm more likely to keep Streaks with the people I am talking to than people I don't know."

At 14 years of age, Cooper uses SnapChat and *Fortnite* to have constant access to his friends using different language patterns that are very different from talking on a phone. Communication is mainly image-based or accomplished through short abbreviated sentences, considered a chat rather than a conversation. In *Fortnite* it is all about the strategy of game play, but it is a significant way in which Cooper communicates and maintains friendships. Cooper noted that it was typical to manage multiple chats, but there needs to be a reason, otherwise Cooper wouldn't bother. Friends are valuable. It seems that the better the friend, the more effort is made in SnapChatting.

When exploring Cooper's use of social media, I asked him to relate these practices to his classroom learning. I asked him what he values doing/not doing, and what other approaches to learning would help him, motivate him and keep him on task. After discussing this idea of teaching and learning on and off over a couple of car rides, he identified three important practices that I will build on in the next section. Cooper did not mention a greater use of technology or the incorporation of social media in his lessons. I asked why, and he said that it was just not what he considers schooling. He has not used technology in ways he has enjoyed. If he did use technology, then he used a laptop computer to access content via the internet or a school subject site, which meant lots of reading, which he was not interested in doing. It seems for Cooper he may have been educated out of the creative use of technology (Robinson & Aronica, 2016). Here is his wish list:

1.   Maintaining supportive relationships: "I think teachers if they don't like you they just block the kid out and if you don't understand they just ignore you."
2.   Valuing contributions: "I like my English teacher. She included us in the actual class. She doesn't write anything on the board, it all comes from us. She also isn't negative about something we have to say. She'd include all our ideas. If we said something that didn't really make sense or was not really relevant she wouldn't just brush it off, she doesn't put us down."

3.   Group work with friends: "Group work. I kinda like group work. It depends
     on who I'm working with. I work better with my friends 'cause I know
     how to communicate with them. When it's people I don't know, I don't
     know how to talk to them. They usually don't let us work with friends."

What does all this mean: what do we want? Teachers want tweens to be motivated to learn. For children who are motivated by social media and gaming
practices, how can we understand and make use of these practices for school-
based learning. In school, we want to try to think about what contemporary
teaching and learning looks like, being informed by these out of school practices and knowing that transforming pedagogies for an emerging curriculum is
our best opportunity.

I just really want Cooper to enjoy learning and have a sense of success. For
this, I have developed a response to what could be considered a way forward.

5   Tweens as "Contributors" in an Emerging Curriculum: Designed by
       a Mum, Educationalist and Researcher

I have gained great insight in observing and talking with Cooper over the
last eighteen months. He has been my teacher as I have taken the role of the
learner. He has taught me how he uses social media and how games make him
feel and think. Through our discussions, we have been co-learners. We have
built ideas together around tween life and communication practices, exploring
the "what for" and the "because" phrases. He has told me he wants to be valued
as a learner, work with his friends and develop good relationships with teachers and his peers. Knowing what Cooper wants and knowing the importance of
communication through social media and games outside the classroom, I want
to consider what his learning could actually look like in the classroom. In this
section I draw heavily from my experiences of being a classroom teacher and a
teacher of (pre-service) educators, with a research focus on online professional
development of continuing teachers for their effective use of technologies in
the classroom. In making this a very pointed idea, one that will be remembered and hopefully adopted by teachers of tweens, I will focus on the word
contribution.

Cooper wants his contributions valued. He wants to participate and be
active in his learning. He is active when he plays *Fortnite* and his contributions
matter to his friends, which helps achieve team victories. In classrooms, his
contributions often don't seem to matter and he knows this. Often in classrooms we see teachers in control of the learning, "brushing off" ideas that are
not in the direction they want the lesson to take. Cooper has seen his teachers

control the whiteboard and the content. Technology in the teacher's hands is used in teacher-centric ways. This is the same as, for example, when YouTube clips are chosen by the teacher. They are teacher-centric. Teachers use them in ways to illustrate *their* ideas about the concept/content. If we try to reverse this, we would consider the technology in the child's hands working with their friends in interest-based groups with the teacher guiding the students' generated ideas and directions. In this way, Cooper, for example, would be *contributing* his ideas valued by his peers and by the teacher as he would have control of the technology and the learning pathway. Technologies need to be more in the child's hands where learning takes place rather than in the teacher's hands. If we shift the control to the child, then we redesign the act of learning. It is in the action of *doing* something with the technology, along with the discussion around these actions, that new knowledge is formed. Therefore, youth in small groups working with technology with boundaries guided by the teacher affords more active student-centric learning to take place.

Technology can become the conduit for critical discourse for collaborative learning activities that stimulate discussion. And here is the second *contribution*, where the child is a co-teacher and co-learner explaining and sharing his or her ideas and building new ones with peers and the teacher. It is in the discussion, in the communication process, in which the child contributes his or her understandings that stimulates further thinking and problem solving. Tweens explain, validate ideas, shape and re-shape each other's thinking. Tweens working in collaborative teams contribute to the discussion of actions and thinking processes (Abrams, 2017). Through guided collaborative learning where technologies and learning pathways are in their hands, tweens have the opportunity to contribute their ideas/concepts and also have the opportunity to talk about those ideas, where they work as a team for a common goal, which is an authentic approach to collaborative learning.

Cooper is valued amongst his friends for the contributions he makes to conversations and game play. SnapChat and *Fortnite* are the current technologies in vogue but these will change. What is important is what Cooper does with these technologies and this needs to be the focus for building an emerging curriculum. In other words, we need to think about what underwrites the engagement more so than the tool. For Cooper, he feels valued through communication and team work. He builds ideas better when active with technologies on a small team. He also learns by watching others play. For Cooper, a collaborative "team approach" with common goals and outcomes is more productive.

In more formal teacher-centric models of learning, in whole class groupings, asking tweens to contribute by providing content they see as relevant to the topic, such as an article in their News Feed or an image or meme, positions the content as more relevant and controlled by the child. Deconstructing this content with the tween together with the class group again demonstrates a valuing of what the tween has brought to the lesson. A teacher colleague recounted to me that she asks her tweens to find a meme on a history concept as a way to stimulate discussion; another colleague showcased a news report that a student had emailed her on the topic they were exploring. These simple approaches to using tween-generated content proposed in these examples demonstrates the valuing of content that is meaningful to the tween. But also, and more importantly, as teachers we should be trying to help our tweens make meaning of the content presented to them every day through various technologies and have them make links to what is learnt in and outside of school. Our tweens are living in a media saturated world. We cannot do this unless they provide some content. We as teachers have a role to play in helping them make clear links to curriculum concepts and draw on skills to deconstruct and make meaning of texts. Therefore, when using content contributed by tweens, teachers are underscoring the value and relevance of tweens' learning practices.

Contributing should also be considered in terms of creating content, creating games, creating YouTube clips on how to play, being producers in this social media world rather than only users or consumers. In one way, we see tweens as consumers of other people's content. However, with such high-productivity software available on the Internet or in the palms of their hands through mobile phones, everyone can be producers of content. I would love to see Cooper developed in this way at school. I see Cooper watching YouTube clips of gamers. I would like to see Cooper making YouTube clips and be the gamer. I know he and his team of 4 mates strategise very well; they are often victorious. Explaining collaborative game play and creating video excerpts to teach other players how to strategise makes for an authentic procedural text. But this YouTube clip per se would only be authentic in the context of outside school game play. What needs to happen in school is the shift from being a consumer of content to a creator of content that is valued in the education community. This could happen through authentic problem-based or project-based work. These kinds of approaches have happened in schools and have been successful when tweens have been able to explore interests that are relevant to them (Prestridge, Tonduer, & Ottenbreit-Leftwich, 2019). In other words, it has to be meaningful for the tween.

An example of a project-based learning approach that a colleague shared with me recently was through the adoption of the term used by Apple—the Genius Bar—to label a project-based period at his school called The Genius Hour. During the Wednesday afternoon period, groups of tweens worked on projects that were interest-based. These projects were sometimes completely open or could have some boundaries, such as "must require a community benefit" or "focus on a particular multi/disciplinary topic." Other schools are developing an entrepreneurial curriculum in which teams of students pitch a commercial idea to a board of experts who fund the development of the product; examples are easily found within Australian Education Departments.[1] The board of experts plays an important role in providing ideas, supporting the re-design of prototypes, as well as guiding product development and marketing. These approaches position the tween as a creator and innovator able to make real contributions. Team work involves using technologies, and critical thinking underpins such activities. This required a contributing mindset.

Cooper made a point that he did not like the way he uses computers at his school. He doesn't know how it could be used in a more interesting way. Over the years of working with teachers in professional development programs and with pre-service teachers in their course work, I have found that teachers tend to mirror approaches they experienced in their own school years. In a way, education is known as a profession which continually replicates practice. This is evident when tweens are asked to make PowerPoints to summarise their knowledge or a Glogster used as repositories for displaying and presenting information. As identified earlier, these uses of technology do not support the learning process; rather they are tacked on at the end when all the learning is completed. This is similar to the use of electronic textbooks, which again do not make learning better or easier. Electronic textbooks may help accessibility but not necessarily learning. For an emerging curriculum, Cooper needs to use technologies beyond representation or curation of information. He needs to act as a designer using technologies as an intellectual partner to construct knowledge.

David Jonassen claimed back in 1995 that computers were mind tools or cognitive tools that should be considered as unintelligent in that the user provides the planning, decision-making and self-regulation of learning. Computers and digital tools have functions that students can activate for specific purposes that support their learning. For example, the computer can store, retrieve and calculate information performing basic functions that free up the student to think critically. Engaging in higher order thinking processes of judging, analysing and conceptualising information supports students to turn information into knowledge, with the technology acting as a partner. In Middle Years schooling, there are many easily accessible technologies that can act as intellectual partners that support the learning process. A rule of thumb that guides the choice of an App or digital tool is that it needs to be content-free and the student can do something within it (Prestridge & Finger, 2017). Mind maps or semantic networking tools provide verbal and visual representations of multidimensional relationships within concepts that can be built and developed further over the space of the investigation of the concept; databases and spreadsheet functions are available to test what-if thinking to examine relationships and patterns in the data; simulations provide spaces for if-then thinking and experimentation. Thinking about the use of technologies in this way positions the learner in control, "doing" something purposeful with the technology around which discussion and experimentation is taking place. Jonassen's (1995) idea of being a "designer" with technology aligns to being a creator or producer with tweens *contributing* to their learning. He reminds us of why being a contributor rather than a consumer is so important: "The people who learn the most from the design and development of instructional materials are the designers, not the learners for whom the materials are intended" (p. 42).

If Cooper could be more of a *contributor* in school, providing ideas that were valued in class, have more control over the direction of his learning, use technologies in ways that he provides the content, analyses, evaluates, experiments and creates, while collaborating with his friends on authentic projects, then he might see that these learning behaviors are required for being a part of a community of learners, inside and outside school.

6   Future Research and Ethical Considerations

With regard to this naturalistic ethnographic study, I want to stress that I have learnt a lot by talking with my tween. The insights I have gained and reconciled as a co-learner, listening *to* and understanding *not* from my point of view but from Cooper's, has really changed the way I think about using technologies with tweens. It has also shaped my understanding of conducting research, especially research with a child-participant. I have come to understand two significant propositions that will inform my approach to qualitative research in general and more specifically parent-child research. The first message is in regard to the depth and quality of the interview data. There was a richness to the data that was in direct connection with my position as a co-learner, where I adopted a "seeking to understand" stance in which my ignorance supported a more enriching flow of dialogue. In other qualitative studies with teachers, for instance, my position as a researcher might have affected their responses given that my knowledge of technology might have contributed to my power within the inquiry. This is not to say that having a mother-relationship provided greater access to gaining insights; it did in this case, but I can see that such a power-hierarchical mother-child relationship could also restrict conversation. To me the co-learner relationship led to rich data collection. The second message, which I think is a major strength of ethnographic research is the *in situ* longitudinal approach, which provides opportunities for anytime conversations and observations, such as in the car or across the dining table. Having those opportunities is a great advantage which relates to other ethnographic studies where school corridors and staffrooms become the "aha" data collection moment of studies.

In closing, the simple opportunity to talk to my son has led to new educational understandings and paved further research directions. Instead of adding SnapChat into the classroom or a game like *Fortnite* to motivate the tween to engage, I now realise this is the wrong way to understand technology integration. This would not be authentic. I now know it is not the technology that needs to be "transferred." Rather, it is the behavior principles of practice, being able to *communicate* and learn with friends and being valued as a *contributor*. Our role as educators is to help our tweens activate these behavior principles into learning actions so that they can be empowered in any outside school or future work space. These understandings are significant for future professional development of teachers and foundational principles to apply to on-going research in effective use of educational technologies in learning. Thank you, my Cooper.

Note

1 Search: www.australiancurriculum.edu.au + entrepreneurs

References

Abrams, S. S. (2017). Cooperative competition, reflective communication, and social awareness in public high school math classes. In Y. Baek (Ed.), *Game-based learning: Theory, strategies and performance outcomes* (pp. 357–370). Hauppage, NY: Nova Science Publishers.

Abrams, S. S., & Lammers, J. C. (2017). Belonging in a videogame space: Bridging affinity spaces and communities of practice. *Teachers College Record, 119*(12), 1–34.

Australia, Department of Education and Training. (2018). *Through growth to achievement: Report of the review to achieve educational excellence in Australian schools.*

Autor, D. H., & Price, B. M. (2013). *The changing task composition of the US labor market: An update of Autor, Levy, and Murnane (2003).* Cambridge, MA: MIT Press.

Catholic schools Office Lismore, Australia. (2016). Retrieved June, 2012, from http://clf.lism.catholic.edu.au/

Davidson-Shivers, G., & Rasmussen, K. (2006). *Web-based learning: design, implementation, and evaluation.* Upper Saddle River, NJ: Pearson/Merrill/Prentice Hall.

Deutsch, M. (1949). An experimental study of the effects of cooperation and competition upon group process. *Human Relations, 2*, 199–231.

Ertmer, P. A., & Ottenbreit-Leftwich, A. T. (2013). Removing obstacles to the Pedagogical changes required by Jonassen's vision of authentic technology-enabled learning. *Computers & Education, 64*, 175–182.

Ertmer, P. A., Ottenbreit-Leftwich, A. T., Sadik, O., Sendurur, E., & Sendurur, P. (2012). Teacher beliefs and technology integration practices: A critical relationship. *Computers & Education, 59*, 423–435.

Fullan, M. (2013a). Commentary: The new pedagogy: Students and teachers as learning partners. *Learning Landscapes, 6*(2), 23–29.

Fullan, M. (2013b). *Stratosphere—Integrating technology, pedagogy, and change knowledge.* Toronto: Pearson.

Green, B., & Bigum, C. (1993). Aliens in the classroom. *Australian Journal of Education, 37*(2), 119–141.

Harasim, L. (2012). *Learning theory and online technologies.* New York, NY: Routledge.

Horst, H., Herr-Stephenson, B., & Robinson, R. (2009). Media Ecologies. In M. Ito et al. (Eds.), *Hanging out, messing around, and geeking out: Kids living and learning with new media.* Cambridge, MA: MIT Press.

Hsu, P. S. (2016). Examining current beliefs, practices and barriers about technology integration: A case study. *TechTrends, 60*(1), 30–40.

Johnson, D. W., & Johnson, R. T. (1996). Cooperation and the use of technology. In M. Spector, M. D. Merrill, J. Elen, & M. J., Bishop (Eds.), *Handbook of research for educational communications and technology: A project of the association for educational communications and technology* (pp. 1017–1044), New York, NY: Springer-Verlag.

Jonassen, D. H. (1995). Computers as cognitive tools: Learning with technology, not from technology. *Journal of Computing in Higher Education, 6*(2), 40–73.

Krause, K., Bochner, S., Duchesne, S., & McMaugh, A. (2010). *Educational psychology for learning and teaching* (3rd ed.). South Melbourne: Cengage Learning.

Lankshear, C., & Bigum, C. (1998). *Literacies and technologies in school settings: Findings from the field.* Paper presented at the Australian Association for the Teaching of English and the Australian Literacy Educators' Association Conference, Canberra, Australia.

Lenhart, A. (2015). *Teens, social media & technology overview 2015.* Pew Research Centre, Internet & Technology. Retrieved from http://www.pewinternet.org/2015/04/09/teens-social-media-technology-2015/

Luckin, R., Clark, W., Graber, R., Logan, K., Mee, A., & Oliver, M. (2009). Do web 2.0 tools really open the door for learning? Practices perceptions and profiles of 11–16 year-old students. *Learning, Media and Technology, 34*(2), 87–104.

Niederhauser, D. S., Howard, S. K., Voogt, J., Agyei, D. D., Laferriere, T., Tondeur, J., & Cox, M. J. (2018). Sustainability and scalability in educational technology initiatives: Research-informed practice. *Technology, Knowledge and Learning, 23*(3), 507–523.

Poitras, E., Doleck, T., Huang, L., Li, S., & Lajoie, S. (2017). Advancing teacher technology education using open-ended learning environments as research and training platforms. *Australasian Journal of Educational Technology, 33*(3).

Prestridge, S. (2012). The beliefs behind the teacher that influences their ICT practices. *Computers & Education, 58*(1), 449–458.

Prestridge, S. (2017). Examining the shaping of teachers' pedagogical orientation for the use of technology. *Technology, Pedagogy and Education, 26*(4), 367–381.

Prestridge, S., & de Aldama, C. (2016). A classification framework for exploring technology-enabled practice—FrameTEP. *Journal of Educational Computing Research, 54*(7), 901–921.

Prestridge, S., & Finger, G. (2017). Chapter 15-using ICT in middle years classrooms. In N.Bar, D. Pendergast & K. Main (Eds.), *Teaching middle years: Rethinking curriculum, pedagogy and assessment.* Crows Nest, NSW: Allen & Unwin.

Prestridge, S., Tondeur, J., & Ottenbreit-Leftwich, A. T. (2019). Insights from ICT-expert teachers about the design of educational practice: The learning opportunities of social media. *Technology, Pedagogy and Education, 28*(2), 157–172.

Project Tomorrow. (2016a). *From print to pixel: The role of videos, games, animations and simulations within K-12 education. Speak up 2015 national findings.* Retrieved May 5, 2016, from http://www.tomorrow.org/speakup/pdfs/SU15AnnualReport.pdf

Project Tomorrow. (2016b). *Ten things everyone should know about k-12 students' digital learning.* Retrieved May 5, 2016, from http://www.tomorrow.org/speakup/pdfs/10things_students2015.pdf

Robinson, K., & Aronica, L. (2016). *Creative schools: The grassroots revolution that's transforming education.* New York, NY: Penguin Books.

Scherer, R., Siddiq, F., & Teo, T. (2015). Becoming more specific: Measuring and modelling teachers' perceived usefulness of ICT in the context of teaching and learning. *Computers & Education, 88*, 202–214.

Schunk, D. (2008). *Learning theories: An educational perspective.* Upper Saddle River, NJ: Pearson Merrill Prentice Hall.

Steinberg, S. R. (2011). *Kinderculture: The corporate construction of childhood.* London: Hachette.

Velding, V. (2017). Depicting femininity: Conflicting messages in a "tween magazine. *Youth & Society, 49*(4), 505–527.

Wang, S., Hsu, H., Campbell, T, Coster, D., & Longhurst, M. (2014). An investigation of the middle year school science teachers and students use of technologies inside and outside of the classroom: considering whether digital natives are more technology savvy than their teachers. *Educational Technology Research and Development, 62*, 637–662.

Yang, H. (2012). ICT in English schools: Transforming education? *Technology, Pedagogy and Education, 21*(1), 101–118.

CHAPTER 4

High Anxiety: A Collaborative Autoethnographic Inquiry

Kathleen M. Alley and Cassandra R. Skrobot

Abstract

This chapter shares a parent-child interaction tied to autoethnographic research that used a co-operative inquiry approach—a way of working with someone who shares similar concepts and interests. Research is often thought of as something done on people, rather than with people. Instead of this traditional model, the authors discuss a shared exploration—a journey of inquiry—to better understand an anxiety disorder Cassandra developed during her late teens and early twenties. The researchers sought to make sense of their entwined relationship as parent and child, and to develop new and creative ways to look at what Cassandra was experiencing and how to improve her outcomes.

1 Introduction

Cassandra felt like she couldn't breathe. She couldn't stop shaking, began to gasp for air, and started to black out as her body went numb and she fell to the ground. When this happened in the fall of her freshman year of college, Cassandra was on her way back to her dorm room. She'd just finished band practice after a full day of classes. Seeing what happened, other students rushed to her aid, calling campus police, who brought her to the university health care center; the first of many trips to come. Panic attacks and blacking out became commonplace as Cassandra tried to cope with increasing stress that fall.

About one third of U.S. college students have difficulty functioning due to depression, and almost one-half share that they feel overwhelming anxiety (American College Health Association, 2013). I see this at my own university, where many of my teacher candidates share their feelings of anxiety each semester. My students often state they are overwhelmed, trying to keep up with the work load from their courses, homework, extracurricular activities, and part-time work responsibilities. They don't seem to be able to organize their time effectively or efficiently, lacking the skills to cope with ever-increasing demands on their time and attention. When I suggest they might need to cut back, my students seem surprised, not recognizing that no one is able to finish 30+ hours of work in a 24-hour day! Additionally, they seem to be measuring what they can and cannot achieve against unrealistic expectations, trying to achieve what is ultimately impossible for anyone.

I have also witnessed the debilitating effects of anxiety experienced by my daughter Cassandra. Though we now recognize Cassandra began to struggle with anxiety during her middle and high school years, those difficulties were compounded ten-fold when she left home for a southeastern university her freshman year of college. In my daughter's case, I believe the education system, obsessed with a narrow definition of success and a one-size-fits-all approach that negates individuality, is at least partially at fault—but so am I, and so is the greater community supporting our youth. As I searched for answers and became an advocate for my own daughter, I began to understand it is up to the adults in students' lives—parents, teachers, community leaders, educational researchers, everyone—to discover ways to reduce the pressure young people experience.

This chapter explores the experiences of my daughter Cassandra and I as she developed an anxiety disorder during her late teens and early twenties. The experiences we share occurred between 2012 and 2016; however, this study was conducted in the past year (2018–2019) in response to our recent discussions as we sought understanding and closure. We used collaborative autoethnographic (CAE) inquiry as a means to "discover in the eruption of a story, the soft reminiscent light of accidental talk, in a burst of memory overstepping forgetting—a world of hope" (Poulos, 2009, p. 15). Our "burst[s] of memory" about our experiences sprung forth from those dialogic conversations. In narrating our experiences, we were able to represent the complexities of grappling with anxiety disorder as a subjective whole (Denzin & Lincoln, 2011), as well as the parent-child relationship in our stories because autoethnography is a knowledge building practice that goes beyond storytelling. The question we created to guide our process was: In what ways have our respective experiences influenced our understanding of college students who experience anxiety disorder?

2   Review of Literature

To better understand the complexity of anxiety experienced by emerging adults, we explored the literature, focusing specifically on college students and anxiety disorder. We explored recent research sharing the scale of this issue, the number of college students affected, and factors contributing to their development of anxiety. We also examined research related to inquiry that involved intimate others, since Cassandra and I had a well-established prior relationship as mother and daughter.

2.1   *College Students and Anxiety*

The primary reason that college students seek counseling today is anxiety (Tate, 2017). More than one-half of college students who visited their campus counseling centers during the 2015–2016 academic year reported symptoms of anxiety, according to a survey conducted by the Association for University and College Counseling Center Directors (Reetz, Bershad, LeViness, & Whitlock, 2017). Anxiety disorder is a class of mental illnesses that include generalized anxiety disorder, panic disorder, obsession/compulsive disorder, and social anxiety, as well as several other types (Reetz et al., 2017).

Since 2009, anxiety has been cited as the primary concern among college students (Reetz et al., 2017). Analysis of mental health data for high school and college students between 1938 and 2007 revealed that an increasing number of young people have reported symptoms of mental illness in general, and anxiety disorder in particular (Reetz et al., 2017). More than 60,000 young people self-reported emotions and symptoms in response to multiple surveys. Researchers found across this time frame that teenagers described themselves in changing terms, including increased feelings of isolation, sensitivity, being misunderstood, narcissism, worry, sadness, low self-control, and general dissatisfaction.

2.2   *Factors Contributing to College Students' Anxiety*

Research findings indicate that several factors contribute to this rise in symptoms of anxiety disorder, including: academic stress (e.g., Kariv & Heiman, 2005; Lester, 2014; Misra, McKean, West, & Russo, 2000); separation from family and/or parental pressure (e.g., Pomerantz, Kim, & Cheung, 2012; Raftery, Grolnick, & Flamm, 2012; Ratelle, Duchesne, & Guay, 2017); financial stress (e.g., Archuleta, Dale, & Spann, 2013; Callender & Jackson, 2008); constant connectivity via cell phone (e.g., Lu, Watanabe, Liu, Uji, Shono, & Kitamura, 2011; Rosen, Whaling, Rab, Carrier, Cheever, 2013) and social media (e.g., Calancie,

Ewing, Narducci, Horgan, & Khalid-Khan, 2017; Mander & Young, 2017); and culturally prevalent beliefs regarding success (Wormeli, 2018).

2.2.1   Academic Stress

While there is a solid body of research on stress, academic stress is a newer and more nuanced area of study. Wilks (2008) defined academic stress as "the product of a combination of academic related demands that exceed the adaptive resources available to an individual" (p. 107). According to research findings, several demands comprise academic stress: course requirements, time management issues, interaction with faculty, personal goals, adjustment to campus environment, and lack of support networks (Kariv & Heiman, 2005; Misra, 2000). If students are unable to cope effectively with these and other stressors, then psycho-social-emotional health consequences may result (MacGeorge, Samter, & Gillikan, 2005; Tennant, 2002). In addition to these effects, academic stress can interfere with academic performance, which in turn may be harmful considering the competitive job market and emphasis on undergraduate academics (Elias, Ping, & Abdullah, 2011).

2.2.2   Separation from Family and Parental Pressure

We live today in a very competitive environment, including academics. A lot of students come from successful parents who put a high premium on their child being successful, and in a university setting success equates to grades (Benner, Boyle, & Sadler, 2016). Therefore, many college students feel inordinate pressure from parents and society to be successful in school, as evidenced through excellent grades. Although research findings have indicated that parent factors can have a positive association with, or facilitate, children's achievement, there is also concern that unrealistic parental expectations will create pressure and foster performance anxiety (Raymo, Somers, & Partridge, 2018). For example, it can be extremely detrimental when parents pressure their children to achieve academically at unrealistically high levels. Researchers (Benner, Boyle, & Sadler, 2016) who study parental guidance versus pressure share that parents' values and beliefs concerning achievement might be at the heart of this issue. Common pressures students share that their parents place on them include parents who want their children to go to a specific college, and those who want children to stay close to home.

2.2.3   Financial Stress

Emerging adulthood involves significant life transition and increased financial responsibility, which has been shown to influence college students' mental health (Roberts et al., 2000). College prices have risen beyond what most families can afford—more than 2.5 times as high as they were 30 years ago (Ma, Baum, Pender, & Welch, 2017). Students at public four-year institutions paid an average of $3,190 in tuition for the 1987–1988 school year, with prices adjusted to reflect 2017 dollars. Thirty years later, that average has risen to $9,970 for the 2017–2018 school year; a 213% increase (Ma et al., 2017).

A review of literature on mental health and financial concerns of college students suggested there needs to be an increased focus on their financial and psychological wellbeing (Roberts et al., 2000). Findings indicated there was a link between college students' adverse financial situations and a negative impact on mental and physical health. Financial stressors have also been positively associated with increased anxiety and depression (Andrews & Wilding, 2004), and academic performance (Joo, Durband, & Grable, 2008). Further, students who considered leaving the university prior to completing their program of study due to financial strain reported poorer psychological health (Roberts, Golding, Towell, & Weinreb, 1999). In contrast, financial satisfaction is an integral component of overall life satisfaction and wellbeing (Plagnol, 2011).

2.2.4   Constant Connectivity

Research investigating cell phone use and anxiety is limited, and measures of anxiety vary from study to study, but there is evidence of a positive relationship between cell phone use and anxiety, particularly among individuals identified as problematic cell phone users (Beranuy, Oberst, Carbonell, & Chamarro, 2009; Bianchi & Phillips, 2005; Lu, Watanabe, Liu, Uji, Shono, & Kitamura, 2011). Problematic cell phone use has been described as an addiction-like behavior leading individuals to use the cell phone compulsively (Takao, Takahashi, & Kitamura, 2009). However, it is not clear whether the relationship between cell phone use and anxiety exists independently of problematic behavior. Nonetheless, even typical cell phone users experience some level of anxiety as a result of a perceived obligation to remain constantly connected with others (Merlo, 2008). Research findings indicate not being able to connect with technology, particularly Facebook, text messages, and cell phone calls, as frequently as desired can be associated with feelings of anxiety (Rosen et al., 2013). Technology use and technology-related anxiety have also been seen to be predictive of mood and personality disorders (Rosen et al., 2013).

Increasingly, there is a diversity of media-related technologies accessible through cell phones as well; thus, when exploring behavioral impacts of cell phones, there is a need to consider other uses such as gaming, Facebook, Instagram, surfing the Internet, and so forth. Researchers have explored many of these activities in relation to anxiety independent of cell phone use (i.e., with other electronic devices), but not the influences of these activities when used via cell phones, which imply a 24/7 connectivity. However, there is research to suggest that it is not the amount of time a person spends online but rather what they are doing online that affects these variables (Chen & Tzeng, 2010). For example, Chen and Tzeng found that women high Internet users who engaged in information seeking and chatting had better academic performance, but they were more depressed than were low users of the Internet.

2.2.5   Social Media

Social media and young peoples' need to maintain a certain image is another factor influencing anxiety among youth today. Individuals born in the 1990s and later grew up in a world where home computers and social media are common (Seemiller & Grace, 2016), with two lives they view as being equally real: digital and analog (in person). In their digital lives, which are often dominated by social media interaction, they are constantly trying to maintain an image by painting pictures of their lives through posts of photographs and stories. Further, young people compare their own realities with the images that others paint on social media—images of what they want others to think, but that might or might not be founded in reality. Additionally, cell phones and computers have been shown to be addictive in and of themselves (Lepp, Barkley, Sanders, & Karpinski, 2014). Students are not just occasionally thinking about how they match up with others; they keep checking and checking, displaying addictive behavior, in the hopes of increased good feelings they are craving. Unfortunately, they are far more likely to receive feelings of anxiety and depression (Primack et al., 2017).

Comparing themselves to others on social media is compounded by the fact that youth spend, on average, 4 hours a day on social media, thereby constantly comparing themselves to people they follow on Snapchat, Instagram, and more. Young people spend at least one quarter of their waking lives on social media, which leads to more emotional distress (Mander & Young, 2017). Findings from research indicate a direct link between the quantity of time spent on social media and levels of anxiety and depression (Lin et al., 2016). Additionally, the more anxious young people feel, the more tempted they become to search social media for information about their social status, which creates a never-ending, vicious cycle (Lin et al., 2016). Exacerbating this issue is that the time youth now spend checking social media used to be spent hanging out with friends, which generally contributed to a more positive outcome. Chatting in person, unlike reading about friends on social media, builds social connections between youth and others, which, in turn, builds young peoples' self-confidence. In contrast, social media creates anxious feelings while also decreasing the amount of oxytocin-induced good feelings generated by actual friend-to-friend contact (Calancie et al., 2017).

2.2.6   Culturally Prevalent Beliefs

Many young people today, including my daughter, believe they must be perfect to be happy and successful. Our education system, with its heavy focus on grades, sends the message to students, families, and the greater community that good grades equal success and bad grades equal failure (Wormeli, 2018). Unfortunately, buying into this belief that grades are the most important factor determining success and happiness in life promotes significant issues with anxiety. Students are terrified they will not be able to measure up, seeing themselves as a failure if they do not get *all A's*. Although students should be encouraged to work hard, seek advice and tutoring, and strive to learn, serious problems can develop when they adopt a belief that grades are everything. As a society, we need to shift our beliefs to a perspective that focuses on learning because of interest in a subject, which, in turn, might decrease stress and allow learners to gain more education from studies (Wormeli, 2018).

3   Method

This qualitative study sought to answer the question: In what ways have our respective experiences influenced our understanding of college students who experience anxiety disorder?

To do so, we adopted the Collaborative Auto Ethnographic (CAE) methodology (Chang, Ngunjiri, & Hernandez, 2013), which is an approach to autoethnographic research. Chang et al. define CAE as "a qualitative research method in which researchers work in community to collect their autobiographical materials and to analyze and interpret their data collectively to gain a meaningful understanding of sociocultural phenomena reflected in their autobiographical data" (pp. 23–24). Using CAE, researchers are "simultaneously the instrument and the data source" (Chang et al., p. 22). Thus, CAE research allows for a deeper understanding about self and other, and fosters collaboration among researchers. In our case, the CAE approach allowed Cassandra and me to better converse about our experiences, providing a rich description of our recollections, and highlighting similarities and differences between our experiences. We share our stories in the findings section, juxtaposing our recollections with each other and creating a new understanding jointly.

3.1   *Participants*

We are a mother (Kathleen) and daughter (Cassandra) who live in the south-eastern United States. As a college student, 18 to 22 years of age (2012–2016), Cassandra experienced symptoms of anxiety and was eventually diagnosed with an anxiety disorder. During this same time, I (Kathleen) was a new assistant professor at a different southeastern university, supporting my daughter during this time of discovery as the family searched for understanding and answers. Though we discussed what we both were experiencing multiple times during this period, we did not initially consider these interactions research. However, in the past few years we have each individually researched anxiety disorders, discussing our experiences and trying to make sense of and find closure together.

During her high school years, my daughter and I were jointly involved in research for my doctoral dissertation. At that time, I sought to understand the text-based role-play-games Cassandra and her friends engaged in online. I wanted to investigate the social and literacy practices supporting these interactions–an interesting form of online, collaborative writing, where participants created stories through role-play on a text-based forum (Alley, 2013, 2018). For this research, Cassandra and I established the ability to engage in dialogic conversations and to use other methods of inquiry (Alley, 2013, 2018). Thus, working together was something we were already comfortable doing as co-inquirers, so it was natural for us to approach this new situation collaboratively, using an autoethnographic model in a similar fashion.

3.2   *Theoretical Framework*

We chose to use a person-centered approach (Rogers, 1957) as a theoretical frame for this inquiry; this is a non-directive form of talk therapy that evolved from the work of Carl Rogers, which allows the client to lead the discussion and is not steered in any way by the therapist, or in our case by the lead researcher (myself). Rogers defined six conditions that he felt needed to exist between individuals (client and therapist), and continue over a period of time: (1) two persons are in a minimal relationship, a psychological contact (client/participant, therapist/researcher); (2) the client is in a state of incongruence, being vulnerable or anxious; (3) the therapist is congruent or integrated in the relationship; (4) the therapist experiences unconditional positive regard for the client; (5) the therapist experiences an empathic understanding of the client's internal frame of reference and endeavors to communicate this experience to the first; and, (6) this communication is to a minimal degree achieved.

Two concepts among these conditions were paramount for our inquiry: (1) the genuineness of the relationship, and (2) unconditional positive regard

(Rogers, 1957). Though I am not a therapist, within the construct of this theory as lead research I took that role and thus it was important for me to be freely and deeply myself: genuine and unafraid. Likewise, I needed to provide Cassandra with unconditional positive regard. There were no conditions of acceptance—a feeling that I would only accept her if she acted or said thus. I had to care for Cassandra as a separate person, with permission to have her own feelings, her own experiences. In essence, I needed to foster her possession of her own experience—thinking, feeling, wanting, and fearing what she did (Rogers, 1957).

We also borrowed from Dr. Carolyn Ellis's (2007) concept of relational ethics, which requires researchers to: (a) act from their hearts and minds, (b) acknowledge interpersonal bonds to others, and (c) take responsibility for actions and their consequences. Researchers must repeatedly ask themselves what their ethical responsibilities are towards those involved in their research. On a fairly traditional level, researchers must monitor how participants are treated in humane, non-exploitative ways. Further, researchers should ask themselves, "What are our ethical responsibilities toward participants when they are intimate others in our research?" And, "How can we be mindful of the various roles we take on as researchers when intimate others are implicated in the stories we write?" (Guillemin & Gillam, 2004). In addition, researchers should be mindful that they create currents of relation and reverberations from those relationships. Although there are no absolutes, other researchers' experiences can help researchers to consider possible solutions to the quandaries they might face (e.g., Adams, 2006; Ellis, 2001, 2004; Kiesinger, 2002; Rambo, 2005). This was a particularly important focus for me, as I had taken an authoritative role much of Cassandra's life; I didn't want to remain in that role now.

3.3   *Researching with Intimate Others*

Although working with intimate others in research can be a cause for concern (Etherington, 2007), it should not stop researchers from engaging in this type of research. Qualitative research can be inherently problematic from an ethical stand point. Etherington (2007) described ethics as a balancing act "between our own needs as researchers and our obligations toward care for, and connection with, those who participate in our research" (p. 614). However, as Maguire (1987) stated, "Without close, empathetic, interpersonal interchange and relationships, researchers will find it impossible to gain meaningful insights into human interaction or to understand the meaning people give to their own behavior" (pp. 20–21). Maguire demands researchers' active involvement in the research processes and presumably the products that result from relational and intimate research. Busier et al. (1997) defined intimate relationships as those that "include qualities of mutual care and friendship as well as revelation of, and respect for, personal vulnerabilities" (p. 165). Thus, we are not isolated, but instead we are "relational beings" who grow through our connections with others (Jordan, Kaplan, Miller, Stiver, & Surray, 1991, p. 167). This was the foundation I chose to build from when exploring topics with my daughter.

Narratives of fieldwork intimacy are supported by multiple research philosophies that help to unmask the researcher, showing him or her as a human being to participants (Ellis, 2007; Goodwin, Pope, Mort, & Smith, 2003; Guillemin & Gillam, 2004). However, there is still a certain level of concern in the research community regarding the use of data obtained through researchers' intimate relationships in the field. To address these concerns, researchers have explored multiple dimension of ethics, including: procedural ethics (Guillemin & Gillam, 2004), ethics of practice (Goodwin, Pope, Mort, & Smith, 2003), and relational ethics (Ellis, 2007). Procedural ethics (Guillemin & Gillam, 2004) involves the type of ethics demanded by an Institutional Review Board (IRB) committee to ensure informed consent, confidentiality, rights to privacy, deception and protecting human subjects from harm were all adequately handled. Ethics of practice (Goodwin, Pope, Mort, & Smith, 2003), also known as situational ethics, deals with the unpredictable, yet ethically important moments that come up in the field. Relational ethics (Ellis, 2007) is a third dimension closely related to ethics of care (Noddings, 1984) that means doing what is necessary to be "true to one's character and responsible for one's actions and their consequences on others" (Slattery & Rapp, 2003). Of these three dimensions, relational ethics in particular require researchers to recognize the interpersonal bonds they have with others, and to consider the relationships they create over time with research participants.

3.4 Positionality and Power

"Research positionality encompasses both societal ascribed and achieved identities that confer status on an individual researcher, such as race/ethnicity, or level of education attained" (Muhammad et al., 2015, p. 1051). In addition, positionality involves relationships between the researcher and others in the community being researched; negotiated through life experiences, connections and motivations for all parties involved (Muhammad et al., 2015). Power also impacts multiple aspects of the research process and must be mediated, beginning with how a team constructs the research process, through data collection and analysis, to knowledge creation.

To tackle issues of positionality and power, my daughter and I sought to be aware and reflexive, sharing insider status equally as we each represented a unique experiences and perspective, drawing on family and cultural backgrounds during knowledge creation (Martin, 2008). During this informal inquiry, my daughter and I positioned ourselves as partners and co-researchers. We each intentionally shared our authentic lack of knowledge about anxiety disorders and what might best support our family as we traveled this new path together, which minimized the perception that one of us might be in a knowledge-privileged position. As part of the collaborative autoethnographic process, we "gazed inward on the self, while maintaining the outward gaze of ethnography, looking at the larger context wherein self-experiences occur" (Denzin & Lincoln, 2011, p. 227).

We regularly engaged in discussions regarding our internal motivations and goals throughout data collection, analysis and knowledge creation. We both came to this inquiry with many questions and concerns, and we wanted to explore the existing research and possible options we could pursue to better support everyone. However, if I ever sensed any resistance, I quickly offered Cassandra an opportunity to talk with me at a later time or not at all. I also encouraged Cassandra to disagree with me and challenge my understandings, as I would hers. Ultimately, we considered our work mutually beneficial and were successful in creating opportunities wherein we could discuss ideas and seek solutions.

3.5   Data Collection and Analysis

Cassandra and I are family. As her mother, it is my job to support her needs—particularly when she is not well. We have always both loved discourse and writing, so it is natural for us to talk regularly, and we often email, text and message one another. We also both keep journals off and on, which are generally confidential; we do not normally share them with each other. However, we were able to use these and other resources to spark discussion retroactively when we began this inquiry, interrogating our feelings and emotions as expressed in those earlier writings. Our data collection methods, commonly used in CAE research, involved an iterative approach: preliminary data collection; subsequent data collection; data analysis and interpretation; and lots of conversations and writing. We revisited the data several times throughout the research process, sharing and reflecting on our contributions.

As we both considered the past several years and what we'd learned from the journey we'd been on, Cassandra and I engaged in ongoing conversations about research goals, developed a timeline for this project, and divided the workload. Because Cassandra was expecting her first child the end of 2018, it was decided I would contribute the review of literature and share my findings with her. By the end of summer, 2018 we both had written an individual narrative about our experiences with Cassandra's anxiety disorder her first two years in college. Once we completed these narratives, we exchanged them, took notes, and discussed them together. We talked about next steps, including a second draft of our narratives. After reflecting and commenting on each other's drafts, we each wrote a new draft of our narratives, partially provided in this chapter.

We shared our revised narratives with each other, discussing any adjustments that might need to be made. I then coded our narratives thematically. We met after I completed that initial coding at the end of 2018 to discuss similarities and differences I had identified in our stories. This meeting was audio-recorded. We focused our discussion on our research question and on the information that emerged to answer it (based on grounded theory methodology; Corbin & Strauss, 2015). During this time, I spoke to Cassandra often so that I could receive her input regarding the connections I was finding across our narratives and with the existing literature.

4   Findings—Our Stories

To answer our inquiry into the ways our respective experiences have influenced Cassandra and my understanding of college students with anxiety disorder, we looked across our narratives using collaborative autoethnographic practices; discussing commonalities across these stories generated the social construction of our reality and knowledge (Geist-Martin et al., 2010). Both our stories offer insights about facets of our shared experience, but it is the juxta-positioning of these facets that crystalized and created something new conceptually. Herein we share the beginning of our stories, as well as three themes that emerged when analyzing our data. We have named these three themes "the three E's" and used them as a heuristic to think about what we learned from our shared experiences: the influence of expectations, emotions and environment on college students' development of anxiety disorder.

4.1   *The Beginning*

Cassandra's anxiety and subsequent depression came on slowly, beginning most likely in middle school, and worsening during high school and college. Kathleen shared, "Initially, her father and I noticed she seemed to be overly concerned about typical teenage issues, like how peers might perceive her, what she looked like." Though she was a strong student with a high IQ who had always done well in school, Cassandra also began to exhibit frustration and anxiety prior to being assessed, especially during district and state testing windows, and later with Advanced Placement and AP/College Entrance exams. In essence, though she really had nothing to worry about, Cassandra was obsessing prior to tests of any kind about how to prepare, and whether she would remember what she had learned. This test anxiety was the first thing to be diagnosed, about the time she was fifteen years of age.

Additionally, as Cassandra began to date in high school, she experienced social anxiety to the extent that it made her physically ill either prior to or after a date. As Cassandra shared:

> When I was in high school, I had anxiety during dates so bad I would come home and throw up everything I'd eaten. I couldn't hold food down when I was dealing with those feelings, and I lost a lot of weight. Eventually I did learn to deal with that better in high school, but my stomach issues came back immediately when I went to college.

By the time she was heading off the college, Cassandra felt ready to take on new challenges and that she'd gotten these problems under control, but they would resume, and new issues would join *them* as she experienced new stressors.

4.2   *Expectations*
Many different types of expectations held by multiple stakeholders in Cassandra's life, as well as the perceptions Cassandra held regarding those expectations, contributed toward the stress she felt and her development of anxiety.

4.2.1   Academic Expectations
Looking across our narratives and conversations, it was apparent that expectations played a big part in Cassandra's developing anxiety and depression. Like other college students, Cassandra struggled with an image of success she felt she couldn't attain, as well as parental and peer pressure, in additional to pressure she placed on herself. Kathleen shared:

> By the time Cassandra had entered the university her freshman year, she felt an ever-increasing burden because she was unable to measure up to an image she came to accept as "success"—further aggravated because Cassandra felt it was the image her father and I held, and what we expected her to achieve.

Cassandra struggled to feel confidence academically, having a difficult time deciding on a major, completing classwork, and successfully finishing a full load of classes each semester. She shared, "Summer classes were actually easier for me to handle because they were more manageable. I liked taking fewer classes and having a shorter time to focus on them." However, even with a lighter load, Cassandra found it difficult to achieve at a level she felt equated to success. When she didn't earn an A or B in a class, Cassandra felt defeated. Additionally, she was overly concerned about sharing that news with her parents, believing they would feel she wasn't applying herself and fault her for not doing her best. Further, Kathleen shared, "Cassandra struggled during this time to understand why something that seemed so easy for many of her friends was so difficult for her to manage." Cassandra felt her friends weren't sharing these struggles, though she admitted she'd never really talked about it with most of them. Cassandra also grappled with the knowledge that school was no longer as easy for her as it had once been in high school, just a few short years ago.

4.2.2   Social Expectations

Socially it was also difficult for Cassandra to meet expectations she set for herself. She had an idealized version of what college would be like playing in her head prior to and when she first started. Cassandra shared, "I was so excited about going away to college. I looked forward to the freedom I knew would come with it, and to new opportunities." However, she didn't realize that with this new freedom would also come new responsibilities, and that she would have to rise to several challenges, juggling academics and her social life to keep up with expectations.

Cassandra wanted to feel a part of the university community, so she decided to try out for marching band; something she had participated in since middle school, and that gave her great joy and confidence previously. She shared, "At the end of the summer, I tried out for the marching band and was very happy when I was selected; it is a very competitive process, but now I had a whole new family—about 300 strong." At the same time, being a band member would prove to be very challenging since, as Cassandra put it, "I was expected to be at practice every afternoon in the fall, and my weekends on home games were pretty much taken up by band 24/7. Sometimes that was tough because I didn't have time to get my classwork done." Juggling band, classes, and her social life became quite overwhelming as the fall semester progressed and more responsibilities were added each day. Additionally, though she was becoming friends with band members, Cassandra wasn't able to get involved in social activities beyond band because it took up so much of her time. This made her feel somewhat isolated.

4.2.3   Parental Factors

Cassandra also experienced anxiety when separated from family—more than she expected she would feel. She shared:

> I was accepted by two universities during my senior year and decided to attend one of them, though the other offered me more scholarship money. However, that one was closer to home and a university my mother had attended…it just didn't feel like "my" university. Mom was also working there, and I didn't want to go to a school where she worked; I'd experienced that in middle school. I wanted something of my own. I love my Mom, but it was time to get away from home.

Going to a different university from where Kathleen worked was a good choice in many ways, but it did involve being a further distance from home (a 5-hour drive), as well as additional stress since Cassandra lost some of her scholarships because her grade point average decreased, which caused a greater financial burden.

Kathleen also shared:

> Cassandra seemed to think we expected her to get all As, but that was never the case. She is an A/B student generally, so her father and I were happy if she kept her grade point average at or above 3.0. We did worry when she was struggling so much in classes we thought she should have been able to handle, but were not sure how to help her.

Although Cassandra's parents didn't expect her to earn As or even Bs all the time, they did hope she would learn content and be able to move forward, eventually graduating with an undergraduate degree. For whatever reason, it took a long while for Cassandra to accept these were her parents' actual expectations, and that she wasn't required to do more to receive their approval and praise.

4.2.4   Peer and Self-Pressure

Though Cassandra did not experience anxiety related to measuring up to an ideal on the Internet she'd created for herself with friends, as seen in related research, she did struggle with being "available" through constant connection via social media, texting and messaging through her smart phone. Kathleen shared, "Cassandra always had her cell phone out when I went to visit her. She had to be connected to friends all the time. Many of these friends were not physically in that geographic area however, which I found interesting." Cassandra confirmed, "I couldn't put my phone away. I even fell asleep with it in my hand. I had to keep checking it to make sure I wasn't missing something." In conversations, we both realized that part of Cassandra's feelings of being overwhelmed were exacerbated by these actions. Cassandra never disconnected from her friends; she never just stepped away to rest and recharge, which was exhausting.

4.3   *Emotions*

A second theme that emerged across our narratives and conversations was the impact that emotions played in Cassandra's development of anxiety. Cassandra did feel very excited initially about going away to college, as shared earlier, but she also felt extremely overwhelmed with the many new responsibilities she juggled. This was made worse because Cassandra lacked organization and study skills to manage her academic and social worlds. For example, keeping up with class assignments for five classes that didn't meet every day, as had her high school classes, was difficult to get accustomed to at first. Cassandra shared:

> I tried to use a planner, but that didn't work. I would write everything in it, but then not go back and look at it several times a day to make sure I was getting things done. I was great at the planning stage, and not too good with follow through and using the planner.

Although Cassandra made efforts to stay on top of things, she struggled and really needed some guidance. In retrospect, she could have benefitted from taking a study skills class and being connected to university resources that would possibly have supported her needs and reduced this stressor.

Cassandra began to feel overwhelmed more of the time, mostly from over scheduling herself and from waiting too long to begin assignments. She felt worried a majority of the time, struggling with feelings of failure as she tried to keep up with an increasingly hectic schedule. When her anxiety became overwhelming to the extent that it began to cause physical and emotional symptoms, Cassandra was scared. Initially, she experienced difficulty eating and keeping food down, as she had when she dealt with social anxiety in high school. Cassandra shared, "It was hard to make myself go to the cafeteria because food smells made me feel sick. I never wanted to eat, and when I did, I had severe stomach pains."

Cassandra began to experience severe stomach pains, which often sent her searching for help at the health center on campus. Cassandra shared, "They gave me a GI cocktail and monitored my vital signs, giving me fluid and getting me stabilized." This happened a half-dozen times before Cassandra decided to come home, which her parents and the university supported. Cassandra shared:

When the stomach attacks would hit me, it was very scary. I didn't know what to do and I wasn't able to be alone to deal with the pain because I had a roommate. Particularly in the middle of the night when this would often hit, I had nowhere to go. I would cry in a bathroom stall or sit in the hallway talking to my Mom in the middle of the night on my cell phone, trying to calm down and get through the attack. And this dorm was not the nice one I had stayed in during the summer; my dorm was one of the oldest on campus, with very small rooms and hallway bathrooms shared by everyone. No privacy.

Cassandra also was often dizzy and fainted a few times. Kathleen shared:

Cassandra often felt lightheaded, experiencing migraines and vision difficulties during high school, which accelerated in college. Cassandra told me she would begin to hear a buzzing noise, see spots in her vision, become lightheaded, and then lose consciousness. She would come to lying on the ground a minute or so later, with people trying to help her or standing above her staring; something that was acutely embarrassing.

In retroactive conversation, Kathleen and Cassandra discussed that she was probably often dizzy because she wasn't eating much and was becoming dehydrated as well. This scared Cassandra quite a bit more than she ever let Kathleen know. Cassandra shared:

I didn't know why it was happening, and I never knew when it would happen, which was frightening at the time. I wasn't sure if I should tell my Mom because I didn't want her to worry; I knew she'd be up immediately if she knew, and I wanted to handle it myself.

As these dizzy periods and fainting spells continued, along with her stomach problems and in general not feeling well, it became harder for Cassandra to make herself get out of bed and go to class each day. Cassandra shared:

I started to find it difficult to get to classes. Eventually, there were days I just couldn't make myself get out of bed—especially in the morning. Even when I could get myself up and going, I was only making it to afternoon classes and band practices, and I began to miss some of them as well, pleading illness.

After several months of struggle, Cassandra finally began to discuss the possibility of returning home to consult specialists and find out if there was anything medically causing the issues she was experiencing, as well as to seek counseling to support her emotional needs. Cassandra stated:

> After several attacks like this, as well as my many trips to the doctor and health center, my parents and I decided it was time for me to go home and figure out what was going on. My father came up to withdraw me from school; a medical withdraw my Dean was happy to support. I am not sure even today how I felt about leaving...I guess I felt like I'd failed, but I didn't know what else to do.

These feelings of failure plagued her for years to come, and she still struggles today. Cassandra returned home and attended the local junior college for the spring semester, reconnecting with some of her high school friends. However, they'd moved on and she felt somewhat isolated and disconnected. Eventually she was diagnosed with stomach issues resulting from stress, but no serious physical condition emerged at that time to account for her symptoms. However, she was later diagnosed with ulcerative colitis as well as social anxiety disorder. Cassandra shared, "Being diagnosed helped, because I was finally starting to figure out what was happening, but it didn't provide me with answers to make things alright again. I am not sure they were ever 'alright' to begin with though."

4.4   *Environment*

A third theme that emerged as contributing to Cassandra's stress and feelings of anxiety regarded the university environment and built-in support systems for students. Cassandra realized that attending the summer program prior to her freshman year was extremely supportive. She shared, "I got to live in a really nice dorm on campus and enjoyed all the activities the university planned to help students feel a part of the community." She also enjoyed the activities that were constantly sponsored by various entities on campus, including student organizations and facilities like the student union and movie theater, as well as the things being offered through student housing. However, one difficulty Cassandra experienced as a result of her involvement in band was that these activities were often held at conflicting times during band practice or other required band events, so she wasn't able to take advantage of them as much during fall semester as she had done in the summer. This limited her ability to make friends outside of band members, and to experience many of the things a first-year student would experience living in student housing—important supportive elements developed for new and transfer students to acclimate to university life.

The university Cassandra chose to attend was also very large (~45,000 under-graduates), so she often felt lost in a sea of students, making few connections that would have helped her to develop a sense of belonging. She was often in lecture hall classrooms with several hundred students as well, rather than a more intimate context that would have been conducive to getting to know other students who shared that course. This made it difficult for her to focus when she attended classes as well, which also made it easier for Cassandra to skip class if she felt overwhelmed and didn't want to attend. As Cassandra put it: "I'd never be missed anyway." Further, the campus itself was very large and was located in a large metropolitan area. Though this was initially exciting, it also caused Cassandra to feel overwhelmed.

Cassandra completed her sophomore year at this university, but she continued to struggle with anxiety and depression; at times attending counseling and trying medications to alleviate symptoms. In the end she decided not to stay for a third year. Cassandra stated:

> The summer before I started my junior year, I decided I wanted to be with my family so I transferred to the university where my Mom worked; something I never thought two years before I would want to do. It was a good decision though, because I was able to feel supported while I continued to work out what I was dealing with, which made it easier for me.

Though being closer to family and taking classes at a smaller university (~20,000 undergraduates) provided some support, Cassandra continued to struggle through decisions about her major, completing classes, and moving toward a degree.

5   Discussion—Putting the Pieces Together

In her narrative, Kathleen shared:

> Looking back now, I try to identify how this came to be...how could my incredible daughter who had graduated high school with honors and struggled so little with honors and AP coursework then, be struggling so much now to believe she was "worthy" and "successful"? What could I have done differently to support her and help her to view herself through my eyes—to see the amazing person I saw?

As we considered what might have contributed to the development of Cassandra's lack of confidence and sense of belonging, as well as her growing social anxiety and depression, a few things became obvious. First, during K-12 years,

Cassandra felt a great deal of stress from mandated assessments, and she was seldom secure in her relationships with peers, even then. Cassandra was also heavily influenced by the need to be constantly connected to others through digital means. Additionally, Cassandra held distorted beliefs about what her parents expected of her; however, as her parents, we had not clearly articulated our own expectations and unconsciously added to her anxiety by not doing so.

Cassandra had grown up in a culture of testing in the Florida public school system, graduating high school in 2012. Consequently, she developed anxiety in relation to testing initially and then other forms of mandated course assessment, like many of her peers. Although Cassandra was able to score at acceptable levels, she became physically ill leading up to testing, including fluctuations in vital signs (blood pressure, pulse, respiration, and temperature) and intense migraines. She also experienced light-headedness and fainting spells, which further complicated her situation by causing embarrassment and additional anxiety. Although test anxiety was the most obvious symptom with which Cassandra initially dealt, it was unfortunately the tip of the iceberg. These symptoms reappeared during the college years in response to the same and new stressors.

Cassandra also developed social anxiety, feeling the need to be connected with friends 24/7, both digital and analog; even sleeping with her cell phone in her hand in case someone tried to reach her, or something happened that she *needed* to know. Her need to be connected at all times caused additional stress and anxiety, in that she was constantly distracted and multi-tasking, regardless of whether she was actively engaged in cell phone use or not; her mind at least was divided, thinking about what she might be *missing* because she was not able to check her phone. As well, Cassandra measured herself against an image of *success* being painted by others in this digital world. The image, however, was an illusion to which she would never be able to measure up, and so the concept of being inadequate in comparison was constantly reinforced. This image of success was partially created based on culturally prevalent beliefs as explained earlier, but also on images painted by others that didn't exist in reality; they were illusions of success that others projected, but they were not founded in truth and did not include full disclosure.

This mismatch between Cassandra's expectation of what warranted the label *success* for academic performance as well as in her private world spilled over onto how she understood my husband and my expectations as well. Although, as Cassandra's parent, I completely admit my husband and I held high expectations for our daughter; we also understood fully that she was not perfect and in our mind as parents, *success* meant doing your best. For whatever reason, unfortunately, this understanding was not translating to our daughter. Cassandra thought we expected "all A's" or "A's and an occasional B" in coursework. She believed we held unreasonable expectations for her; something she would never be able to achieve. In Cassandra's mind, our expectations would continually increase as she met them; thus, she believed we would always expect more from her than she was capable of delivering, no matter how much she achieved. This was very destructive for our relationship with our daughter, until counseling helped us talk through our expectations and her understanding as a family. Eventually, she came to believe that we only wanted to support her to do her best, no matter how that was measured. Cassandra also came to accept that we were not going to change our love or our attitude towards her as well as how we interacted with her, based on how others measured her achievement.

6   Parent–Child Research

Parent–child research involves investigations done with, for and/or on your own child, which can be disconcerting because of the taboos surrounding the involvement of intimate others in research. However, intimate relationships can serve as a catalyst forcing us to deeply interact with others, and therefore help us to develop a greater understanding of ourselves and others. Busier et al. (1997) define intimate relationships as those that "include qualities of mutual care and friendship as well as revelation of, and respect for, personal vulnerabilities" (p. 165). According the human and feminist development theorists, we are not isolated; we are "relational beings" who grow through our connections with others (Jordan et al., 1991). Maguire (1987) said, "Without close, empathetic, interpersonal interchange and relationships, researchers will find it impossible to gain meaningful insights into human interaction or to understand the meaning people give to their own behavior" (pp. 20–21). In contrast to the restraint required by positivism, Maguire demands researchers' active involvement in the processes and products that result from relational and intimate research.

When conducting research with intimate others, it is important that researchers put several conditions in place to ensure they deal with research intimacy suitably. As we work with our children, either as co-researchers or as subjects, we must remember that we play multiple roles: parent, researcher, expert, learner. However, we can employ methodologies that will help us in processing this complex relationship to remain conscious of how our relationship with our child(ren) might influence data collection, analysis, and research findings. "Understanding involves intimacy and quality between self and [other]" (Belenky, Clinchy, Goldberger, & Tarule, 1986, p. 101). Power ineq-uities in the researcher–participant relationship can be addressed to generate a foundation of equity and to underpin mutual understandings. To these ends, Busier et al. (1997, p. 167) suggest researchers ask the following questions when considering engaging in research intimacy:

1. What are the sociocultural power relationships (age, gender, race, class, educational level, professional roles, etc.)? As mother, I held a pow-er-based position in our relationship. As a researcher, I shared the deci-sion making in the research process. Also, since my daughter was the insider in the context we were researching, she held unique power-based positionality (Harré & van Langenhove, 1999).

2. Are researcher and research participant on somewhat equal footing? If not, can inequities be bridged? As researchers, my daughter and I con-tinuously attempted to bridge perceived inequities by naming them and discussing their possible impacts. This bridging was not unlike how we addressed differences we encountered as mother and daughter in other aspects of our relationship as well.

3. Can researcher and research participant engage in critical dialogue about the role of power in their relationships? As indicated in point #2, my daughter and I were in the habit of discussing inequities and conflict that occurred within our relationship and the various roles it afforded.

"Power is a part of intimate relationships, so exploring and discussing power issues is critical in developing a solid research design and research processes when we involve intimate others, not to mention a solid baseline for a familial relationship" (Alley, 2018, p. 1473). To ensure we consider power and position-ing with all of my participants, researchers can use several methods to interro-gate their awareness of situated power/authority and their understandings of the various roles they play in the research process.

6.1   *Researcher Reflexivity*

According to Welch (1994), "We create our own stories, but only as coauthors" (p. 41). Relational reflexivity is one way to think about ourselves as research-ers and as individuals involved in relationships with our research participants, providing the means to include the voices of all participants, including our dia-logue about these relationships. Revealing the interplay between researcher and researched helps us better understand how an intimate relationship might influence fieldwork and interpretation. Busier et al. (1997) call for a "costory," defined as "a collaborative construction of a historical event, episode, or per-sonal story created by dialogue among the participants" (p. 167). Dialogic con-versation is one method that can be used to support the development of a co-story, as at least two participants (researcher and researched) become co-researchers and co-writers when engaged in conversation. Keeping a researcher reflective journal is another way we consistently interrogated our thoughts throughout the research process. We should acknowledge relationality within the research process, recognizing the connectedness between our participants and ourselves.

In addition to this thoughtful consideration of our role during data collection and analysis, we should also include two areas in the research design to address researcher reflexivity: the need for reciprocity and the question of validity. To attain reciprocity, we could employ several procedures including: conducting interviews in an interactive, dialogic manner, requiring self-disclosure as researchers; conducting sequential interviews of individuals to facilitate collaboration and a deeper probing of research issues; and, to negotiate meaning with participants by recycling descriptions, emerging analysis, and conclusions. We can also use several procedures to check the credibility of data, increasing validity and minimizing the distorting effect of personal bias upon the logic of evidence (Kamarovsky, 1981), including triangulation, reflexivity, and member checks (Lincoln & Guba, 1985). One method I utilized was "face validity," through the recycling of description, emerging analysis and conclusions with my daughter during multiple member checks (Reason & Rowan, 1981).

6.2   *Our Stories Continue*

6.2.1   Cassandra

I am now 26 years old, I am married and the mother of an 18 month old, and I am pursuing a masters degree in professional writing, focusing on creative writing, composition and rhetoric. I realize now that I have lived with anxiety and subsequent depression for several years—since I was about thirteen—and that I will live with this condition for the rest of my life. However, I think I have better coping skills now and a support system to deal with my feelings when things get overwhelming. I talk with my doctor regularly, go to counseling when needed, and I follow a treatment program that seems to be working well for me right now. I don't feel like dealing with anxiety and depression will keep me from doing the things I want to do in my life, but I know it will be something I have to deal with to achieve my goals; and it doesn't feel insurmountable to me now.

Working with Mom on various research projects in the past did have a big influence on our relationship, as it evolved over time. Mom treated me like an adult more than like a child most of the time, which helped me to act like one too. Instead of being the one with all the answers, Mom searched for the answers with me, listening to my ideas and making me a part of the process.

I think being co-inquirers helped us to be on a more level playing field—for both of us to contribute to the solutions we were seeking together. That made me take ownership and helped me to feel empowered to find answers; I felt like I was at least working towards trying to make things better, even when I wasn't sure how that was going to happen. Today I continue to use many of those skills I learned researching topics with Mom, in my education and in my every-day life. I think I am a better problem-solver and communicator now because of those experiences, and that I have more confidence to go after answers to my questions.

6.2.2   Kathleen

I believe whole-heartedly that the stance Cassandra and I took as co-inquir-ers many times throughout her teen and emerging adult years supported our journey as parent and child, helping us to successfully traverse the bumps we met along the way and resulting in the strong adult friendship that is now blos-soming between us. I tried very hard to not be the font of all knowledge—to co-construct understanding with my children, so they knew I didn't have all the answers, or think I should provide them with all their answers.

Although I know that being involved together in my dissertation research (Alley, 2013, 2018) influenced the way I interacted with my daughter as she was growing up and going through situations like those described in this chapter, it was also very natural for me to engage with my daughter this way because my own mother had treated me in much the same manner. My mother was not college educated and would never have considered herself a researcher, but she valued my insight and opinions growing up and encouraged me to voice my thoughts. She wanted me to be a strong woman, able to communicate my thinking and to stand comfortably on my own when needed, and I wanted the same for my own daughter. I doubt I would have positioned myself and my daughter in exactly the same way had I not been a trained researcher, but I would have valued my daughter's voice and engaged as a partner with her to solve issues regardless.

It took Cassandra a long time to develop her own definition of *success* and to believe her efforts were worthy of that label. Today Cassandra still deals with anxiety; something I regret because I feel partially responsible for its develop-ment. However, I know that engaging with me to explore her condition, and to find ways to better support all our needs, allowed Cassandra to feel some con-trol during these experiences when she often struggled to feel any control at all. For many people who struggle with anxiety disorders, including my daugh-ter, this diagnosis need not be a meaningless curse. When you are experienc-ing anxiety, it might feel absolutely horrible, but anxiety can transform into a blessing that helps people to find peace and purpose when they learn to cope with it and to seek solutions.

6.3   *Ethical Considerations and Future Directions*

When conducting future research, one way to ensure ethical behavior is to use dialogue to support equal footing during conversations about data as part of analysis. In this context I define dialogue as a form of communicative interaction between people in an exchange of utterances (Bakhtin, 1981). "Through dialogue, people engage each other out loud and themselves silently in order to articulate and express ideas" (Alley, 2018, p. 1475). As co-researchers, parent and child can jointly examine, question, wonder, and reflect on various issues, and these two-way exchanges help them to understand one another, as well as listen for the meaning in another person's perspective (Anderson, 2012). Dialogue seeks alignment instead of being focused only on identifying facts. It is an interactive, responsive process that supports understanding through conversation.

This understanding of dialogue, knowledge, and language is grounded in the belief that identities are relational and constructed through recursive dialogue and conversation (Gergen, 2009). We speak, think, and act as the "multiplicity of voices" residing in each of us (Anderson, 2012). Thus, narrating in recursive dialogue holds the power to shape and reshape who we are and what we think about ourselves and others; relationships and conversations are entwined in a circle of influence. As relational beings, influenced by and influencing one another, we cannot be separated from relationships and their contexts (Shotter, 1984). In this and other research with my daughter, I use various competencies to engage in dialogic communication, uncovering interactions, including: dialogic storytelling (holding and describing your perspective); dialogic listening (being profoundly open); and dialogic interaction (maintaining the tension between telling your own story and being open to others). Dialogic storytelling, listening and interaction can foreground participants' voices and help researchers consider relational elements during the research process.

As researchers who interact with intimate others in our lives, we must be guided throughout the research process by the same moral compass we use when we make ethical decisions in our personal lives. "We should question more and engage in more role taking than we normally do because of the authorial and privileged role that a researcher gives us" (Ellis, 2007, p. 23). In my own research, I ask many questions, including sharing my interpretations and asking my daughter if I am representing her experiences accurately. I realize the increased importance and change in depth of member checking when working with my daughter; I ask myself questions and use a reflective journal and anecdotal notes to constantly interrogate my understanding of the data being collected and analyzed. Facing my own writing when journaling in this manner forces me to face the underlying moral reasoning propelling my narrative.

This type of research is often emergent as well, so researchers need to understand that relational and ethical considerations might change. I use process consent for this reason when working with intimate others in particular, ensuring throughout the research process they are still interested in being a part of the research (Etherington, 2005). Even when I have consent initially, because relationships change over time, it is possible they will change their minds. In the case of intimate participants, we know the relationship is life-long, so we must be ready to witness and respond to changes in the relationship. Finally, I consider how much I ask of my daughter as a participant and/or co-researcher. As researchers, we must be careful to not cross the line by asking too much. Overall, we need to remember that intimacy in research carries responsibilities and considerations, and these must be provided for in our methodology and scrutinized throughout the research process.

7   Conclusion

When young people are experiencing anxiety and depression, they often feel ashamed—like they are alone in a sea of despair. They think that no one else is experiencing what they are experiencing, and they do not have a clue what to do to make these feelings go away. If young people have no one with whom to talk, they feel isolated, hopeless, stuck in feelings that embarrass them, and these feelings increase over time (Primack et al., 2017). In our situation, this is exactly what Cassandra was experiencing, although as parents we did not realize it for some time. We did know Cassandra was not acting happy, however, and that she was distant and disconnected, which troubled us. These were important warning signs I am grateful we heeded.

Rather than stay in this state of anxiety, young people need to learn coping skills, so they can learn to problem-solve. For example, through counseling, my daughter learned how to put into words the anxious feelings and negative thoughts she was having, which enabled her to listen to herself and voice the thoughts and fears in her head. When young people are able to identify negative feelings and concerns affecting them, they can learn to respond in alternative ways and discover new solutions to the situations they face. In counseling, talking about their feelings and thoughts with a listener who takes them seriously is important. That person can then encourage them to seek solutions. Many resources are available today for students, free of charge, on college campuses. I often send my students who voice these feelings and concerns with me to the student counseling center for either group or private therapy. As an instructor and advisor of students, I am in a position to notice when student behaviors change at times. Taking advantage of opportunities to share resources on our campus and in our community is one way I can reach out to my students when I notice something that makes me feel concern.

If you are interacting with a young person you suspect is experiencing anxiety, there are several things you can do to respond positively. First, it is important to tell them they are not alone—that the anxiety they are experiencing at this time in their life is normal, even if that sounds like we are making light of their feelings initially. Additionally, regardless of age, everyone feels anxiety from time to time. This is a good thing because anxiety can be helpful if we share our feelings and concerns with others and if we try to problem-solve to find solutions; anxiety is actually a wonderful warning signal that something important needs our attention.

Adult others in young people's lives can also be helpful by inviting them to share what is going on inside their heads. Asking young people "What…" and "How…" are the best question-starter words as they engender open-ended, full responses. In contrast, "Do you…" or "Have you…" invite short, defensive responses. Adults who interact with young people also need to be willing to respond with interest, not criticism, whatever they might hear.

References

Adams, T. (2006). Seeking father: Relationally reframing a troubled love story. *Qualitative Inquiry, 12*, 704–723. doi:10.1177/1077800406288607

Alley, K. M. (2018). The roles we played: Exploring intimacy in research. *The Qualitative Report, 23*(6), 1470–1482. Retrieved from https://nsuworks.nova.edu/tqr/vol23/iss6/13

Alley, K. M. (2013). *Playing in Trelis Weyr: Investigating collaborative practices in a Dragons of Pern role-play-game forum.* (Doctoral dissertation). University of South Florida. Retrieved from ProQuest Dissertations & Theses. (Accession Order No. 1417072690)

American College Health Association. (2013). *American College Health Association-National College Health Assessment II: Reference group data report spring, 2013.* Hanover, MD: American College Health Association.

Anderson, H. (2012). Collaborative relationships and dialogic conversations: Ideas for a relationally responsive practice. *Family Process, 51*(1), 8–24.

Andrews, B., & Wilding, J. M. (2004). The relation of depression and anxiety to life-stress and achievement in students. *British Journal of Psychology, 95*, 509–521.

Archuleta, K. L., Dale, A., & Spann, S. M. (2013). College students and financial distress: Exploring debt, financial satisfaction, and financial anxiety. *Journal of Financial Counseling and Planning, 24*(2), 50–62.

Bakhtin, M. (1981). *The dialogic imagination: Four essays by M. M. Bakhtin* (M. Holquist, Ed., C. Emerson & M. Holquist, Trans.). Austin, TX: University of Texas.

Belenky, M. F., Clinchy, B. M., Goldberger, N. R., & Tarule, J. M. (1986). *Women's ways of knowing: The development of self, voice, and mind.* New York, NY: Basic Books.

Benner, A. D., Boyle, A. E., & Sadler, S. (2016). Parental involvement and adolescents' educational success: The roles of prior achievement and socioeconomic status. *Journal of Youth and Adolescence, 45*(6), 1053–1064.

Beranuy, M., Oberst, U., Carbonell, X., & Chamarro, A. (2009). Problematic Internet and mobile phone use and clinical symptoms in college students: The role of emotional intelligence. *Computers in Human Behavior, 25*, 1182–1187. doi:10.1016/j.chb.2009.03.001

Bianchi, A., & Phillips, J. G. (2005). Psychological predictors of problem mobile phone use. *CyberPsychology & Behavior, 8*, 39–51. doi:10.1089/cpb.2005.8.39

Busier, H. L., Clark, K. A., Esch, R. A., Glesne, C., Pigeon, Y., & Tarule, J. M. (1997). Intimacy in research. *International Journal of Qualitative Studies in Education, 10*, 165–170. doi:10.1080/095183997237250

Calancie, O., Ewing, L., Narducci, L. D., Horgan, S., & Khalid-Khan, S. (2017). Exploring how social networking sites impact youth with anxiety: A qualitative study of Facebook stressors among adolescents with an anxiety disorder diagnosis. *Cyberpsychology: Journal of Psychosocial Research on Cyberspace, 11*(4), Article 2. doi:10.5817/CP2017-4-2

Callender, C., & Jackson, J. (2008). Does the fear of debt constrain choice of university and subject of study? *Studies in Higher Education, 33*(4), 405–429.

Chang, H., Ngunjiri, F. W., & Hernandez, K. C. (2013). *Collaborative autoethnography.* Walnut, CA: Left Coast Press.

Chen, S. Y., & Tzeng, J. Y. (2010). College female and male heavy internet users' profiles of practices and their academic grades and psychosocial adjustment. *Cyberpsychology, Behavior, and Social Networking, 13*, 257–262. doi:10.1089/cyber.2009.0023

Corbin, J., & Strauss, A. (2015). *Basics of qualitative research: Techniques and procedures for developing grounded theory* (4th ed.). Thousand Oaks, CA: Sage.

Denzin, N. K., & Lincoln, Y. S. (Eds.). (2011). *The Sage handbook of qualitative research.* Thousand Oaks, CA: Sage.

Elias, H., Ping, W. S., & Abdullah, M. C. (2011). Stress and academic achievement among undergraduate students in University Putra Malaysia. *Procedia – Social and Behavioral Sciences, 29*, 646–655.

Ellis, C. (2001). With mother/with child: A true story. *Qualitative Inquiry, 7*, 598–616. doi:10.1177/10778004010070005

Ellis, C. (2004). *The ethnographic I: A methodological novel about autoethnography.* Walnut Creek, CA: AltaMira Press.

Ellis, C. (2007). Telling secrets, revealing lives: Relational ethics in research with intimate others. *Qualitative Inquiry, 13*(1), 3–29. doi:10.1177/1077800406294947

Etherington, K. (2007). Ethical research in reflexive relationships. *Qualitative Inquiry, 13*(5), 599–616.

Geist-Martin, P., Gates, L., Wiering, L., Kirby, E., Houston, R., Lilly, A., & Moreno, J. (2010). Exemplifying collaborative autoethnographic practice via shared stories of mothering. *Journal of Research Practice, 6*(1), 1–14.

Gergen, K. J. (2009). *Relational being: Beyond self and community.* New York, NY: Oxford University Press.

Goodwin, D., Pope, C., Mort, M., & Smith, A. (2003). Ethics and ethnography: An experiential account. *Qualitative Health Research, 13*, 567–577. doi:10.1177/1049732302250723

Guillemin, M., & Gillam, L. (2004). Ethics, reflexivity, and "ethically important moments" in research. *Qualitative Inquiry, 10*, 261–280. doi:10.1177/1077800403262360

Harre, R., & van Langenhove, I. (Eds.). (1999). *Positioning theory: Moral contexts of international action.* Malden, MA: Wiley-Blackwell.

Joo, S., Durband, D. B., & Grable, J. (2008). The academic impact of financial stress on college students. *Journal of College Student Retention, 10*(3), 287–305.

Jordan, J. V., Kaplan, A. G., Miller, J. B., Stiver, I. P., & Surrey, J. L. (Eds.). (1991). *Women's growth in connection.* New York, NY: Guilford Press.

Kamarovsky, M. (1981). Women then and now: A journey of detachment and engagement. *Women's Studies Quarterly, 10*(2), 5–9.

Kariv, D., & Heiman, T. (2005). Task-oriented versus emotion-oriented coping strategies: The case of college students. *College Student Journal, 39*(1), 72–85.

Kiesinger, C. (2002). My father's shoes: The therapeutic value of narrative reframing. In A. P. Bochner & C. Ellis (Eds.), *Ethnographically speaking: Autoethnography, literature and aesthetics* (pp. 95–114). Walnut Creek, CA: AltaMira Press.

Lepp, A., Barkley, J. E., Sanders, G. J., & Karpinski, A. C. (2014). The relationship between cell phone use, academic performance, anxiety, and satisfaction with life in college students. *Computers in Human Behavior, 31*, 343–350.

Lester, D. (2014). College student stressors, depression, and suicidal ideation. *Psychological Reports, 114*(1), 293–296.

Lin, L. y., Sidani, J. E., Shensa, A., Radovic, A., Miller, E., Colditz, J. B., Hoffman, B. L., Giles, L. M., & Primack, B. A. (2016). Association between social media use and depression among U.S. young adults. *Depression & Anxiety, 33*, 323–331. doi:10.1002/da.22466

Lincoln, Y. S., & Guba, E. G. (1985). *Naturalistic inquiry.* Newbury Park, CA: Sage Publications.

Lu, X., Watanabe, J., Liu, Q., Uji, M., Shono, M., & Kitamura, T. (2011). Internet and mobile phone text-messaging dependency: Factor structure and correlation with dysphoric mood among Japanese adults. *Computers in Human Behavior, 27,* 1702–1709. doi:10.1016/j.chb.2011.02.009

Ma, J., Baum, S., Pender, M., & Welch, M. (2017). *Trends in college pricing 2017.* New York, NY: The College Board.

MacGeorge, E. L., Samter, W., & Gillihan, S. J. (2005). Academic stress, supportive communication, and health. *Communication Education, 54,* 365–372.

Maguire, P. (1987). *Doing participatory research: A feminist approach.* Amherst, MA: University of Massachusetts.

Mander, J., & Young, K. (2017). *Gen Z: Examining the attitudes and digital behaviors of internet users aged 16–20.* Retrieved from https://blog.globalwebindex.com/chart-of-the-day/gen-z-now-spend-4-hours-daily-online-via-mobile/

Martin, K. L. (2008). *Please knock before you enter: Aboriginal regulation of outsiders and the implications for researchers.* Tenerife: Post Pressed.

Merlo, L. (2008). Increased cell phone use may heighten symptoms of anxiety. *Primary Psychiatry, 15*(5), 27–28.

Misra, R. (2000). Academic stress of college students: Comparison of student and faculty perceptions. *College Student Journal, 21,* 1–10.

Misra, R., McKean, M., West, S., & Russo, T. (2000). Academic stress of college students: Comparison of student and faulty perceptions. *College Student Journal, 34*(2), 236–246.

Muhammad, M., Wallerstein, N., Sussman, A. L., Avila, M., Belone, L., & Duran, B. (2015). Reflections on researcher identity and power: The impact of positionality on Community Based Participatory Research (CBPR) processes and outcomes. *Critical Sociology, 41*(7–8), 1045–1063. doi:10.1177/0896920513516025

Noddings, N. (1984). *Caring, a feminine approach to ethics & moral education.* Berkeley, CA: University of California Press.

Plagnol, A. C. (2011). Financial satisfaction over the life course: The influence of assets and liabilities. *Journal of Economic Psychology, 32*(1), 45–64.

Pomerantz, E. M., Kim, E. M., & Cheung, C. S. (2012). Parents' involvement in children's learning. In K. R. Harris, S. Graham, T. Urdan, S. Graham, M. J. Royer, & Z. Moshe (Eds.), *Individual differences and cultural and contextual factors. APA handbooks in psychology: APA educational psychology handbook* (Vol. 2, pp. 417–440). Washington, DC: American Psychological Association.

Poulos, C. N. (2009). *Accidental ethnography: An inquiry into family secrets.* Walnut Creek, CA: Left Coast.

Primack, B. A., Shensa, A., Escobar-Viera, C. G., Barrett, E. L., Sidani, J. E., Colditz, J. B., & James, A. E. (2017). Use of multiple social media platforms and symptoms of depression and anxiety: A nationally-representative study among US young adults. *Computers in Human Behavior, 69,* 1–9.

Raftery, J. N., Grolnick, W. S., & Flamm, E. S. (2012). Families as facilitators of student engagement: Toward a home-school partnership model. In L. S. Christenson, L. A. Reschly, & C. Wylie (Eds.), *Handbook of research on student engagement* (pp. 343–364). New York, NY: Springer Science + Business Media.

Rambo, C. (2005). *Handing IRB an unloaded gun* (Unpublished manuscript). University of Memphis, Memphis, TN.

Ratelle, C. F., Duchesne, S., & Guay, F. (2017). Predicting school adjustment from multiple perspectives on parental behaviors. *Journal of Adolescence, 54,* 60–72.

Raymo, L. A., Somers, C. L., & Partridge, R. T. (2018). Adolescent test anxiety: An examination of intraindividual and contextual predictors. *School Mental Health,* 1–16.

Reason, P., & Rowan, J. (1981). Issues of validity in new paradigm research. In P. Reason & J. Roawn (Eds.), *Human inquiry* (pp. 239–252). New York, NY: Wiley.

Reetz, D. R., Bershad, C., LeViness, P., & Whitlock, M. (2017). *The association for university and college counseling center directors annual survey.* Retrieved from http://www.aucccd.org/assets/documents/aucccd%202016%20monograph%20 -%20public.pdf

Roberts, R., Golding, J., Towell, T., Reid, S., Woodford, S., Vetere, A., & Weinreb, I. (2000). Mental and physical health in students: The role of economic circumstances. *British Journal of Health Psychology, 5*(3), 289–297.

Roberts, R., Golding, J., Towell, T., & Weinreb, I. (1999). The effects of economic circumstances on British students' mental and physical health. *Journal of American College Health, 48*(3), 103–109.

Rogers, C. R. (1957). The necessary and sufficient conditions of therapeutic personality change. *Journal of Consulting Psychology, 21,* 95–103.

Rosen, L. D., Whaling, K., Rab, S., Carrier, L. M., & Cheever, N. A. (2013). Is Facebook creating "iDisorders"? The link between clinical symptoms of psychiatric disorders and technology use, attitudes and anxiety. *Computers in Human Behavior, 29,* 1243–1254. doi:10.1016/j.chb.2012.11.012

Seemiller, C., & Grace, M. (2016). *Generation Z goes to college.* San Francisco, CA: Jossey-Bass.

Shotter, J. (1984). *Social accountability and selfhood.* Oxford: Blackwell.

Slattery, P., & Rapp, D. (2003). *Ethics and the foundations of education: Teaching convictions in a postmodern world.* Boston, MA: Allyn & Bacon.

Takao, M., Takahashi, S., & Kitamura, M. (2009). Addictive personality and problematic mobile phone use. *CyberPsychology & Behavior, 12,* 501–507. doi:10.1089/cpb.2009.0022

Tate, E. (2017, March). Anxiety on the rise. *Inside Higher Education.* Retrieved from https://www.insidehighered.com/news/2017/03/29/anxiety-and-depression-are-primary-concerns-students-seeking-counseling-services

Tennant, C. (2002). Life events, stress, and depression. *Australian and New Zealand Journal of Psychiatry, 36,* 173–182.

Welch, D. D. (1994) *Conflicting agendas: Personal morality in institutional settings.* Cleveland, OH: Pilgrim Press.

Wilks, S. E. (2008). The moderating impact of social support among social work students. *Advances in Social Work, 9,* 106–125.

Wormeli, R. (2018). *Fair isn't always equal: Assessing and grading in the differentiated classroom.* Portsmouth, NH: Stenhouse Publishers.

CHAPTER 5

Remixing Digital Play in the Early Years: A Child-Parent Collaboration

Alaina Roach O'Keefe and "E" O'Keefe

Abstract

How do young children experience digital play in the 21st century? The purpose of this exploratory case study was to examine one child's play in non-digital and digital contexts for three years. The research was theoretically grounded in socio-cultural theories of learning, and nested ecological systems and early childhood pedagogy. The author conducted this study with her son from age two to five in the context of his nested ecological networks (home, daycare, extended family). Findings (a) illuminate how digital technology provided affordances to multimodal play; (b) challenge warnings found in research and policy regarding impact of screen time on young children; and (c) offer new insights into the emerging digital citizenship of one child, through use of digital technology, construction of learning stories, and adoption of a co-research approach. This study makes a significant contribution to unravelling some of the complexities of the meaning of play in the digital age.

1   Introduction

When my son was roughly ten months old (and crawling for my iPhone), the National Association for the Education of Young Children (NAEYC) released a position statement about the use of technology and interactive media for children from infancy through eight years. I was interested in learning more about what advice the statement authors were giving early childhood practitioners *and* I was also interested in it from a parent's perspective. The story about what I learned over a three-year period is shared with you here.

The purpose of this parent-child case study research was to examine my son's play in the context of our family and nested networks (i.e., home, the Early Learning Centre [ELC], and extended family) over the span of three years. Very little research has examined the use of digital technology with children from two to five years longitudinally, especially with the child as a co-researcher. Wang et al. (2010) explored Bronfenbrenner's theory of bio-eco-logical development to help them make sense of children's emerging practices online, but few researchers have explored it over time, a concept important to Bronfenbrenner's later work (2005). Given a dearth of longitudinal, in-depth research about the digital play of children, aged 2–5, coupled with a surfeit of diverse views about digital play in the lives of young children, there emerged a strong rationale for this timely research (Alper, 2011, 2012; Bers & Kazakoff, 2013; NAEYC, 2012; Plowman et al., 2012; Roach O'Keefe & Moffatt, 2013; Wang et al., 2010). Therefore, this research conducted from a parent-researcher per-spective makes a significant contribution to the literature.

The goals of the research were threefold. I wanted to explore and under-stand: (1) how my son (henceforth known as "E") used a variety of digital tools in our home context in his play activities with our family; (2) how proximal processes and bio-ecological systems influenced his play with and without dig-ital tools; and, finally, (3) how he played a part in the co-analysis of the research with me. The learning stories shared in this chapter are part of a larger disser-tation and contributed to findings that answer these three questions.

The research involved my son and me, along with other family members, including my husband, E's maternal and paternal grandparents, and our extended family. It included hours of multimodal play that involved E and our family learning together. We shared activities, such as art making, read-ing together using print and digital resources, playing outside, playing with *Lego* and looking up further *Lego* instructions on the iPad/internet, cooking together from recipe books (as well as finding online recipes), taking videos/ photos (prompting discussions about memories made) to create digital books of family stories, creating art (both online and offline), making music (and watching concerts on YouTube), and watching TV and movies together. All the while, E was engrossed in environments that supported the development of early literacy skills and included artistic play, block play, socio-dramatic play, and outdoor play.

Based on my pedagogical perspective, including recommendations from research (Berson & Berson, 2010; Cope, & Kalantzis, 2000; Deitz & Kashin, 2012; Lankshear & Knobel, 2003; Mitchell & Dunbar, 2006; NAEYC, 2012; Plow-man et al., 2012; Van Scooter Boss, 2002; Wang et al., 2010), the goal of this research and practice for three years was to include digital technology in our lives as a natural and meaningful practice and to examine ways in which E used it in his play. While statements from the NAEYC and Fred Rogers Centre warn about the use of digital technology with young children, I also entered into the research with intent aligned with the stance on the importance of interactivity and intentionality, and with what Guernsey (2012) considers the three C's—content, context, and the child—when choosing to use digital technology with young children. Several years of research also suggested that the learning opportunities for both children and adults are greater when technology is used together (between adult and child) in social, natural, and integrated ways.

Data analysis led to the creation of learning stories, which provided rich opportunities to explore and analyze play, a concept that some call elusive (Harwood, 2017; Sutton-Smith, 1997). Play is usually engaged in for enjoyment and recreation, often defined as creative, make believe, voluntary, and universal (Golinkoff, Hirsch-Pasek, Russ, & Lillard, 2013) and involves representation of ideas through games and actions (Sutton-Smith, 2008). The play episodes documented weaved together both concrete (traditional) play and digital play that was fluid as E made meaning of his experiences. In this chapter, I discuss the findings based on the theoretical frameworks (Bronfenbrenner, 2005; Clark & Moss, 2005; Farrell, 2005a; Vygotsky, 1978) and the research literature that informed the study.

2   The Early Years, Digital Play, and Research with Young Children

2.1   *The Early Years*
The early years (0–8) are a time when children learn and explore their environments socially and play with various digital literacy tools (Carrington & Marsh, 2005; Harwood, 2017; Marsh et al., 2017; Plowman, McPake, & Stephen, 2012; Rowsell, 2017; Van Scoter & Boss, 2002). Traditional notions of play have taken on new meanings in the digital age, with early multiliteracies and play practices continuously changing as digital technology is woven into the daily lives of both children and adults (Cope & Kalantzis, 2000; Leu, 2000; Marsh et al., 2017; New London Group, 1996; Pahl & Rowsell, 2012; Wohlwend, 2015a, 2015b, 2017). These play practices have transformed how children interact with their peers, parents, and educators (Wang et al., 2010), with little known about their social interactions with family members using these technologies in play (Verenikina & Kervin, 2011). Wohlwend (2017) suggested that given this shift and extension of what multiliteracies now consider, the definition of play has become even more "slipp[ery]" (p. 162) than previous "unruly literacy" definitions of play suggested (Sutton-Smith, 1997). Berson and Berson (2010) asserted that learning environments without technology are disconnected from some children's realities, suggesting that digital technologies needed to be examined to fully understand young children's early literacy development and their play

practices (National Association for the Education of Young Children, 2012; Wolhwend, 2015).

2.2   *Digital Play*

We now have a generation of preschoolers recently characterized as *digitods* or *high-tech-tots* as technology is integrated into the daily routines and 21st-century family's life (Berson & Berson, 2010). There is also a deep sense of hesitancy and fear over the potential risk of using digital tools with young children. Despite these concerns, many studies also show the potential of digital technologies to build and enhance multiliteracies (Berson & Berson, 2010; Cope & Kalantzis, 2000; Gee & Hayes, 2011; Leu, 2000; Lopez, Caspe, & Weiss, 2017; Luke, 2000; Marsh et al., 2017; Pahl & Rowsell, 2011; Plowman et al., 2012, 2016; Bers & Horn, 2010; Yelland, 2010).

Play theory has a history spanning two centuries with definitions, uses, and research to illustrate how its presence has contributed to the healthy socio-emotional and cognitive capacity of both children and adults (Froebel, 1887; Montessori, 1912; Pellegrini, Dupuis, & Smith, 2007; Sutton-Smith, 2008). Various modes of play served as foundational and fundamental experiences that were part of this research (Ginsburg, 2007). In this research, I defined "Digital play" as playful behaviours or play events involving digital technology of some kind, where digital technology provides various affordances or sits alongside more traditional play activities.

2.3   *Research with Young Children*

An important thread in this research was the diligence and ethical contexts within which research should be conducted with young children. The current literature on the ethics of doing research with young children calls for researchers to understand and consider *the role of the child in the research* when they are designing their studies (Abbott & Langston, 2005 ; Fargas-Malet et al., 2013; Farrell, 2005a, 2005b, 2005c; Jipson & Jipson, 2005 ; Sargeant & Harcourt, 2012; Skånfors, 2009; Talyer, Farrell, Tennet, & Patterson, 2005; Walsh, 2005).

Over the past decade, there has also been a general trend toward research *with* children as co-researchers instead of *on* them as subjects (Allen, 2005; Corsaro, 2005; Darbyshire et al., 2005; Fargas-Malet et al., 2013; Farrell, 2005b; Kellitt, 2010; Mayall, 2000; O'Kane, 2000; Sargeant & Harcourt, 2012), a philosophy which was adopted in this study that involved me, a parent, researching *with* my child. The *Mosaic Approach*, coined by Clark and Moss (2005), also encouraged research with children that focused on meaning making in respectful early childhood pedagogy. Therefore, there was potential for re-imagining how research is conducted with children, and this question was further explored in the methodological approach to the research and subsequent methods of data analysis.

3   Theoretical Foundations

3.1   *Theory of Bio-Ecological Development*

Bronfenbrenner's (2005) theory asserts that children (humans) develop within ecological systems (see Figure 5.1). The first system is the microsystem (the immediate environment surrounding a child, e.g., home, preschool). The second is the mesosystem, which is about interactions and what links microsystems (like home or preschool) together. The third is the exosystem—environments in which a child might not be actively involved but which would have significant influence on them (e.g., ideologies, community, public policy). The fourth is the macrosystem that includes broader cultural or sub-cultural settings in which both microsystems and exosystems are embedded (e.g., how technology influences communication; society's understanding of children). The chronosystem is the evolution of the systems and reflects cumulative experiences and notable transitions over three types of time: micro, meso, and macro (which mirror the systems). Bronfrenbrenner's theory is drawn upon as

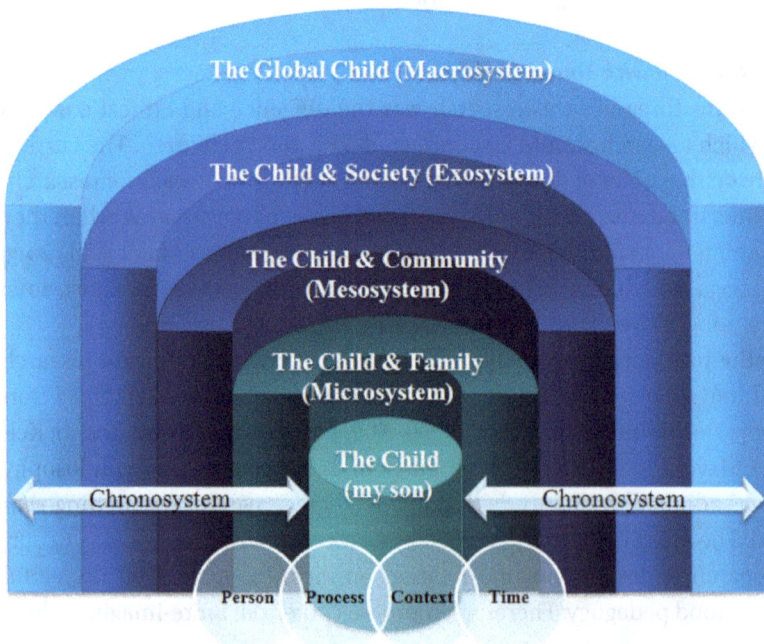

FIGURE 5.1   Bronfenbrenner's theory of bio-ecological development

a framework for investigating the way in which my son ("E"), and our family experienced digital play together, therefore focusing on the mesosystem and how the proximal processes took place across three years.

As a working mom, I felt the tensions that Bronfenbrenner (2005) described in his writing about the changing family, and particularly about the "conflict between work and family roles reducing the quantity and quality of parent-child interaction" which was also associated with lower achievement, particularly among boys (p. 205). Therefore, Bronfenbrenner's (2005) theoretical perspective was helpful in framing the study's structure. The conceptual framework that anchored this study was comprised of the nested system surrounding my child, E, who was two years old when the study began. Many researchers have used Bronfenbrenner's theories to guide their research, but rarely had it been examined through the person, process, or context over time.

3.2   Social Constructionism, Funds of Knowledge, and Socio-Cultural Theories of Learning

This research was conducted with my son, inspired by an epistemological stance of social constructionism (Dewey, 1938/1963; Piaget, 1926/1929; Vygotsky, 1978). I used theoretical underpinnings of my child as capable and competent (Clark & Moss, 2005; Corsaro, 2005; Danby & Farrell, 2005; Dewey, 1938/1963; James, 2007; Malaguzzi, 1994; Montessori, 1912) and we brought our own funds of knowledge to each experience (Moll, Amanti, Neff, & Gonzalez, 1992). I drew upon socio-cultural theories of learning that suggest that children learn best in collaboration with others and that the co-construction of knowledge and understanding can occur while being playful together as a family (Clark & Moss, 2005; Gee & Lankshear, 1997; Heath, 1983; Lankshear & Knobel, 2006; Pahl & Rowsell, 2012; Street, 1999; Vygotsky, 1978) and that the relationships and environments in which this happen are crucial to learning experiences (Montessori, 1912). The research is inspired by the *Te Whariki Worldview* that emphasizes the critical role of "socially and culturally mediated learning; reciprocal and responsive relationships for children with people, places, and things; collaboration with adults and peers; guided participation and observation of others; and through individual exploration and reflection" (New Zealand Ministry of Education, 1996, p. 9).

The study also built on these socio-cultural theories of learning and development (Bronfenbrenner, 2005; Rogoff, 2003) by taking a reflexive and emergent approach to learning that is cyclical (Piaget, 1953; Stacey, 2008, Wien, 2006). Play itself was also culturally situated, with mother and father being involved in play interactions in multiple ways across culture and time (Göncü & Gaskins, 2011; Roopnarine & Davidson, 2015). How this socio-cultural approach was evident in digital play within my son's nested bio-ecological system (his world) was central in understanding how he developed important playful early literacy behaviours (Bronfenbrenner, 2005; Pahl & Rowsell, 2012).

4   Methodological Considerations and Design

This was a longitudinal ethnographic case study, firmly entrenched in a framework that honors early childhood pedagogy and ethical approaches to research with children. The study was informed by the *Mosaic Approach*, originally developed and designed to investigate the daily experiences of young children in early years' settings (Clark & Moss, 2005). The case at the centre of this study was the process by which my son and our family experienced play together, often with various digital tools. It was a single, descriptive, and exploratory look into the real-life context in which multimodal play occurred within and across nested ecological networks over three years.

I chose a case study approach, particularly ethnographic case-study research; this approach is useful when the focus of the study is to answer "how" and is philosophically underpinned by a constructivist paradigm and, as in this case, rooted in socio cultural learning and systematic ethical methodologies (Baxter & Jack, 2008; Pollard, 1987; Stake, 1995; Yin, 2014). I used what Purcell-Gates (2004) called a "phenomenological approach" (lived experience) to ethnography. This study particularly aligns with the work of Andrew Pollard from the 1980s and 1990s, who used case study as a longitudinal strategy, to inquire into the nature of learning over three years with a complex set of perspectives (parent, child, and reflective teacher) and with a multitude of tools.

4.1   *Ethical Considerations*

For this research to be rooted in a truly ethical approach with young children, then the child as co-investigator must be authentically and collaboratively engaged with the data analysis (Sargeant & Harcourt, 2012) and not just with the data collection. One of the key features of researching with children often involves an attempt to gain insight into what their experiences are like and what their thoughts and ideas are (Farrell, 2005; Sargeant & Harcourt, 2012). Farrell also suggests that research with young children should only be conducted where: (a) the research is important to their health and well-being; (b) their participation is indispensable to the research; (c) the research method is child-appropriate; and (d) the research conditions provide for their physical, emotional, and/or psychological safety (2005, p. 168). In addition, listening to children and distinguishing issues of power in practice during the process is crucial and "related to the process of making decisions *with* children, not just *for* them" (Roberts, 2000; Clark et al., 2003; as cited in Farrell, 2005, p. 170). These conditions were met and ethical approval for this study was granted from the University of Prince Edward Island.

4.1.1   Co-Researching with E

While he was quite young (age two) when data collection began and at the age of six-and-a-half, E was capable of helping to reflect and analyse his experiences. Researchers have fused a variety of approaches to co-analyzing data with children. These particular approaches are discussed in the literature: scribing in pencil or digitally recording when children are communicating their thoughts and then verifying the ideas afterwards with the child; summarizing the experience for the child and asking his/her thoughts about it; or helping children describe what the research is all about in real life and why it might be useful (Sargeant & Harcourt, 2012). I chose to weave the first and third process in my co-analysis phase with E, and the learning stories acted as a way to achieve this in the summary. Member checking is an ongoing, ethical process in research with young children and informed how I engaged my son in the analysis phase of the research.

4.1.2   Listening

Listening to children is at the crux of recognizing and valuing their worth as human beings (Farrell, 2005). Therefore, the process of this research was iterative, comprised of talking and listening, and communicating with my son and my husband and extended family as a continual, recurrent process throughout the analysis phase of the research. They all had multiple opportunities to review and communicate contributions to the findings. I communicated results in developmentally appropriate ways (in plain language, art, sometimes hands-on) in order for E to glean the best understanding possible. My husband and mother read multiple versions of the research analysis and were able to ask questions, clarify ideas, and were an integral part of the project.

4.2   *Data Collection*

Data collection took place between April 1, 2013 and April 1, 2016. I organized the data by year and month in digital folders. I spent three years engaged in systematic participant observation and documentation. Each observation included multiple sources of information such as videos, photographs, field notes, and artwork or other artefacts produced. The length of observations varied according to the nature of the play experience, for example, from five minutes during a FaceTime interaction to several hours of *Lego* building and accessing online instructions.

My original intent was to conduct focused observations once a month over the three-year time frame of the study; however, due to the exploratory real-life context, I found myself collecting much more data than intended. The final data set consisted of 130 discrete observations made over 36 months, 80 of which are reported in the findings. These 80 discrete points of observational data collected over three years resulted in 1977 units of data (1184 photographs and 64 videos). Additionally, 12 Shutterfly books (see Figure 5.2 for example), 29 pieces of artwork (see Figures 5.3 and 5.4 for example), and 627 emails to and from the Early Learning Centre were also categorized. In the end, there were approximately 2160 hours of observation documented.

FIGURE 5.2   Shutterfly books

FIGURE 5.3   E painting "blue" and "red"

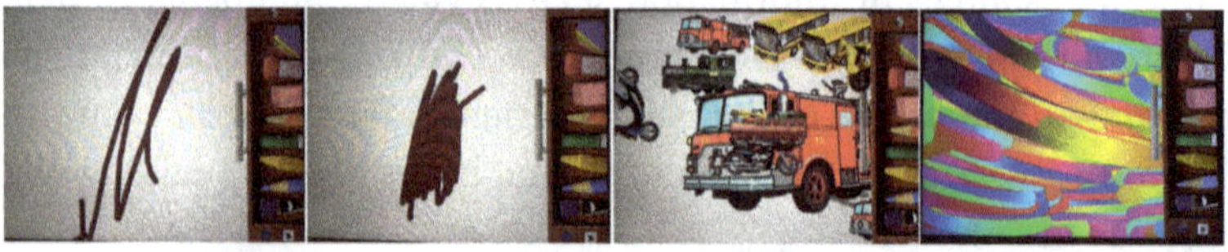

FIGURE 5.4   E's first four Draw Pad creations/paintings

Documentation and learning stories are evolving processes that provide time for a parent or an educator to value learning and make learning visible, often in the form of a story.

The criteria I used to choose what to document was informed by Seitz (2008) and Carr and Lee (2012). I wrote learning stories that described what E did, what it meant, what we should do next, and included family reflections. In formal learning settings, educators sometimes see documentation over time if it is gathered in a portfolio. Usually a learning story might be a page long with some text and a few pictures. Our learning stories ranged from 20–30 pages and included on average 20 photos and/or videos over a three year period.

During the data collection phase, visual methods, documents, and photography/videography were used to enhance understanding and to add to his experiences and stories (Clark & Moss, 2005). Through co-creation of data, it is the intent to reduce "othering" (Johnson et al., 2004) and to work towards representing an equitable power balance and narrative of both my son and myself (Ball, 2005; David et al., 2005; MacNaughton & Smith, 2005; Morrow, 2005).

4.3   *Process for Data Analysis*

Analysis of the case study involved five phases (Figure 5.5). Once the learning stories were compiled and created (in phase 2), I shared them with E in child-friendly language. I asked the following guiding questions as we reviewed each

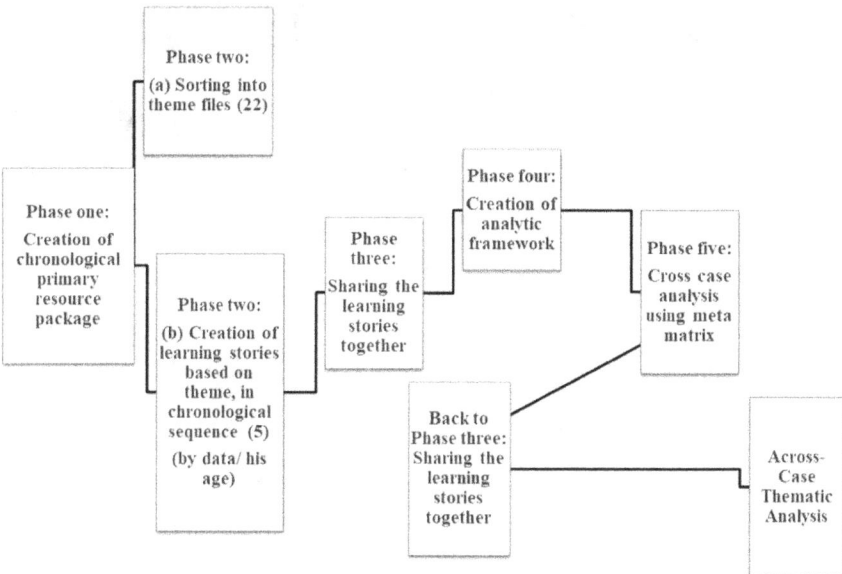

FIGURE 5.5   Analyzing the case

story together to record any of his thoughts, reactions, memories, or questions so that we could begin an initial analysis together.

1.   What do you remember about this?
2.   How does it make you feel? (I included a similar Smiley Face Assessment Scale (Yang, 2004) frequently used in child related research that depicts happy, sad, boring, excited, and angry faces he could point to).
3.   Did I forget anything to tell in this story?
4.   Do you want to add anything to this story? And I took notes.

A descriptive picture of the story of my son's preschool play experiences began to emerge, and the analytic strategy was conceptualized for a meta-matrix for analysis across the learning stories. This type of cross-case analysis proved to be highly systematic; it allowed for inclusion of diverse qualitative data, and aligned with the approach to ethnography I adopted (Miles & Huberman, 1994). The final phase of data analysis involved me reading and re-reading the entire case (Rice & Ezzy, 1999), incorporating my son's analysis, and summarizing and coding these reflections to find emergent themes (Crabtree & Miller, 1999). I searched the case record for patterns, underlying themes, recurring ideas, images, words, and experiences as a thematic/content analysis within the case record in chronological order within and across each learning story, and also across ecological systems using Bronfenbrenner's bio-ecological systems and my research questions as a guide (Figure 5.6).

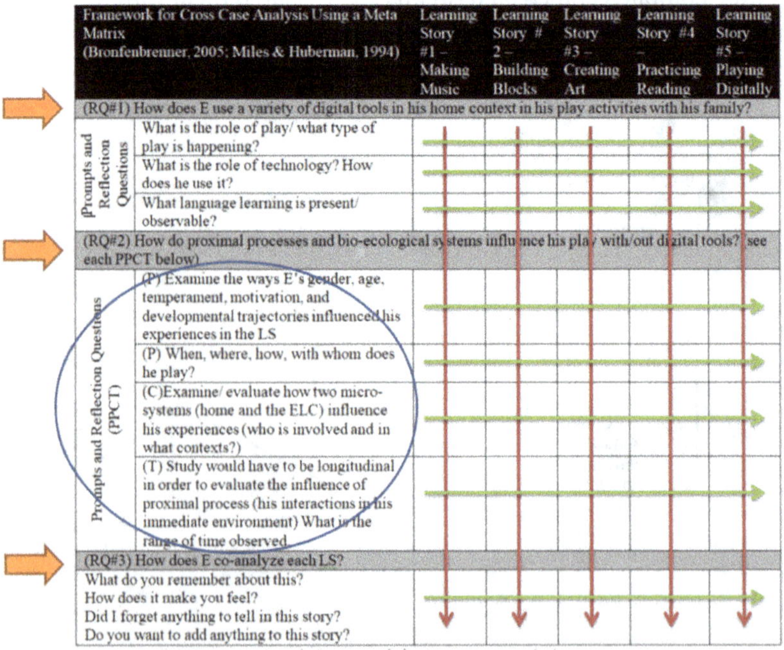

FIGURE 5.6   Meta matrix for cross-case analysis

4.4 *Across Case Synthesis*

I discovered that E developed through several types of play during his pre-school years: creative play, building and block play, socio-dramatic musical play, and literacy play. His nested ecologies provided him with inspired interest at home, and at the ELC and vice versa. I also discovered that as we co-analysed the learning stories together, E began to ask questions about online spaces, namely Facebook. The Mosaic Approach supported this ethical examination with my son and enabled me to honor his space/response in the dialogue:

> One day I was looking at his photos on Facebook, I asked him if he was in the group photo of something he had attended. He said, "no, they took me and two other kids to the side when they took it." I asked, "Did this make you sad not to be in the group photo?" He replied, "No, but why wasn't I?" I explained that I didn't give permission for his face to be online for others to see. I asked if he wanted me to give permission. He said, "No mama, I don't really want to be on Facebook right now, maybe later."

5 How E Used Digital Tools in Play

5.1 *Theme One: Developing Digital Literacies in Play*

E used digital technology in his literacy practices and meaning making by imitating adults, using digitized texts, and representing ideas through photos. He developed digital literacy through the use of multimodal literacy tools. For example, he used a CD player to listen to stories and his digital storybooks, and as a tool to communicate across space and place (Facetiming and texting his

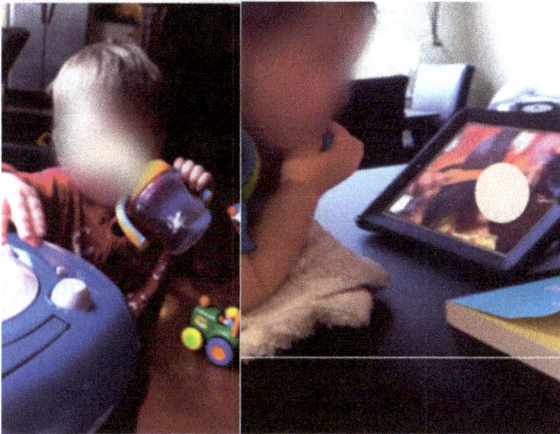

FIGURE 5.7   Listening to stories (left) and Facetiming a read-aloud (right) (screen capture from video)

Nannie), through co-writing with me to email friends or remixing a traditional read-aloud over FaceTime (Figure 5.7).

Digital technology provided affordances and multimodalities to play situations and contributed to the meaning making that transpired in E's play (e.g., FaceTime read aloud, accessible recipes for cooking, family books, storytelling (Abrams, 2015, 2017; Pahl & Rowsell, 2012; Jewitt & Kress, 2003). Digital play was also positioned as a situated social practice, akin to literacy events (Heath, 1983), where technology was involved in social interactions (e.g., FaceTime). Situated social practices would also assume that what E did (or was able to do) *with* the technology was much more important than what technology *did* itself (Hamilton, 2010).

5.2   *Theme Two: Enabled Research Opportunities*

Similar to the findings of Memme and Winters (2017) and Rose et al. (2017), the ways in which E used various digital technologies provided him with diverse learning opportunities. The iPad enabled research and inquiry opportunities for E, and lead to developing his sense of agency in learning (Harwood & Scott, 2017). E used digital technology for research in a variety of ways, including Lego instructions, cruise ship schedule, and exploring letters, numbers, and colours (Figure 5.8).

FIGURE 5.8   Classic Lego and E's search for online instructions

5.3   *Theme Three: Facilitated Perspective Taking*

E's use of the iPad and the learning that occurred using it can be linked to other findings also documented by Winters and Memme (2017). Specifically, these everyday play opportunities and the documentation of them enabled him to take on different perspectives. Through conversations about his personal experiences, he engaged in story-sharing that developed personal memories that contributed to his identity construction (Carr & Lee, 2012; Nelson, 2000). In contrast to Zimmerman, Christakis, and Meltzoff (2007) who warned

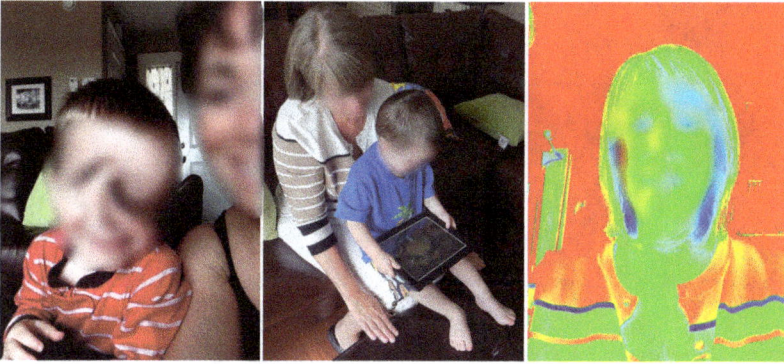

FIGURE 5.9   E takes silly selfies with Nannie on the new iPad

about decreased vocabulary because of (possibly passive) screen time, video documentation showed how E engaged in increased language and vocabulary development and social interaction with other members of his family, like his cousin and his grandmother, "Nannie" (Figure 5.9). This also signals that there is a difference between passive screen time and (inter)active screen time with a trusted and supportive adult.

5.4   Theme Four: Intergenerational Literacies

E's grandparents were an influential element in his experiences and learning, and the relationship was reciprocal, demonstrating how he influenced systems as well. As grandparents were scaffolding his learning and experiences, he also was teaching them about new ways of reading and how to use technology. Intergenerational literacy practices were evident as his grandparents used technology to connect with E to record memories and to create family narratives together (Heydon, 2013; Heydon & O'Neill, 2017). He learned that he could connect with them virtually, share games with them, and use photographs to recount stories of their adventures together.

5.5   Theme Five: Independent Experimentation

E used technology independently as a tool for passive viewing of shows and movies through iTunes and Netflix; as a manipulative to engage in different forms of puzzle play; and as a distraction during long-distance travel. This behaviour is consistent with findings from Ofcom's yearly reports (2015), which highlight the range of devices, internet access, and media viewing that young children engage in. Parallel to findings reported by Harwood et al. (2015), I argue that he also experienced empowerment by his ability to use the tools available to him—tools that fostered a sense of agency to pursue play, learning, or inquiry of his own choosing (see Figures 5.10–5.12).

FIGURE 5.10   New Lego apps for the plane ride

FIGURE 5.11   E narrates an email on the plane

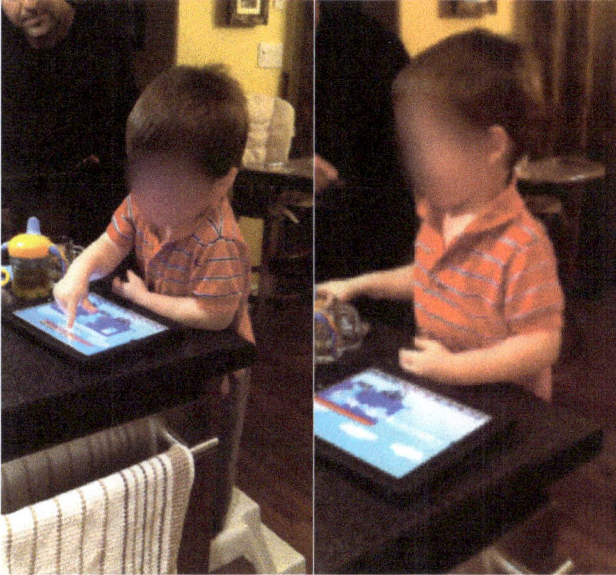

FIGURE 5.12   Video: E plays *Tozzle*, a digital puzzle, on the iPad (screen capture from video)

5.6   *Tensions*

My work also revealed tensions that my husband and I grappled with during the period of the study. Specifically, we questioned what, how much, where, and with whom E should or should not be using digital technology. We also discussed limiting his access to technology according to published warnings and guidelines. In fact, we considered several of the following strategies as identified by researchers (Chaudron, 2015; Livingstone & Helsper, 2008; Livingstone, Haddon, Görzig, & Ólafsso, 2011; Nikken & Jansz, 2014): co-use, active mediation, restrictive mediation, and supervision (see Figure 5.13). Also aligned with the research, the younger E was, the more restrictions we had. Also, because of previous research that positions the digital as a threat to social interactions and outdoor play, we ensured that we offered E many opportunities to play outside.

5.7   *Positionality*

Regardless of the efforts I took to attempt balance, it was "an unescapable fact that a power imbalance will endure" throughout this process by the very virtue of my position as an adult with authority, and thus I held a very privileged position as a researcher (Sargeant & Harcourt, 2012, p. 31). The strategies I used to

FIGURE 5.13   Independent parallel digital play/imitation by E with daddy

mitigate this are woven throughout the theoretical and methodological frameworks I outline in this work. They included the Tri-Council Policy Standards 2:
Core articles, the sociology of childhood, the pedagogy of listening, and multiple points of informed consent and assent with family during the process.
I wanted to document meaningful experiences, not orchestrate experiences
for the sake of the research. Careful planning, communication, and acknowl-
edgment of my position and respectful relationships were essential to negotiating power together.

E may also have perceived or experienced these tensions as a result of his
and our positionality in the ecosystems. He was an only child from a Cauca-
sian, Atlantic Canadian (Prince Edward Island), dual heterosexual parent
family with Irish, Scottish, Francophone, and Métis family heritage. His family
identifies as Catholic, with a high socioeconomic status. E's most immediate
environment (microsystem) at home provided him with love and affection, as
well as opportunities to explore and have autonomy and control over some of
his learning. My husband and I believe in a safe, reliable, routine environment

where child(ren) are loved, respected, and listened to. We had the authority to make these informed decisions based on our position in society as educated parents.

6 Parent-Child Co-Analysis

6.1 *The Role of the Learning Stories*

There are four ways in which E analyzed the data in the learning stories. First, he analyzed his abilities through watching his own participation and mastery of experiences ("Can we do it again? I did a good job!" Research notes, October 14, 2017). His analysis prompted a higher-level thinking and reflection on his own learning. He was able to review his data, reflect on it, and draw conclusions based on this. His own assessment demonstrated "growth mindset" (Dweck, 2013, 2017) through learning stories (Carr & Lee, 2012) that offered him an opportunity to focus on ability and perseverance even if he struggled during the task.

Second, he was participating in what Carr (2005) called an "identity referenced assessment" through learning stories that can become "a jointly owned tool for sustained thinking about learning" (p. 42). Carr also asserted that these shared interactions can set up features of learner agency central to recognition of interest, co-authoring, and self-assessment.

Third, he took the opportunity in the analysis process for his "right to correction" (Sargeant & Harcourt, 2012, p. 88) on two occasions: first, in one instance, he added to a story with a picture of his *My Little Pony* book, and second, when he asked to ensure that it would not be posted online. In the process of his analysis of this learning story, he also accepted his right to verify the data, to also clarify and verify that this has been a positive experience, and to enhance the trustworthiness of the study. It was also an opportunity for him to remix the text and thus the messages that the learning story carries (Pahl & Rowsell, 2012); "To have some control over how other people see us, or how others portray us, is an inherent right afforded to many adults but rarely afforded to children" (Sargeant & Harcourt, 2012, p. 88). E was engaged in sharing the learning stories together with me during the co-analysis. He continued to enjoy and provide his verification that I had captured the stories well and included everything that I should.

The role of the learning stories offered a participatory space (Moss, 2014) and also presented E as the protagonist in his own stories and learning. This is integral to the Reggio Emilia approach to learning that values, honors, and privileges children's meaning making processes and capacities (Edwards,

Gandini, & Forman, 1998; Rinaldi, 1998; Rose et al., 2017). He was beginning to conceptualize the undefined and abstract notion of his own space in the virtual world when we discussed his images and therefore presence online, and in turn, asserted his agency in contributing toward decisions about it. In other words, there were several signals of E's emerging and layered digital literacies (Abrams, 2017) and unfolding sense of digital citizenship.

6.2   *Digital Citizenship*

E began to assert his online rights and identity. Part of his inquiry during the analysis involved whether the data were available to others and videos and photos were online for others to see. I explained that it was part of his learning and the research I had been doing with him so it was just on the computer right now and not online. E's choice and agency and his realization of it emerged from the zone of proximal development that I established with him during the study. This emerged again during our discussion about Facebook, along with his desire to not "be on Facebook right now," and refusing to engage in what Siibak and Ugur (2010) call the "social media online playground" (p. 126).

Finally, we took our responsibility seriously to both protect and empower E when it came to digital technology. The NAEYC (2012) asserts that parents have a responsibility to both expose children to digital tools and media, and to also teach them how to ask questions and think critically about this in their lives. Early childhood research about documentation has encouraged adults to respect the child's desire not to have their pictures taken (Carr & Lee, 2012; Stonehouse, 2010). However, E's example illustrates that it is important for parents not only to have these conversations about photographs and online footprints with their children at a young age, but also to respect their choices.

6.3   *Revisiting Conversations*

E often revisited his analysis and our conversations and took the position of co-owning these stories. The more we engaged in this process together, the more his position of co-researcher strengthened, indicating that there are multiple points along the co-researching with children continuum. In the weeks following the analysis and writing of this work, E revisited his analysis and our conversations in an organic way and demonstrated his ability to self-regulate. In addition, conversely to what Kabuto (2008) realized in her study, E took the position of co-owning these stories:

> E visits me in the office to say hi, gives me a hug and tells me he misses
> me. He peers over my shoulder at what I am writing or looking at, which

often includes pictures or the learning stories that we share together. He asks, "What are you writing about now, Mama?" and I respond, explaining I am still writing "our stories" and his experiences are teaching me more about how young children learn and about digital technology and screen time. I ask him a series of questions including, "Why do you think we need rules around screen time?" to which he responds, "Because when I watch it too much it makes my eyes sore" and "Sometimes it makes me rambunctious!" (laughing). (Research notes, November 25, 2017)

E's insights showed his emerging awareness and personal learning of his strengths and challenges around self-regulatory behaviors (Shanker, 2013; Zimmerman, 1994) with respect to screentime, and how we have continued to talk about digital citizenship with him. Likewise, suggested by Kabuto (2008), the more we engaged in this process of reflexivity together, the more his position of co-researcher strengthened.

Furthermore, including co-analysis in the process was important to the trustworthiness of the study, and reaffirmed that this research was a positive experience for E and that he had agency and voice. He had the opportunity to keep his data, invitations to participate regularly using child-friendly language, opportunities to participate when it did not interfere or overtly disrupt his regular routines, safe and confidential experiences throughout the process, and multiple occasions to engage in the data analysis process. Involving E in the analysis of the research shifted the balance of power so he could exercise his voice and contribute to reflexivity in the case (Mayall, 2000). In support of this, E said that he would like to continue documenting his learning at home. I believe that his desire to continue reinforces the power of including E in the research as a co-researcher rather than an object of study (Corsaro, 2005; Darbyshire et al., 2005; Fargas-Malet et al., 2013; Farrell, 2005; Kellitt, 2010; Mayall, 2000; O'Kane, 2000; Sargeant & Harcourt, 2012). He readily takes on the role of collaborator and is confident asserting his voice—research or not—in our everyday family discussions and lives.

> I told him (fall 2019) that I had written in a book that would have an entire chapter about our research that we did together. For a moment, he looked at me quizzically (it had been a while since we talked about and revisited the research project). Then, in a moment of recognition and remembering dawned on him, and he exclaimed whole-heartedly, "yes! yes! I want to be an author, I'd like that a lot!" It affirmed another point along the continuum of consent and shared power, reinforcing the co-researcher role for him. (Research notes, September 12, 2019).

6.4   *Parent-Researcher Role(s)*

Experiencing multiple subjectivities that encourage one to explore and understand studies like this one is not just about one person (E) but about our collective intellectual and cultural history across nested ecologies (Bronfenbrenner,
2005). Kabuto (2008) also suggested that parent-researchers do not take on
isolated roles of parent and researcher; but that the multidimensional aspects
of being a mother, wife, researcher, and academic constitute me as a whole
person and that the interaction between the multiple roles is what is crucial to
the research product. In fact, these interactions can "lead to paths of inquiry
that evolve into theoretical and conceptual ideas within research" (Kabuto,
2008, p. 183). In addition, Farrell's (2005) ethical guidelines were used to mitigate the potentially conflicting role of caring, protective parent and researcher,
always leaning toward respectful, ongoing, participatory practices and doing
no harm.

There were also times when what I observed challenged what I thought I
knew, and there were also times that this ethnographic perspective allowed
me insight into complex theories about play. While the case study had clear
boundaries, there was also a fluidity that demonstrated Bronfenbrenner's theory of nested systems and taught me how complex it really is.

6.5   *Reflections on Parent-Research*

As parent-researcher, I provide educational, theoretical, and practical insights
into the everyday social processes of learning in our family. Similar to situations reported in other parent-research studies, there were times (e.g., at age
two, when we allowed him to use an iPad and he had little interest) when what
I was observing challenged what I "thought should be" (Kabuto & Martens,
2014, p. 2). There were also times that this ethnographic perspective brought
me insight into complex theories about play and the role that digital technology can take in my son's play. While it is a case study with clear boundaries,
those boundaries were also fluid within the bio-ecological framework, and
they spilled over and influenced one another. In addition, this study provided
insight into early childhood learning in an informal way with an insider perspective that I never would have experienced with someone else's child(ren)
or family because I had access to both systematic and scheduled observations
but also those which happened "in the moment" Kabuto (2008). In so doing,
I aim to contribute to the ongoing discussion about the development of early
learning and how it might best be supported in the digital age.

7   Concluding Thoughts

The roles of technology were both situated and multimodal in E's play experiences in a variety of ways over three years that were rich in meaning making for him. The tensions we felt as parents provide significant insights into critical analysis of what it means to be playing and parenting in a digital age. In addition, the notion of the critical attention to digital citizenship is one for further exploration and discussion with both parents and educators of young children.

Through the specific, unique, and holistic account of how several forms of play unfolded over three years that includes views of myself, E, and our family, we have demonstrated how ecologies and nested systems influence various types of play experiences over time. There was also a level of healthy tension between and within these systems that offers opportunities for strengthening the scaffolding that happened in E's learning, and for personal learning and development of the adults doing the scaffolding.

The exploratory nature of the work provided opportunities for observation and listening (Clark & Moss, 2005; Rinaldi, 1998; Wein, 1998) and in-depth, rich description (Purcell-Gates, 2004) in real-life contexts (Flyvberg, 2001) across nested systems to explain how E engaged in various forms of play (Bronfenbrenner, 2005). Through the systematic use of learning stories, my study honors both early childhood pedagogy (Clark & Moss, 2005) and the sociology of childhood (Mayall, 2000). The methods I used were theoretically and pragmatically motivated and similar to that of Plowman (2014). In addition, involving E in the co-analysis of the research enabled him to collaboratively engage in the data analysis (Sargeant & Harcourt, 2012), and Plowman (2014) asserts that it enables researchers to consider aspects of children's experience that we might otherwise overlook. E was also able to exert agency in multiple ways through the reflexive discussions about learning, digital technology use, and research.

Through an innovative process informed by early childhood pedagogy, and re-examining how research can be conducted with young children, this research demonstrates how learning stories can be an authentic way to conduct research with young children, has offered possible approaches to doing research *with* children, and has contributed to unravelling some of the complexities and possibilities of what it means to play, learn, and parent in the digital age.

8   Future Research and Ethical Considerations

8.1   *Research Recommendations*

Continued research must examine what kinds of technologies young children are using, in what contexts, and whether they are being used in developmentally appropriate ways (interactive versus passive) (Hirschy, 2017) through play to become "multiliterate" (Yelland, 2010, p. 16). There are also implications for how adults (early childhood professionals and/or parents) support this learning (Bers & Kazakoff, 2013). Therefore, the dynamic and hybrid nature of these digital technologies and this study provides evidence that there is a need for further research into how more children experience meaning making using digital technology in their play within and across multiple contexts over time, and how home and extended family, early learning environments, and community influence each other (Bronfenbrenner, 2005; Wang et al., 2010). Therefore, recommendations for future research include:

a   Investigating parents' perspectives on digital play in the early years: how are they using it (or not) with their children? This would build on this single case study;

b   Conducting a larger scale study that involves families (children and their parents), and their early childhood educators in the exploration of possibilities in digital play in the early years, while also including a diverse group of participants in terms of language, ethnicity, and socioeconomic status;

c   Exploring digital play again from a longitudinal perspective starting at age two until age six through the transition into kindergarten; in an attempt to delve into the transition year when there are additional play experiences in a school setting;

d   Exploring digital play with children under the age of two in Prince Edward Island; this is an age that has not been explored in our region;

While the American Academy of Pediatrics (1999) revised its fear-inducing message of "no screens before two," coupled with the collection of research outlined in this study, the fact that the NAEYC last began revisions in 2009 (Schomburg & Donohue, 2009) necessitates a call for re-examination of the NAEYC policy statements on the use of interactive media with young children.

In addition, there are two main recommendations for practice of digital play in the early years. First, although it may not involve future research, there is a need to revive both dialogue and significant work on policy about digital citizenship in the early years centres and reconsider what this means for our youngest 21st century early learners in Canada. This would also include the need for both significant training and professional development in the field of early childhood. Second, there is a need for parent-friendly information and practical, useful and realistic examples of how they could engage in family play practices that respect and protect young children to develop their own emerging digital literacies.

8.2   *Ethical Considerations*

Listening was a key factor of the ethical considerations in this study. Clark and Moss's (2005) framework for listening included six key guiding ideas. They suggested research should be:

> (1) multi-method, and recognise voices of children; (2) participatory, treating children as experts and agents in their own lives; (3) reflexive, and include both children, practitioners and parents in reflecting on meanings and interpretations; (4) adaptable, in that the research would be able to be applied to a variety of early childhood experiences; (5) child-focused: focused on children's lived experiences: looking at lives rather than knowledge gained or care received; and (6) rooted: embedded into practice, that is, a framework for listening which has the potential to be both used as an evaluative tool and to become embedded into early years practice. (2005, p. 13)

While the learning stories acted as a way for me to analyze the data for themes of early childhood learning and development (Flanagan, 2011) and nested ecologies (Bronfenbrenner, 2005), they were also a powerful tool in affirming positive parenting practices as we reflected on how E was learning and growing. Moreover, the learning stories presented an ethical, authentic way for E to co-analyze the data, and for him to assert his power in the study. They offered a deeper ethical opportunity in the research that enabled him to participate in a form of growth mindset (Dweck, 2013), identity referenced assessment, which also involves co-authoring (Carr & Lee, 2012), and exerting his voice and rights to articulate his perspectives (Clark, 2003) as an active participant in the research (Sargeant & Harcourt, 2012). Another example of exerting his voice, was his desire to be referenced as "E" in the study as his pseudonym.

The learning stories were an important contributor in his development of early digital literacies and an evolving awareness of digital citizenship for my son and us as parents. The tensions we felt as parents provide significant insights into critical analysis of co-researching with children. In addition, the notion of the critical attention to digital citizenship is one for further exploration and discussion with both parents and educators of young children. Emerging from this research are possibilities for future research in early childhood digital play, re-envisaging how research can be conducted with preschool children using learning stories, and exploring Bronfenbrenner's model over time.

References

Abbott, L., & Langston, A. (2005). Ethical research with very young children. In A. Farrell (Ed.), *Ethical research with children* (pp. 37–48). New York, NY: McGraw Hill.

Abrams, S.S. (2015). *Integrating virtual and traditional learning in 6–12 classrooms: A layered literacies approach to multimodal meaning making.* New York, NY: Routledge.

Abrams, S. S. (2017). Emotionally crafted experiences: Layering literacies in Minecraft. *The Reading Teacher, 70*(4), 501–506.

Allen, G. (2005). Research ethics in a culture of risk. In A. Farrell (Ed.), *Ethical research with children* (pp. 15–26). New York, NY: McGraw Hill.

Alper, M. (2011). Developmentally appropriate new media literacies: Supporting cultural competencies and social skills in early childhood education. *Journal of Early Childhood Literacy, 13*(2), 175–196.

American Academy of Pediatrics. (1999). Committee on public education. Media education. *Pediatrics, 104*(2), 341–343.

Ball, J. (2005). Restorative research partnerships in Indigenous communities. In A. Farrell (Ed.), *Ethical research with children* (pp. 81–96). New York, NY: McGraw Hill.

Baxter, P., & Jack, S. (2008). Qualitative case study methodology: Study design and implementation for novice researchers. *The Qualitative Report, 13*(4), 544–559.

Bers, M. U., & Kazakoff, E. R. (2013). Techno-Tykes: Digital technologies in early childhood. In O. N. Saracho & B. Spodek (Eds.), *Handbook of research on the education of young children* (3rd ed.). New York, NY: Routledge.

Bers, U. M., & Horn, M. (2010). Tangible programming in early childhood: Revisiting developmental assumptions through new technologies. In I. R. Berson & M. J. Berson (Eds.), *High-tech tots: Childhood in a digital world* (pp. 49–72). Charlotte, NC: Information Age.

Berson, I. R., & Berson, M. J. (2010) (Eds.). *High-tech tots: Childhood in a digital world.* Charlotte, NC: Information Age.

Bronfenbrenner, U. (2005). *Making human beings human: Bioecological perspectives on human development.* London: Sage.

Carr, M. (2005). The leading edge of learning: Recognizing children's success as learners. *European Journal of Early Childhood Research, 13*(2), 41–50.

Carr, M., & Lee, W. (2012). *Learning stories: Constructing learner identities in early education.* Thousand Oaks, CA: Sage.

Carrington, V., & Marsh, J. (2005). Digital childhood and youth: New texts, new literacies. *Discourse: Studies in the Cultural Politics of Education, 26*(3), 279–285.

Chaudron, S. (2015). *Young children (0–8) and digital technology: A qualitative exploratory study across seven countries.* Ipsra: Joint Research Centre.

Clark, A. (2003). The Mosaic approach and research with young children. In V. Lewis, M. Kellet, C. Robinson, S. Fruser, & S. Ding (Eds.), *The reality of research with children and young people* (pp. 157–180). London: Sage.

Clark, A., & Moss, P. (2005). *Spaces to play: More listening to young children using the Mosaic approach.* London: National Children's Bureau.

Cope, B., & Kalantzis, M. (Eds.). (2000). *Multiliteracies: Literacy learning and the design of social futures.* New York, NY: Routledge.

Corsaro, W. A. (2005). *The sociology of childhood* (2nd ed.). Thousand Oaks, CA: Pine Forge Press.

Crabtree, B., & Miller, W. (1999). *Doing qualitative research* (2nd ed.). London: Sage.

Danby, S., & Farrell, A. (2005). Opening the research conversation. In A. Farrell (Ed.), *Ethical research with children* (pp. 49–67). New York, NY: McGraw Hill.

Darbyshire, P., MacDougall, C., & Schiller, W. (2005). Multiple methods in qualitative research with children: More insight or just more? *Qualitative Research, 5*(4), 417–436.

David, T., Tonkin, J., Powell, S., & Anderson, C. (2005). Ethical aspects of power in research with children. In A. Farrell (Ed.), *Ethical research with children* (pp. 124–137). New York, NY: McGraw Hill.

Deitz, B., & Kashin, D. (2012). *Play and learning in early childhood education.* Toronto: Pearson.

Dewey, J. (1938/1963). *Education and experience.* New York, NY: Macmillan.

Dweck, C. (2013). Mindsets: How to motivate students (and yourself). *Educational Horizons, 91*(2), 16–21.

Dweck, C. (2017). The journey to children's mindsets–and beyond. *Child Development Perspectives, 11*, 139–144. doi:10.1111/cdep.12225

Edwards, C. P., Gandini, L., & Forman, G. E. (1998). *The hundred languages of children: The Reggio Emilia approach—advanced reflections.* Greenwich, CT: Ablex.

Fargas-Malet, M., McSherry, D., Larkin, E., & Robinson, C. (2013). Research with children: Methodological issues and innovative techniques. *Journal of Early Childhood Research, 8*(2), 175–187.

Farrell, A. (Ed.). (2005a). *Ethical research with children.* New York, NY: McGraw Hill.

Farrell, A. (2005b). New possibilities for ethical research with children. In A. Farrell (Ed.), *Ethical research with children* (pp. 176–178). New York, NY: McGraw Hill.

Farrell, A. (2005c). New times in ethical research with children. In A. Farrell (Ed.), *Ethical research with children* (pp. 166–175). New York, NY: McGraw Hill.

Flanagan, K. (2011). *PEI's early learning framework*. Retrieved from http://www.gov.pe.ca/eecd/eecd_EYFrWrk_Full.pdf

Froebel, F. (1887). *The education of man*. New York, NY: D. Appleton and Company.

Gee, J. P., & Hayes, E. R. (2011). *Language and learning in the digital age*. London: Routledge.

Gee, J. P., & Lankshear, C. (1997). Language, literacy and the new work order. In C. Lankshear, J. Gee, M. Nobel, & C. Searle (Eds.), *Changing literacies* (pp. 83–102). Buckingham: Open University Press.

Ginsburg, K. (2007). The importance of play in promoting healthy child development and maintaining strong parent-child bonds. *Pediatrics, 119*(1), 182–191.

Golinkoff, R. M., Hirsch-Pasek, K., Russ, S. W., & Lillard, A. S. (2013). Probing play: What does the research show? *American Journal of Play, 6*(1), xi–xiii.

Göncü, A., & Gaskins, S. (2011). Comparing and extending Piaget's and Vygotsky's understandings of play: Symbolic play as individual, sociocultural, and educational interpretation. In A. Pellegrini (Ed.), *The Oxford handbook of the development of play* (pp. 48–57). New York, NY: Oxford University Press.

Harwood, D. (2017). The digital world of young children. In D. Harwood (Ed.), *Crayons and iPads* (pp. 1–5). London: Sage.

Harwood, D., Bajovic, M., Woloshyn, V., Marco Di Cesare, D., Lane, L., & Scott, K. (2015). Intersecting spaces in early childhood education: Inquiry-based pedagogy and tablets. *The International Journal of Holistic Early Learning and Development, 1*, 53–67.

Harwood, D., & Scott, K. (2017). 'Let me show you how to play with the iPad': Young children as teachers. In D. Harwood (Ed.), *Crayons and iPads* (pp. 52–64). London: Sage.

Hamilton, M. (2010). The social context of literacy. In N. Hughes & I. Schwab (Eds.), *Teaching adult literacy: Principles and practice* (pp.7–27). Berkshire: Open University Press.

Heath, S. B. (1983). *Ways with words*. Cambridge: Cambridge University Press.

Heydon, R. (2013). *Learning at the ends of life*. Toronto: University of Toronto Press.

Heydon, R., & O'Neill, S. (2017). Children, elders, and multimodal arts curricula: Semiotic possibilities and the imperative of relationship. In M. J. Narey (Eds.), *Multimodal perspectives of language, literacy, and learning in early childhood: Educating the young child* (Vol. 12, pp. 149–167). Cham: Springer.

James, A. (2007). Giving voice to children's voices: Practices and problems, pitfalls and potentials. *American Anthropologist, 109*(2), 261–272.

Jewitt, C., & Kress, G. (Eds.). (2003). *Multimodal literacy*. New York, NY: Peter Lang.

Jipson, J., & Jipson, J. (2005). Confidence intervals: Doing research with young children. In L. D. Soto & B. B. Swadener (Eds.), *Power and voice in research with children* (pp. 35–43). New York, NY: Peter Lang.

Johnson, J. L., Bottorff, J. L., Browne, A. J., Grewal, S., Hilton, B. A., & Clarke, H. (2004). Othering and being othered in the context of health care services. *Health Communications, 16*(2), 255–271.

Kabuto, B. (2008). Parent-research as a process of inquiry: An ethnographic perspective. *Ethnography and Education, 3*(2), 177–194.

Kabuto, B., & Martens, P. (Eds.). (2014). *Linking families, learning, and schooling: Parent-research perspectives.* New York, NY: Routledge.

Kellitt, M. (2010). *Rethinking children and research: Attitudes in contemporary society.* New York, NY: Continuum International.

Lankshear, C., & Knobel, M. (2003). *New literacies.* Buckingham: Open University Press.

Lankshear, C., & Knobel, M. (2006). *New literacies: Everyday practices and classroom learning* (2nd ed.). Maidenhead: McGraw Hill.

Leu, D. (2000). Literacy and technology: Diectic consequences for literacy education in an information age. In M. Kamil, P. Mosenthal, D. Reason, & R. Barr (Eds.), *Handbook of reading research* (3rd ed., pp. 743–770). Mahwah, NJ: Lawrence Erlbaum.

Livingstone, S., Haddon, L., Görzig, A., & Ólafsson, K. (2011). *Risks and safety on the internet: The perspective of European children.* Retrieved from http://eprints.lse.ac.uk/33731/

Livingstone, S., & Helsper, E. J. (2008). Parental mediation of children's Internet use. *Journal of Broadcasting and Electronic Media, 52*(4), 581–599.

Lopez, E., Caspe, M., & Weiss, H. (2017). Logging in to family engagement in the digital age. In C. Donohue (Ed.), *Family engagement in the digital age: Early childhood educators as media mentors* (pp. 16–29). New York, NY: Routledge & Washington, DC: NAEYC.

MacNaughton, G., & Smith, K. (2005). Transforming research ethics: The choices and challenges of researching with children. In A. Farrell (Ed.), *Ethical research with children* (pp. 112–123). New York, NY: McGraw Hill.

Malaguzzi, L. (1994). Your image of the child: Where teaching begins. *Early Childhood Educational Exchange, 3*, 52–61.

Marsh, J., Mascheroni, G., Carrington, V., Árnadóttir, H., Brito, R., Dias, P., Kupiainen, R., & Trueltzsch-Winjen, C. (2017). *The online and offline digital literacy practices of young children: A review of the literature.* Retrieved from http://digilitey.eu/wp-content/uploads/2017/01/WG4-LR-jan-2017.pdf

Mayall, B. (2000). Conversations with children. Working with generational issues. In P. Christensen & A. James (Eds.), *Research with children. Perspectives and practices* (pp. 120–135). London: Routledge Falmer.

Memme, L., & Winters, K. L. (2017). Digital inquiry and socio–critical negotiations in two early childhood classrooms. In D. Harwood (Ed.), *Crayons and iPads* (pp. 29–41). London: Sage.

Miles, M. B., & Huberman, A. M. (1994). *Qualitative data analysis: An expanded source book* (2nd ed.). Thousand Oaks, CA: Sage.

Moll, L., Amanti, C., Neff, D., & Gonzalez, N. (1992). Funds of knowledge for teaching: Using a qualitative approach to connect homes and classrooms. *Theory into Practice, 31*(2), 132–141.

Montessori, M. (1912). *The Montessori method.* Retrieved from http://www.arvindguptatoys.com/arvindgupta/montessori-new.pdf

Morrow, V. (2005). Ethical issues in collaborative research with children. In A. Farrell (Ed.), *Ethical research with children* (pp. 150–165). New York, NY: McGraw Hill.

Moss, P. (2014). *Early childhood and compulsory education: Reconceptualising the relationship.* New York, NY: Routledge.

National Association for the Education of Young Children (NAEYC) and Fred Rogers Centre. (2012, January). *Technology and interactive media as tools in early childhood programs serving children from birth through age 8.* Retrieved from http://www.naeyc.org/files/naeyc/file/positions/PS_technology_WEB2.pdf

Nelson, K. (2000). Narrative, time, and the emergence of the encultured self. *Culture & Psychology, 6*(2), 183–196.

New London Group. (1996). A pedagogy of multiliteracies: Designing social futures. *Harvard Educational Review, 66*(1), 60–92.

New Zealand Ministry of Education. (1996). *Te Whāriki: Early childhood curriculum.* Retrieved from http://www.education.govt.nz/assets/Documents/Early-Childhood/te-whariki.pdf

Nikken, P., & Jansz, J. (2014). Developing scales to measure parental mediation of young children's internet use. *Learning, Media and Technology, 39*(2), 250–266.

Ofcom. (2015). *Children and parents: Media use and attitudes report.* London: Ofcom. Retrieved from https://www.ofcom.org.uk/research-and-data/media-literacy-research/childrens/children-parents-nov-15

O'Kane, C. (2000). The development of participatory techniques. Facilitating children's views about decisions which affect them. In P. Christensen & A. James (Eds.), *Research with children, perspectives and practices* (pp. 136–159). London: Routledge Falmer.

Pahl, K., & Rowsell, J. (2012). *Literacy and education* (2nd ed.). London: Sage.

Pellegrini, A. D., Dupuis, D., & Smith, P. K. (2007). Play in evolution and development. *Developmental Review, 27*(2), 261–276.

Plowman, L. (2014). Researching young children's everyday uses of technology in the family home. *Interacting with Computers, 27*(1), 36–46.

Plowman, L., McPake, J., & Stephen, C. (2012). Extending opportunities for learning: The role of digital media in early education. In S. Suggate & E. Reese (Eds.), *Contemporary debates in child development and education* (pp.95–104). Abingdon: Routledge.

Piaget, J. (1926/1929). *The child's conception of the world*. New York, NY: Basic Books.

Piaget, J. (1953). *The origins of intelligence in children*. New York, NY: Basic Books.

Pollard, A. (1987). *Children and their primary schools: A new perspective* (Vol. 2). London: Falmer Press.

Purcell-Gates, V. (2004). Ethnographic research. In N. K. Duke & M. H. Mallette (Eds.), *Literacy research methodologies*. New York, NY: The Guilford Press.

Rice, P., & Ezzy, D. (1999). *Qualitative research methods: A health focus*. Melbourne: Oxford University Press.

Rinaldi, C. (1998). Projected curriculum and documentation. In C. Edwards, L. Gandini, & G. Forman (Eds.), *The hundred languages of children: The Reggio Emilia approach—Advanced reflections* (pp. 113–125). Norwich, CT: Ablex Publishing.

Roach O'Keefe, A., & Moffatt, L. (2013, June). *Where to start: Early childhood educators, digital literacies and professional learning*. Paper session presented at 82nd Canadian Society for the Study of Education Congress, Victoria, BC.

Roberts, H. (2000). Listening to children: And hearing them. In P. H. Christensen & A. James (Eds.), *Research with children: Perspectives and practices* (pp. 225–240). London: Falmer Press.

Rogoff, B. (2003). *The cultural nature of human development*. New York, NY: Oxford University Press.

Roopnarine, J. L., & Davidson, K. L. (2015). Parent-child play across cultures. *American Journal of Play, 7*(2), 228–252.

Rose, S., Fitzpatrick, K., Mersereau, C., & Whitty, P. (2017). Playful pedagogic moves digital devices in the outdoors. In D. Harwood (Ed.), *Crayons and iPads* (pp. 16–28). London: Sage.

Rowsell, J. (2017). Be the "I" in the iPad: iPads and children who love them. In D. Harwood (Ed.), *Crayons and iPads* (pp. 6–15). London: Sage.

Sargeant, J., & Harcourt, D. (2012). *Doing ethical research with children*. London: Open University Press.

Seitz, H. (2008). *The power of documentation in the early childhood classroom*. Retrieved from https://www.naeyc.org/files/tyc/file/Seitz.pdf

Shanker, S. (2013). *Calm, alert, and learning*. Toronto: Pearson.

Siibak, A., & Ugur, K. (2010). Is social networking the new "online playground" for young children? A study of Rate profiles in Estonia. In I. R. Berson & M. J. Berson (Eds.), *High-tech tots: Childhood in a digital world* (pp. 125–152). Charlotte, NC: Information Age.

Skånfors, L. (2009). Ethics in child research: Children's agency and researchers' 'ethical radar'. *Childhoods Today, 3*(1), 1–22.

Stacey, S. (2008). *Emergent curriculum in early childhood settings*. St. Paul, MN: Redleaf Press.

Stake, R. E. (1995). *The art of case study research*. Thousand Oaks, CA: Sage.

Stonehouse, A. (2010). A matter of respect: Recognizing young children's right to privacy. *Putting Children First, 35*, 16–17. Retrieved from http://ncac.acecqa.gov.au/educator-resources/pcf-articles/Recognising_chns_right_to_privacy_Sept10.pdf

Street, B. V. (1999). Literacy and social change: The significance of social context in the development of literacy programmes. In D. A. Wagner (Ed.), *The future of literacy in a changing world* (Rev. ed., pp. 55–72). Cresskill, NY: Hampton Press.

Sutton-Smith, B. (1997). *The ambiguity of play*. Cambridge, MA: Harvard University Press.

Sutton-Smith, B. (2008). Play theory: A personal journey and new thoughts. *American Journal of Play, 1*(1), 80–123.

Van Scooter, J., & Boss, S. (2002). *Learners, language and technology: Making connections that support literacy*. Northwest Educational Laboratory. Retrieved February 24, 2005, from http:www.netc.org/earlyconnections/pub/index/html

Vygotsky, L. S. (1978). *Mind in society: The development of higher psychological processes* (M. Cole, V. John-Steiner, S. Scribner, & E. Souberman, Eds.). Cambridge, MA: Harvard University Press.

Walsh, K. (2005). Researching sensitive issues. In A. Farrell (Ed.), *Ethical research with children* (pp. 68–80). New York, NY: McGraw Hill.

Wang, X. C., Berson, I. R., Jaruszewicz, C., Hartle, L., & Rosen, D. (2010). Young children's technology experiences in multiple contexts: Bronfenbrenner's ecological theory reconsidered. In I. R. Berson & M. J. Berson (Eds.), *High-tech tots: Childhood in a digital world* (pp. 23–48). Charlotte, NC: Information Age.

Wien, C. A. (2006). Emergent curriculum. *Connections, 10*(1), 1–4.

Winters, K. L., & Memme, L. (2017). Tablets as invitational spaces. In D. Harwood (Ed.), *Crayons and iPads* (pp. 42–51). London: Sage.

Wohlwend, K. E. (2015a). *Playing their way into literacies: Reading, writing, and belonging in the early childhood classroom*. New York, NY: Teachers College Press.

Wohlwend, K. E. (2015b). Making, remaking, and reimagining the everyday: Play, creativity, and popular media. In J. Rowsell & K. Pahl (Eds.), *Routledge handbook of literacy studies*, (pp. 548–560). London: Routledge.

Wohlwend, K. E. (2017). The expression of multiliteracies and multimodalities in play. In F. Serafini & E. Gee (Eds.), *Remixing multiliteracies: Theory and practice from New London to new times* (pp. 162–175). New York, NY: Teachers College Press.

Yelland, N. (2010). New technologies, playful experiences, and multimodal learning. In I. R. Berson & M. J. Berson (Eds.), *High-tech tots: Childhood in a digital world* (pp. 5–22). Charlotte, NC: Information Age.

Yin, R. K. (2014). *Case study research: Design and methods* (5th ed.). Thousand Oaks, CA: Sage.

Zimmerman, B. J. (1994). Dimensions of academic self-regulation: A conceptual framework for education. In D. H. Schunk & B. J. Zimmerman (Eds.), *Self-regulation of learning and performance: Issues and educational applications* (pp. 3–21). Hillsdale, NJ: Lawrence Earlbaum Associates.

Zimmerman, F. J., Christakis, D. A., & Meltzoff, A. N. (2007). Associations between media viewing and language development in children under age 2 years. *The Journal of Pediatrics, 151*(4), 364–368.

CHAPTER 6

Career Development? What's That: Engaging My Daughters in an Examination of Their Learning Process and How It Can Inform Their Future— Or Not

Lourdes M. Rivera, Nora Rivera-Larkin and Dahlia Rivera-Larkin

Abstract

Career development and school engagement are two concepts that have a significant impact on student outcomes. Research has indicated that addressing students' career development can have a positive impact on helping prepare them for their futures. Research on engagement has demonstrated its importance in understanding and promoting student learning. A positive connection between career development and engagement also has been supported. Together, these two concepts can provide insights on how to help students become more successful. Using narrative inquiry, this study examines the experiences of two adolescent girls, 16-year-old Nora and 13-year-old Dahlia, as they examine their learning experiences in and out of school; what it means to be engaged in the learning process; and the connection to their career development. The data obtained were analyzed using an iterative process which resulted in the identification of two themes: School Learning as Restrictive and Boring and Engagement/Enjoyment. The lead author discusses the findings, and provides recommendations for educators. An examination of the ethical considerations when working with significant others is also provided.

1   Introduction

Given that I am a counselor educator with a focus on career development, facilitating the career development of my two daughters at first might seem like a no-brainer. After all, years of research and work in the area of career development, providing career counseling and teaching in the area, would suggest that I was in a unique position to support, encourage, and facilitate the development of my own children. However, like many situations that reflect the adage

© KONINKLIJKE BRILL NV, LEIDEN, 2020 | DOI: 10.1163/9789004421721_006

"the cobbler's children have no shoes," I found myself at an impasse—push too hard and they disengage; don't push enough and they seem to stagnate. When I was invited to contribute to this book, it seemed like a perfect opportunity to help me help my daughters engage in a more thoughtful examination of their learning process, career development, and themselves. I hoped that by engaging them in this project it would help empower them to become more thoughtful about how they approach their learning processes, and also how their choices impact their learning and their future. This chapter is the story of our journey, how we engaged and negotiated working together, and what has come out of this endeavor for them and for me.

2 Some Background

It is important, I believe, to frame the context and experiences of each of my co-researchers within their uniqueness as individuals. This uniqueness influenced not only the questions addressed, but also the process for each of them. I provide a brief profile of how I see my daughters (both have read and provided feedback on my perspective and for the most part concede that it is reflective of who they are) and they provide one of me.

2.1 Co-Researcher #1: Nora

Since a young child, Nora has been fascinated with reading and writing—she loves books. For the past few years, she's been writing her own stories (not that I get to read them). I would describe my oldest daughter as friendly, but reserved. Although she has a number of friends who get together for movies and Starbucks (mostly Starbucks) she tends to prefer spending time at home, reading, going on online, texting with her friends. I would describe her as someone who keeps things to herself and is reflective and thoughtful about everything, but doesn't open up easily. She has a wicked sense of humor and can often be found cackling out loud as she watches her favorite modes of entertainment (i.e., sitcoms, video bloggers).

Discussions about her becoming a writer, a veterinarian, and a number of other possibilities have been part of our family conversations. Yet, now that Nora is a junior in high school, our conversations about colleges and majors had become more challenging as time went on. Even our college visits seemed to turn into "Mami's college visit" with her, seeming to take little interest. Her level of engagement and enthusiasm, in my opinion, seemed lackluster. She was a junior in high school and yet she seemed no closer to have a sense of what she might want to pursue or where she would like to go to college. I was beginning to feel the press of time and I believe she was as well, which contributed to making our conversations more challenging. Questions including "what are you interested in, what colleges are you considering, what type of setting," were not getting us anywhere. So, I proposed she might want to consider focusing on her process of choosing a college; she'd get a lot of work done on the college exploration process while collaborating with me on this chapter. That did not go well. Instead, we decided that her interest in writing and using digital media to learn about writers and what that experience was like for her, how it influenced her own learning and writing, would work best. Thus, Nora's focus is on her relationship with digital means of learning about writing and writers, while reflecting on what this experience means to her and how it influences her own pursuits.

2.2   Co-Researcher #2: Dahlia

In contrast to her sister, Dahlia has been more physically oriented and active, a perpetual object in motion; for her, keeping still for even a few minutes has been impossible—she's been, as she describes it, a "fidgety" person. Even as a young child she was incapable of sitting still; we'd often find her climbing up chairs, counters, kitchen cabinets. Her first day in day care, as her father and I waited out of sight to make sure she would settle in, we heard the teacher say "Dahlia, there is no running in the class." It seemed as though she had organized a game of catch—mind you, this was just minutes after entering the room! Another aspect of her personality is that she has had an innate ability for taking things apart—toys, books, anything she could get her hands on. Fortunately, as she got older, it turned out she also had an innate ability for putting things back together. So, when it came to deciding what she would focus on for this chapter, it was a matter of picking from a number of self-taught hobbies—solving Rubik's Cubes, performing card tricks, or building skateboards—all of which she taught herself using the internet. She decided on the Rubik's Cube endeavor. Given the level of commitment and time that she dedicated to this interest online and offline, it seemed like a perfect topic to focus on as she explored her learning process and what it means to her.

2.3   Co-Researcher #3: Mami

Our mother is a smart, empathetic and kind person. She can be impatient and annoying at times because while she likes to do things very quickly we tend to procrastinate. However, she is also understanding and adaptable. She always tries to understand different points of views and always looks out for the best interests of those around her. Our mother is very hard-working and has instilled that sense in us all our life. She is very fun and corny and enjoys reading and watching movies with us but she has also taught us to balance work and fun. She encourages us to pursue what makes us happy and has worked to try and find the things that make us happy. While she can be brutally honest, she has shaped us into strong, independent women and we are very thankful to have her as a mother.

3 Conceptual Framework

3.1 *Career Development*
Given my interest and work in the area of career development, particularly among school-aged populations, I wanted to examine how my daughters' learning process contributed to their career development; their understanding or thinking about the type of work they might want to pursue in the future. Granted, at their age, identifying a specific occupation isn't the goal—nor is it realistic. However, we can get a sense of the type of work individuals might pursue based on their interests and abilities.

Within the field of career development, there are many frameworks and definitions that attempt to capture the complexity of this process. Super, Savickas, and Super (1997) provided a developmental framework that identifies life stages individuals progress through during which they learn about themselves and the world of work. Two of these stages, growth and exploration, take place during the school years, a time during which youth are learning about their interest and abilities and are beginning to develop their self-concept (who they see themselves as, the roles that they have in life). During the growth stage (ages 4 to 13), students are acquiring information about themselves and the world around them which will inform the next stage of development, exploration. It is during the exploration stage (ages 14–24) that students begin the process of "crystalizing" in a general way what they might want to do in the future. As individuals progress through these stages, what they learn about themselves and the world around them, the opportunities and options available to them, will eventually inform their future goals and aspirations, educationally and occupationally. According to Super et al. (1997) during these critical years, youth need to begin to develop a sense of self, an awareness of occupational options and begin to narrow down their preferences. This narrowing down of preferences in turn will inform what they devote their energies to and eventually the choices they make, even if tentatively, about the type of work they would like to engage in as adults. The more successfully students progress through these stages, the better prepared they will be to make important decisions about their academic and career pursuits.

Given the significance of this period of time (i.e. school-aged years) in shaping and informing youths' ideas and possibilities for their futures, a number of researchers have made the case that including career development interventions within the classroom curriculum can help increase students' appreciation for the relation between what they are learning in school and their goals for the future (Rivera & Schaefer, 2009; Schaefer & Rivera, 2014).

Research on career development in schools has provided ample support for the positive impact these interventions can have on students (Hooley, Marriott, Sampson, 2011). Based on their comprehensive review of the literature on career development in schools, Hooley et al. (2011) argued that career development efforts can help "students to orient themselves towards their futures and to consider how their actions might shape different life journeys" (p. 4). In a follow up study to examine the impact of career development on student outcomes three years after high school graduation, Lapan, Aoyagi, and Kayson (2007) found that students who had benefited the most from career development interventions were more likely to pursue additional education and tended to report higher levels of life satisfaction.

Career development interventions also have been associated with increased school engagement (Kenny, Bluestein, Hasse, Jackson, & Perry, 2006; Orthner, Jones-Sanpei, Akos, & Rose, 2013; Perry, Liu, & Pabian, 2010). Using a randomized trial Orthner et al. (2013) reported that students who received classroom instruction that included career-related information were more likely to report higher levels of school engagement than students who did not receive the instruction. The relation between career development and school engagement brings us to the second concept that I was interested in examining as part of our inquiry: how do Nora and Dahlia engage in the learning process.

3.2   Engagement

Engagement has been defined in numerous ways and is also considered to be a multidimensional concept that attempts to explicate students' involvement in the learning process (Jimerson, Campos, & Greif, 2003). The focus on engagement as a concept that influences student learning has been examined and researched for over 20 years and continues to garner considerable attention in the field of education. The importance of engagement in understanding and promoting student learning has received support despite the challenges faced in defining and measuring the concept (Boekaerts, 2016; Eccles, 2016). Based on a review of the extant literature, Fredericks, Blumenfeld, and Paris (2004) organized student engagement into three categories: behavioral engagement, emotional engagement, and cognitive engagement. Though the three categories themselves present challenges given the different definitions that have been used for each and how each has been measured (for a detailed discussion see Fredricks et al., 2004), this framework does provide a somewhat basic way of understanding engagement—how do students behave within the learning process (e.g., time spent on tasks), how do they feel while engaging in learning (e.g., enjoyment), and what are they thinking (e.g., self-regulation).

3.3   Career Development and Increased School Engagement

As mentioned previously, a relation has been found between career development interventions and student engagement. Focusing on students' career development within the school setting is about assisting them to become more aware of the things they like, the things they are good at, and making connections between what they are learning in school and their future goals. The more relevance students see between what they are learning in school and their futures, the greater the likelihood that the positive outcomes that have been associated with increased engagement (e.g., academic performance) can be achieved. Thus, career development and school engagement can be seen as two intricately related concepts that can be used to better address student learning. It is within this conceptual framework that I engaged in this collaborative narrative inquiry with my daughters.

4   Methodology

4.1   Initiating the Collaboration

I have two lovely and intelligent daughters (yes, I recognize the inherent bias of a mother in this statement). Nora was a junior in high school and Dahlia was in 7th grade when I approached them about working together on this project. I explained to them that this would provide us the opportunity to work together on better understanding what motivated them and how and why. I also shared with them what I thought to be the benefit of helping them better understand how they learn and work best. I impressed upon them the seriousness of this request and the level of responsibility that it would entail. I shared with them the invitation email and asked them to think about it before they committed. After some initial questions, they both agreed to participate; Nora, the writer, somewhat hesitantly.

4.2   Data Collection

The questions that guided our inquiry and the process of how we would engage in this research were determined in collaboration based on their areas of interest and my interest in career development. The questions aimed at getting them to think about what and how they engaged in learning digitally and non-digitally, and what their personal experience was like. They each spent considerable time pursuing their interests using digital media, yet their school learning seemed to get only as much time as was needed to complete specific assignments. A main goal was to have them tell their stories in their own words using narrative inquiry (Clandinin & Connelly, 2000). I also was interested in examining their sense of engagement with the topics that they chose to pursue (learn about) on their own as opposed to what they were learning in school. The questions for each were slightly different (see Appendix A) because (because I tried) to tailor them to what I understood about each of them and their interests.

Although throughout the process, strategies for achieving our goals changed and evolved, at each step of the process, the decisions of how to proceed were agreed to by the three researchers. And, our process was not straight forward and neat; it was messy. Below is a description of how we went about conducting this narrative inquiry.

Just like many parents, I would ask about school: what they were up to, what they enjoyed, and what their hopes and dreams were for the future. We would discuss different jobs and careers and even what the difference was between the two. This guided our initial attempt at conducting this collaborative narrative inquiry. Thus, we began the process with me interviewing Nora and Dahlia individually in our home. I began by asking them questions about their learning experiences, the things they enjoy doing, what they thought about, and what was important to them. This strategy, however, did not get us very far. Invariably, my attempts at engaging them in this line of inquiry became tense, and Nora and Dahlia seemed to become impatient with me. We just didn't seem to be able to find the right moment, the right mood to conduct the interview; or perhaps it was the setting, or working face to face. I soon gave up on this strategy.

My next strategy was to ask them to write their thoughts and feelings about their experiences based on the questions we had been discussing. This way they could go off on their own and work on the questions without having to answer me directly, face-to-face. This didn't get us very far either. Every time I asked if they had something for me to read, Nora and Dahlia would offer a response to the effect of "I'll get to it." Feeling more and more frustrated with time ticking away, and at a loss for how to get them moving, I thought of another option: why not use technology to get them working on this; after all, part of this project is to better understand their digital and non-digital learning and how they engage best. So, I created a Google doc for each of them with the questions I had developed. This too seemed to sputter. Deadlines weren't met.

My follow-ups were pushed aside. Eventually, however, the approach proved to be successful. I finally had something on paper from each of them. At last, we had found a strategy that, despite its limitations, seemed to help us move forward.

4.3   Data Analysis

I used an iterative process to review and analyze the responses provided by Nora and Dahlia in order to identify themes (Berkowitz, 1997; Clandinin & Connelly, 2000). After reading the girls' initial responses to the questions on the Google doc, I asked them to respond to some follow-up questions, mostly to seek clarification on what they were communicating. The follow-up questions and their responses were also done via the Google document. Once I had all of their follow-up responses, I read through them again, first all of Nora's, then all of Dahlia's, all the while making notes about what seemed of interest to me (for example, Dahlia's statement about boredom and how long things took). After reading through their responses multiple times and taking notes as I went along, I created a table in which I organized excerpts from their responses and compared them to each other. As I reviewed their responses again, I identified and labeled themes that seemed to emerge from my reading of both of their responses.

Through this iterative process, I initially extrapolated four themes that seemed to permeate both of their experiences and their sense of what mattered to them. At this point, I shared with Nora and Dahlia the excerpts I used, the analysis I conducted, and the themes that emerged; I asked each of the girls to review the themes and provide feedback. Then, the three of us met to discuss their feedback together. Based on our discussions, the girls reported that two of the themes were representative of their experiences. The other two, they felt, were somewhat redundant and could be eliminated or were already represented in the two themes they endorsed. Once we agreed on the two themes, we went over their responses again and, together, selected which excerpts they felt were most representative of their experiences within the identified themes. The two themes that we finally agreed upon are reflective of their thoughts, feelings and experiences and what they were trying to convey in their responses.

5   What We Learned

Despite the difference in questions, in their responses, there emerged some commonalities among their experiences and perceptions about learning online versus learning in school as well as their sense of engagement. In what follows are the two themes that Nora, Dahlia, and I found to resonate in their writing.

5.1   Theme: School Learning as Restrictive/Boring

Both Nora and Dahlia are high performing students; I base this statement on the fact that throughout their formal educational experience, they have brought home grades in the 90s. Yet, despite their academic success in school, both reported that learning in the school setting was restrictive and boring.

Nora:

> In school I often get bored because what we learn there is not something I am particularly interested in and it doesn't engage me enough which has been a growing problem through the years...I am not very good in math and science subjects and those tend to bore me...i do enjoy english and social studies subjects because i like to learn about literature and writing and the world.

And, although she is aware that she needs to spend time and energy in the areas that she is not "interested" in, it is still difficult for her and she doesn't feel as productive:

> i usually prefer to do more creative activities...because it interests me more and i have more fun doing it...I need to work on my balancing of activities and time planning but i usually feel more productive and creative when doing my own things and working on my own projects.

For Dahlia, when writing about her learning to solve the Rubik's Cube using the internet as compared to her learning experience in school, she writes:

> This experience was different from my learning experience in school because some of the things I learn in school do not interest me as much. It is also different because in school we do not get to decide how long our breaks are or how long we work for...I can take a week to learn one step while at school I would only have 45 minutes...Instead of having to learn certain lessons by a certain time I was able to take things at my own pace which helped me understand the steps better.

In Dahlia's writing about her experience, what emerges is her preference for managing her own time, spending as little or as much time as she feels comfortable. Another interesting piece of information that came across in Dahlia's responses was her sense of school learning or non-digital learning, taking too long. I was particularly struck by this as it provided me some insight into her sense of time, particularly when she is asked to do something that she does not consider to be of interest to her (e.g., cleaning her room). Below is an excerpt that speaks to this:

> The internet made it a lot faster for me to find the information that I was looking for at that point in time instead of me having to spent five or ten minutes trying to find each step in a book.

This statement is particularly curious because this is the same person who spent hours creating a handwritten notebook containing all the algorithms she learned online which she then used to practice solving the Rubik's Cube. This does not include the number of hours that she actually spent practicing—according to her estimate, she spent over 200 hours over the course of the year solving the Rubik's Cube and bringing her time down to about 17 seconds. Yet, spending five minutes looking something up in a book is too time consuming.

In both their experiences, having to spend time on things that do not "interest" them and having to do it within specific time constraints not of their own making—having others dictate how they spend their time—seems to contribute to this sense of school learning being a "restrictive" exercise.

5.2   *Theme: Engagement/Enjoyment*

The themes of engagement and enjoyment came up repeatedly in their answers to the questions posed and in our conversations. Although initially I had these two as separate themes, the girls felt that the two went hand-in-hand, that one was intricately tied to the other and should be combined into one. After much discussion, I agreed to keep it as one theme. As they described it, their enjoyment, having "fun," kept them engaged in the activities that they pursued digitally. And it seemed the more they enjoyed what they were doing, the more time they spent on these activities. Having fun kept them engaged and motivated them to seek more information and to spend more time learning about the things that interested them. Unlike the school learning, which they spent the minimum of time needed to complete a task or assignment (and at that, grudgingly), when they were having fun or learning about something that they cared about, they willingly spent more time on task.

In discussing her experience watching and learning from the writers whose videos she watches online, Nora writes:

> I followed them and others because they were inspiring, made me laugh, and made me happier...When I watch videos, not only on BookTube, but of people who make me laugh, inspire me, are my favorite artists, it makes me happier, it shows me what I like in other people, what I like in books, and helps me add on to my own creativity (themes, character types/qualities, quotes, scenes, etc.).

Although watching these online videos can be thought of as entertainment, a source of pleasure and fun, Nora is also learning about writing and communicating her ideas. This experience informed her own writing and character development.

For Dahlia, the engagement and enjoyment seemed to emerge from being able to achieve something, to meet a challenge. In discussing her experience with using the internet to solve the Rubik's Cube, she writes:

> I felt excited because I was learning about something new that interested me and kept my brain active...Since I am a very competitive person, each time I solved the Cube faster I felt like I was winning a competition against myself which is something I enjoyed throughout the experience. My competitiveness is the thing that drives me to succeed. I always want to win and i always want to prove people wrong so it drove me to succeed in solving the cube.

In addition to her sense of accomplishment, being able to solve the Rubik's Cube and get faster at it, she also reports that "Once I solved it I felt extremely accomplished and happy." Dahlia also derived much enjoyment solving the Rubik's Cube for friends and family members—particularly experiencing their amazement and their inability to do it themselves was and continues to be a source of enjoyment for her.

5.3   Connecting Their Experiences to Career Development

When asked about how their experiences and what they learned about themselves related to their thoughts about what type of work/career they might want to pursue in the future, Nora and Dahlia had difficulty seeing the connections or relevance. Despite the relation between the skills and abilities embedded in their pursuits and possible future work areas, they saw these as separate endeavors—what I do because I enjoy it and what type of work I might do in the future. Though in Nora's responses there was some indication that she was making some connection between the things she enjoyed and her future pursuits, for Dahlia the disconnect was complete. In light of Super et al.'s (1997) model of career development, this lack of clarity or connection between their interests and abilities and what they might do in the future is to be expected.

For example, Dahlia can be placed in the "growth" stage; although she has many interests that can be related to different career fields, she's not ready to make these connections. And, when I pointed out for Dahlia that the skills, abilities, and interests that she displayed in solving the Rubik's cube (and her other activities) indicated that she might like work in the fields of mathematics or engineering, she was adamant in her rejection of these as possibilities. She even accused me of taking away the "fun" in what she was doing.

Nora, however, can be described as having entered the "exploration" stage as she is beginning to identify career options that are related to what she is interested in and seeing these as possibilities for herself. In describing her experience and engagement with her favorite online resources, she writes that when watching these video blogs online:

> I can see myself as a more confident person, as a person that creates their own business, creates a successful book, becomes successful, etc. because I see them doing it and they help me believe that I could do it too.

Although she may not be able to express a clear intent of what she might want to do in her future, her words clearly address how she is beginning to identify possible career pursuits related to her interests.

The disconnect between what youth enjoy and are good at and their future possibilities is something that educators need to be aware of as they attempt to prepare students for the future. Even if students do not have an idea of what career they might want to pursue (and this might be developmentally appropriate), helping students recognize and understand the connection between what they are learning and future opportunities is still needed. Integrating information about careers within the curriculum is one way of providing information to broaden students' awareness of possibilities and fostering greater engagement (Orthner et al., 2013). If we want students to be actively involved in their school learning and be planful, we need to help them see the connection between what they are learning in school and future learning and work opportunities. This is something I will continue to do with my daughters and I encourage educators to do with students—draw the connection between classroom learning and its application in the world. But let me be clear, students might resist this connection, as I experienced with Dahlia—but the effort is worth making. Perhaps Dahlia is rejecting this now, but the awareness that there are fields in which her abilities can be utilized might some day in the future inform her choices.

6   Summary and Final Thoughts about Our Collaboration

Below we each provide a brief summary of what working on this chapter was like for us.

6.1   *Nora*

Working on this chapter was a difficult process because I'd never really realized or thought much about how much I used the internet for my creative process or to motivate me. I had to really think about how internet shapes myself and I also thought about my friends and other people online who enjoyed the same content I did and how we had similar interests and how they must feel about creators as well. I am happy to share some Youtubers I watch who I believe to be great role models and inspirations and who I believe have truly shaped me as a person. Through the internet I have learned about new music that I have come to truly love, new books that I can't wait to read, new shows and movies to watch, and especially a new mindset of productivity and pursuing happiness and doing something with my life that I love.

6.2   *Dahlia*

Working in this chapter was a fun and difficult project. I was able to reminisce on a very fun part of my life. It was difficult because I am not the most skilled writer so this task was difficult for me especially with the deadlines. One of the things that I had the most difficulty with was the reaching deadlines. This was difficult for me because I have a very hard time focusing on things I don't perticulary want to work on. This was the most difficult at the beginning because I didn't want to have to sit down and work on the google doc for an extended period of time. Overall this was a very fun experience to be able to work on something with my mother and sister.

6.3   *Responses*

After reading their responses, I asked them to say a little about what they learned about themselves as learners. This is what they had to say:

> Nora:
> I learned that I am a visual learner and I retain information better when writing/seeing notes and being able to review them. I am also a procrastinator but I have found that I do some of my best work at the last minute even though I know I shouldn't. I prefer to do work that interests me and

I am more engaged when I am having fun and learning the things I want, when I want to.

Dahlia:
Throughout this experience I have realised that I am a visual learner. I have realised this by going through different methods of learning that were digital and non-digital. I eventually realised that the method that worked for me was watching youtube videos that had a visual explanation to the steps of solving the rubik's cube. This made it easier for me to recreate the steps with my own hands on my own cube.

In both their experiences, the ability to use digital media and particularly the ability to watch others engage in, demonstrate, or discuss the topics that they had an interest in, seemed to enhance their experience in general, and their learning in particular.

6.4   *Lourdes*

First, let me say: It was not as easy as I thought it would be. Since being invited to contribute this chapter, we (my daughters and I) had been discussing what the process would be like and on what aspects of their learning experiences each might focus. Of course, I had ideas, I had plans. I had no clue. The process of negotiating what each would focus on was relatively easy with my youngest co-researcher, while the older one proved a bit more challenging. The process itself was bumpy to say the least. On multiple occasions we would seem to be moving along only to stall or totally stop dead in the water. Our working rhythms never seemed to be in sync—other demands would pull my focus from monitoring their progress. Their other interests would take precedence over working on the chapter. Deadlines I would impose seemed to mean nothing—deadline, what is a deadline? So, I would say that this process was an ongoing rediscovery, recreation, renegotiation, reinvention of how we would work together to get the task done. I must admit, there were moments when I had my doubts that we would complete this project. Clearly, we made it through the ups and downs, a little worse for the wear—at least on my part.

Another challenge was that of figuring out how to write this chapter. Throughout the entire process I felt the pull between making it a "scholarly" piece when the more natural route seemed telling our story. I still struggle with whether I could have made it more "scholarly" but the story wouldn't have been the same. This narrative, this story telling, seemed the most appropriate and genuine way to present the inquiry that my daughters and I engaged in, individually and together.

On a more personal note, this has been a tremendous learning experience. I learned things about my daughters that, although I sort of knew, I didn't realize they knew about themselves. In many ways, though many of the questions I hoped would be answered through this process weren't (e.g., what college would Nora pick) many others were. This collaborative inquiry with my daughters has left me more confident that they will find their way and that maybe I don't need to be as engaged and worried about every aspect of the choices they make. My girls have it a little more together than I give them credit for—I think most kids probably do. We, as adults, just need to provide them with the tools, the opportunities and the space to do their thing (with a bit of oversight, of course). In the end this experience has left me with a sense that maybe their father and I have done a better job of preparing them to become independent, self-motivated, and engaged learners than we give ourselves credit for—even if they can't see it or are not able to articulate it just yet. So, I need to have a bit more faith in them and in the process of growing up.

7   Conclusion and Recommendations

Preparing students to be active and informed participants in their learning process and planning for their futures takes more than teaching them content, giving them assignments and testing what they have learned—it takes engaging them in the learning process, identifying what interests and motivates them and finding ways of relating this to the learning process and their future opportunities. Educators need to understand and, yes, differentiate how they teach students in a manner that best meets students' needs. Career development is a life-long process, one that encompasses not just what we learn in school, but what we learn about ourselves—our interests and abilities, our passions, and how these can be applied or utilized in the endeavors that we pursue in life, specifically work. By incorporating a greater focus on career development, we may be able to engage students in the learning process more effectively and, in so doing, address the apparent boredom and irrelevance that seems to prevail in their classroom experiences.

With the example of my two daughters, I see two very different approaches to engaging them. One thrives on competition, and the other does not. One needs time to reflect and process her experiences, and the other needs to be actively engaged and challenged with an outcome or prize at the end of her efforts. The one thing that they have in common is their passion for the activities that they dedicate a considerable amount of time to, and these activities are relevant and related to their learning and possibly future work lives. Both Nora and Dahlia need guidance in helping them make connections between what they enjoy and are good at and the future educational and occupational opportunities available to them. Although they may not see their learning experiences (in and out of school) as part of their career development, this learning is informing their future college and work-related decisions. And maybe they don't have to see the connections just yet, but we as adults and educators need to fill in the gaps for them; we need to be vigilant that they are gaining an understanding and awareness of the larger world that we are preparing them to inhabit—the world that they will become productive, working members of, contributing to the larger society and ideally being happy, satisfied and fulfilled.

8   Future Research and Ethical Considerations

Conducting research with family members requires researchers to not only carefully consider the traditional ethical considerations that we have for study participants, but also be attuned to the complexities that arise given the personal relationships that we have with them. The researcher must be constantly vigilant to effectively balance the ethical challenges that might arise due to the dual role we play as professionals working with intimate others (Ellis, 2007; Etherington, 2007). In this section, I address some of these ethical considerations and how they differ when working with family members and discuss some of the challenges that I faced as I conducted this research with my daughters.

First, let me begin by stating that when conducting research with family members, issues of consent, confidentiality and privacy become murkier, and navigating these waters is a constant challenge as the boundaries between the personal and the professional become blurred. Perhaps one of the more pressing ethical considerations is that of participant consent.

8.1   *Consent*
Obtaining consent from prospective research participants is one of the most important steps before collecting data. Once institutional review boards approve a study, the researcher identifies potential participants and provides them information on the study and what they can expect. The individual then either agrees to participate or does not. If the individual agrees to participate,

then the researcher begins the relationship and eventually that relationship ends; if the participant refuses, the researcher moves on to someone else. When working with family members, however, this clear-cut process is not so clear. First, there is an established familiarity. Once the research is completed the relationship continues, perhaps somewhat altered, but it does continue. This personal relationship can introduce myriad nuances to what can be considered consent which warrants the question: What constitutes consent when one is asking one's own child to participate in collaborative research? And do they understand what they are consenting to (Ellis, 2007).

When I invited my daughters to participate in this project, I provided them with information, described what they could expect and what I believed to be the benefits of having them engage in this project. I gave them time to think about it and eventually they agreed to work with me. But what does their consent really mean in this situation? After all, I am their mother and there is a power differential at play—am I as a parent being seen by my daughters as really giving them a choice? Did they feel a sense of obligation? Did they feel a need to please me when they consented to participate in this project? Although I repeatedly communicated that it was their choice throughout the process (particularly when they were not meeting deadlines), did they truly feel that they could say "no" to me?

As I have mentioned previously, there were times when I had to prod them to get the work done. How did they balance the wanting to do it on the one hand, but not wanting to actually sit down and do the work when the work needed doing? Did my efforts to keep them on task ever become (or were perceived as) coercive? And, if so, did they feel that they could push back, say no and withdraw their consent? These types of considerations need to be examined by researchers working with family members throughout the entire process. This is especially more critical when working with minors who might not feel that they can say no to an adult, much less a parental figure.

8.2 *Privacy and Confidentiality*

The issue of privacy and confidentiality also emerged as important considerations that impact this type of collaborative research with family members. After all, our personal relationship meant that I knew things about them that I would not have known of a traditional research participant. This knowledge influenced how I worked with them because I had information about them that they might not have shared with a stranger. An example of this tension became evident in my attempts to get Nora and Dahlia to think more critically, to examine more deeply, to question more rigorously. I needed to constantly monitor and balance how my prior knowledge of them—which they had not directly shared as part of this inquiry process—influenced how I directed our

discussions. In what ways did my prior knowledge and my goals and expectations influence the trajectory of our work? It is difficult to say, but I am sure
that it played a role in the process—how could it not?

Another ethical consideration that emerged for me during this process
related to privacy and confidentially is the extent to which my daughters realized that their experiences would be made public. Yes, they "understood" that
we would be writing a chapter that would be published and, therefore, made
public. But, did they really understand what that meant? After all, they were
only 13 and 16 at the time (and given that they are identified as my daughters, there is no anonymity). This issue became particularly salient as we were
nearing the end of this project and I asked the girls to provide a brief bio that
would be included as part our chapter. I provided examples they could use to
guide them. Whereas Dahlia's provided some details that conveyed information about herself, Nora's was two sentences that didn't really say much about
her. When I asked her if she would like to provide a little more detail about herself, her response was: "no, people don't need to know things about me." Will
she at some point regret that she participated in this process? I do not regret
engaging in this research with my daughters—I hope that they never do either.

Researchers working with family members also need to be thoughtful and
reflect upon how their dual roles (i.e., researcher and family member) are playing out in the work itself. Etherington (2007) addresses the need for researchers to take a reflexive stance and be aware of how their own values influence
the work with study participants. I would add to this the need to reflect on how
one can effectively balance the role of researcher with that of mother/father/
grandparent. It is a delicate, and I would venture to say, fragile line that can easily be crossed even with our best intentions. Throughout this process, I experienced a tension between the "Mom" and the "researcher" role. The back and
forth that I felt emotionally was being a mother trying to help my daughters
become more aware of their learning process so that hopefully it would enable
them in leading happy and productive lives and the professional role of the
researcher. Given some of the challenges that I faced working with and getting
the girls to do their part, were there times when the researcher role superseded
the motherly role? Did my need to meet my commitment to others perhaps
influence how I negotiated these moments with Nora and Dahlia? If I had not
been accountable to the editors of the book, would I possibly have dropped
the project? I don't have answers to these questions, but these are the types of
delicate dynamics that future researchers working with family members need
to consider and reflect upon. Although there are guidelines and frameworks
(Ellis, 2007; Etherington, 2007) that can assist researchers pursuing this type of
work, the burden of being constantly vigilant to the blurring of boundaries is
still a considerable challenge.

References

Berkowitz, S. (1997). Analyzing qualitative data. In J. Frechtling & L. Sharp (Eds.), *User-friendly handbook for mixed methods evaluations*. Arlington, VA: Division of Research, Evaluation and Communication, National Science Foundation. Retrieved from https://www.nsf.gov/pubs/1997/nsf97153/chap_4.htm

Boekaerts, M. (2016). Engagement as an inherent aspect of the learning *process. Learning and Instruction, 43,* 76–83.

Clandinin, D. J., & Connelly, F. M. (2000). *Narrative inquiry: Experience and story in qualitative research.* San Francisco, CA: Jossey-Bass.

Eccles, J. S. (2016). Engagement: Where to next? *Learning and Instruction, 43,* 71–75.

Ellis, C. (2007). Telling secrets, revealing lives: Relational ethics in research with intimate others. *Qualitative Inquiry, 12*(1). doi:10.1177/1077800406294947

Etherington, K. (2007). Ethical research in reflexive relationships. *Qualitative Inquiry, 13*(5), 599–616. doi:10.11.77/1077800407301175

Fredericks, J., Blumenfeld, P. C., & Paris, A. H. (2004). School engagement: Potential of the concept, state of the evidence. *Review of Educational Research, 74*(1), 59–109.

Hooley, T., Marriott, J., & Sampson, J. P. (2011). *Fostering college and career readiness: How career development activities in schools impact on graduation rates and students' life success.* Derby: University of Derby. Retrieved from https://www.researchgate.net/profile/Tristram_Hooley2/publication/261991118

Jimerson, S. R., Campos, E., & Greif, J. L. (2003). Toward an understanding of definitions and measures of school engagement and related terms. *The California School Psychologist, 8,* 7–27.

Kenny, M. E., Blustein, D. L., Hasse, R. F., Jackson, J. & Perry, J. C. (2006). Setting the state: Career development and the student engagement process. *Journal of Counseling Psychology, 53*(2), 272–269. doi: 10.1037/002-0167.53.2.272

Lapan, R. T., Aoyagi, M., & Kayson, M. (2007). Helping rural adolescents make successful postsecondary transitions: A longitudinal study. *Professional School Counseling, 10,* 266–272.

Orthner, D. K., Jones-Sanpei, H., Akos, P., & Rose, R. A. (2013). Improving middle school student engagement through career-relevant instruction in the core curriculum. *The Journal of Educational Research, 106*(1), 27–38.

Perry, J. C., Liu, X., & Pabian, Y. (2010). School engagement as a mediator of academic performance among urban youth: The role of career preparation, parental career support, and teacher support. *The Counseling Psychologist, 38*(2), 269–295.

Rivera, L. M., & Schaefer, M. B. (2009). The career institute: A collaborative career development program for traditionally underserved secondary (6–12) school students. *Journal of Career Development, 35*(4), 406–426. doi:10.1177/0894845308327737

Schaefer, M. B., & Rivera, L. M. (2014). Working collaboratively in a small secondary school to facilitate career development. *American Secondary Education, 43*(2), 51–68.

Super, D. E., Savickas, M. L., & Super, C. M. (1997). The life-span, life-space approach to careers. In D. Brown, L. Brooks, & Associates (Eds.), *Career choice and development* (3rd ed., pp. 121–178). San Francisco, CA: Jossey-Bass.

Appendix A: Questions for Nora and Dahlia

Nora:

1. How did you become engaged with the online blogs/videos and what motivated you to follow them?
2. What have you learned, in general, about your own learning process by engaging in your own self-directed learning online?
3. Are there ways in which your engagement with the online resources you access help you in pursue other interests (e.g., other things you're interested in) and learning/school (engaging in other activities); are there ways it gets in the way of your pursuit of other interests?
4. Discuss your experience learning online vs learning in school.
5. What was your experience as co-researcher like for you? Do you think you've learned anything that will help you as a learner?

Dahlia:

1. How did you become interested in finding information online about the Rubik's Cube?
2. What have you learned, in general, about your own learning process by engaging in your own self-directed learning online?
3. Describe your process in learning how to solve the Rubik's Cube, particularly your learning and practicing the algorithms.
4. Discuss your experience learning online vs learning in school.
5. What was your experience as co-researcher like for you? Do you think you've learned anything that will help you as a learner?

CHAPTER 7

Researching and Parenting in the iWorld:
The Dialogism of Family Life

Joanne O'Mara and Linda Laidlaw

Abstract

As literacy researchers, the authors' roles as parents have continued to provide
a pervasive influence on their work, particularly in informing their perspectives on children's digital practices and meaning making. In this chapter, the
authors draw on three key examples to examine the ways in which their observations at home, together and individually, informed their digital literacies
research. The authors address the relationships across their parental observations and their professional and scholarly work, as well as considerations
for youth, and for research, in the digital era. The authors draw on the work
of Bahktin (1984) to describe these processes as dialogic, and present methodological and ethical considerations for researchers who might choose an
autoethnographical path.

1 Introduction

Digital culture is intertwined in children and young people's literacy practices
and ways of meaning making. As researchers who have been studying children's
digital media use in schools and out-of-school contexts in relation to literacy
for the past decade, we have noted tectonic shifts in media and communication practices within our own research, in the growing corpus of research literature (e.g., Dezuanni, Dooley, Gattenhof, & Knight, 2015; McPake, Plowman,
& Stephen, 2013; Marsh, 2017; Merchant, 2015), and in our home lives with our
own children. Most recently we have noticed that the boundaries between the
digital and offline realms are blurring, following Carrington (2017) who suggested that the metaphors for online/offline may no longer be valid.

In our roles as parents and literacy researchers, the intertwining and blurring of boundaries between our home and professional lives is similarly
constant, as we try to adopt practices we know to be educationally sound in
our parenting, as well as bringing our knowledge of young people's literacy

practices from home into our professional and theoretical understandings. We see these dialogic conversations as weaving across our discussions with each other, and across our own family lives, the literatures we take up in the field, our collective and individual research, and the professional practices we model and examine in education.

In this chapter, we explore our shared work in researching and parenting and in our interconnected journeys which have provided a dialogic approach to our teaching and research. We use Bahktin's (1984) term *dialogism* to describe both the processes and products of our work, as this work is produced through our endless dialogues with each other, our children, the literature, and our professional and academic worlds. Bahktin described "[t]ruth is not born nor is it to found inside the head of an individual person, it is born between people collectively searching for truth, in the process of their dialogic interaction" (p. 110). In framing this discussion around Bahktin's dialogism, we are not ascribing to the notion of a single truth; rather, we are using this notion because of the open-ended, multiple points of view, and messy, unresolved nature of much of our experience and collective searching. Our research about the changing nature of young people's literacy practices is an iterative process of dialogic interaction—among ourselves, texts and experiences—that looks both forward and backward, the process itself in conversation with our separate and combined worlds, and the products of this work—such as this chapter—also taking up dialogic practices in our text production.

As literacy researchers, our roles and experiences as parents have had an ongoing and pervasive influence on our work, particularly through informing our perspectives on children's digital practices and meaning making, and the dialogism (Bahktin, 1984) of family life contributes to our understandings of research in literacy pedagogy in the digital age. While we are located in different countries, different hemispheres—Jo in Australia and Linda in Canada— our work together typically has converged along similar discursive approaches, where our conversations bring together experiences from family life and the questions and discussions we have engaged with our children. Conversely, we bring to our children insights from our research and professional discussions, providing us with an opportunity to test theories and digital research practices, and where meaning making becomes a dialogic and recursive dance (Sumara, 2002).

1.1   *A Background Note on Our Contexts*
In our chapter, we address areas of shared interests, observations and roles— we are both academic women of "a certain age" working in university positions as researchers and educators, and we share interests in dialogic processes

and understandings and literacy research in the digital realm. However, it is important to note some of the differences we bridge across our work and our dialogues. Most obviously is that Jo is located in Melbourne, Australia, while Linda is situated in Edmonton, Alberta, Canada. Our geographic, climactic and cultural contexts frequently lead us to comparative examinations, which in turn generate complex conversations and opportunities to examine areas of difference in our individual contexts. In our roles as literacy researchers, we engage in such comparisons with intentionality, as we compare teaching and learning practices, curricula, and cultures of schooling in relation to our projects focusing on digital mobility. These sorts of comparative analyses also enter our informal conversations about our family lives and our experiences as parents. While we both situated as academic parents of two children, the details of our lives are quite different, with Jo in a shared parenting/spousal family structure—her husband is Canadian. Linda is a single adoptive parent and her family is transracial. Linda's children (both girls) are now teenagers and Jo's (a girl and a boy) are now entering the tween and teenage years— although our dialogues of parenting began when our children were infants. Across our collective children, they represent a number of diverse positions in connection to health, heritage, and disability, yet for the purposes of this chapter, and in response to their own desires not to have the details of their lives "over-shared" we choose not to reveal that which could identify them individually, and we focus our shared gaze on our autoethnographic interpretations as researcher-educator-parents.

2   The Dialogism of Family Life

While this chapter focuses on the dialogism of family life, our research has always been in conversation and dialogue with others: between ourselves, with family and friends, with colleagues in our departments, with the scholars we read—with our everyday lives in the world. As parents, our conversations with our children and Jo's partner have mixed into this, and following Bahktin (1984), we "live in a world of others' words" (p. 143). From the beginning of our shared work, where we drew on Barthes' work on writerly texts (Barthes, 1975) to frame drama workshops (O'Mara & Laidlaw, 2004), we have woven together literary theory, research and teaching influences, and autobiographical experiences from home.

Dennis Sumara (2002) suggested that reading literature can provide rich focal practices that create "the possibility for deep insight" (p. xiii) and that these also might make connections to autobiographical experiences. Similarly, for us, the sharing and dialoguing across our experiences in parenting and observations of literacy for our children provides rich and generative focal opportunities for insights that we bring into the realm of research and through which we also read and interpret research and texts. While our work in research and teaching is highly visible, on the surface of our academic work, our family lives are situated as the larger, rich, 'below the surface' influences, similar to the metaphor of an iceberg.

As we have written elsewhere (e.g. Laidlaw, O'Mara, & Wong, 2019), our shared work takes up autobiographical, participatory and ethnographic methods, and we call ourselves *accidental ethnographers*, "finding our way into participatory, ethnographic methods through both serendipity and unexpected divergence from initial research plans" (p. 184). Along this path we have been informed by ethnographers such as Behar (1996), Clifford and Marcus (1986), and Heath, Street, and Mills (2008), as well as autobiographical writers and theorists (Richardson, 1997). Our shared work often begins with "small stories" (Behar, 1996) or examples from home and our lives as parents, branching outward to create new dialogues with our professional and theoretical understandings.

In this chapter, we describe three different research/writing examples we have produced, each of which takes a different approach to our research through dialogue with our family lives. The first of our examples focuses on how dialoguing about and documenting home literacy practices informed the creation of the first of our articles addressing digital practices for literacy and schooling. Our second example shares how we used approaches from fiction to address topics of difference and that we blended autobiographical examples from home with research data. Our third example explores the application of ideas that blend knowledge from research and home, demonstrating a dialogic merging of theory and practice. Along the way, we address methodological and ethical considerations for researchers who might choose a similarly autoethnographic path, as well as particular considerations for youth and for education.

3 Documenting Home Practices: Shared Toys and Conversations

Our first example is derived from a paper we wrote in 2011, *Living in the iWorld: Two Literacy Researchers Reflect on the Changing Texts and Literacy Practices of Childhood* (O'Mara & Laidlaw, 2011). At that time, the usage of mobile touchscreen devices such as iPhones and iPads was just becoming more widespread. Significantly for early childhood, these devices are very accessible for young children because of the touchscreen, ease of use, and mobility aspects. We were in the process of setting up a new research project together, and Linda had come to Australia on a sabbatical with her children. Our four young (at the time) children spent several weeks together, and our observations and conversations during this extended visit marked a point where we started using our understandings of what was happening at home to frame our investigations 'in schools'. From this point on we began to note the important role our informal observations were playing for our work in school settings: "the informal observations we have made via our own children offer insights from the "micro" perspective in looking forward to the "macro" possibilities for classroom work with children and technologies and our work with teachers" (p. 151).

We also noticed through our literature review for the new project we were developing that, at that point, there was "very little analysis of how 'home practices,' where the children often have relative openness and freedoms with their device usage, might be different from subsequent school activities" (p. 151) in academic articles as well as in more popular publications aimed at parents or the general public. We also had observed that in many schools, both within the contexts where we researched and also in the settings where our children were attending, the devices were very new to early years education; there was a great deal of teacher worry as well as surveillance around touch screen devices, such as iPads, in connection to access, protection (from the 'evils of the internet'), and around organization as classroom objects and the learning potential of these devices.

Spurred on by our conversations, we documented what our own children were doing with iPads in their time at home, paying close attention to the ways our children were engaging with iPads and how these were mediating other experiences, such as individual and shared play. As we observed our children playing together in Australia, we were struck by how our children learned from each other and also noted that, in our own home contexts, our children had "relative freedom of usage and open-ness of approaches to using the devices, in contrast with the ways in which the devices are domesticated in the practices of schooling" (p. 151).

During this time together we spent many hours drinking coffee and talking into the night once children were asleep and we had time for developing our "iWorld" paper and furthering our shared research plans. The questions we developed as central to this first "iWorld" writing began to reveal the path towards our larger, shared research program, beginning with our own "wonderings" about the implications of what we had observed in our family contexts:

> We ask how might these technologies and practices be changing the understandings and usage of texts and literacies of the children who enter into classroom spaces? What transformative possibilities might these home technology practices announce for teaching and learning within classroom environments? (pp. 151–152)

Importantly to our work, we had noted the ways in which our children were deeply engaged with meaning making in a range of ways, and how this was connected to their self-identity. We saw them as active participants in this process, not as passive responders, and our documentation of these processes in this paper and our ongoing discussions around our own children's digital agency and pursuit of their own interests shaped the research we did in schools and communities. We also documented with photographs and descriptions the ways that the interactions with touch screen mobile devices had entered the language and framing of our children's play. This included some examples that were important to our understanding of how the digital was being incorporated into children's everyday worlds of play. These observations have been significant to our growing understanding as literacy researchers of the place of the digital in young people's everyday lives. The suggestion from Carrington (2017) that the young people she was working with no longer distinguished between online and offline aligns with our observations of our own children growing up and mixing digital play with pretend play in a seamless way. We documented our children playing with digital and nondigital toys together and moments such as this:

> Our children were playing at the dollhouses and the 3-year-old realised that a tiny pretend laptop was missing. After everyone looked around for a bit, he returned to play and sat the mother doll at the computer desk. "She's going to Google to find out where the little computer is." (p. 153)

FIGURE 7.1   The dollhouse Mum Googles to find the dollhouse boy's computer

In illustrating this example, we photographed the set up and the children playing in ways that preserved their anonymity, but brought the story to life for the reader. Returning to this paper and photograph for this chapter, we see the intimate and familiar revealed through this image (the quilt Jo made, the much-loved dollhouse desk, and the 3-year-old's hands), but also note that the way the photograph is presented and the chapter written, our children were not exposed, which has been an integral part of our discussions and ethical considerations in this work.

Dialoguing about and documenting home literacy practices from our perspectives as parents informed the creation of the first of our shared articles addressing digital practices for literacy and schooling, and further, led us toward a path that brought us into three large, government-funded research projects. Our second example shares how we continued to take up issues we noted in our roles as parents and extended these to use approaches from fiction to address topics of difference. This work brought together autobiographical examples from home alongside data from our Canadian and Australian research projects.

4   Fictionalizing the Real: Writing Text

Our second example emerged several years later from our conversations about experiences our own children were having at school in connection to the topic of handwriting, and that often drifted into home experiences. Linda and her children had travelled to Australia for a conference in the Australian summer, which overlapped with the Canadian winter university break. As we chatted about our shared research projects and began to develop writing for a later Canadian conference presentation, we did so while our children were in view and engaging in a range of activities: circus class, backyard play on the trampoline and monkey bars. These observations of physical play and out of school learning contrasted with our discussions of particular school activities—with both of us finding similarities, despite very different school systems—in how challenges with handwriting were addressed. We were both quite surprised to notice in our own contexts that, at that point, handwriting struggles were not particularly being addressed through any technological solutions in spite of iPads and laptops being more common by this point in our local schools. Over the preceding term, we had both encountered separate situations where our research and professional knowledge of digital assistive technologies met up with what we experienced, through our parental roles, as frustrating resistance to provision of technology and a dogged determination to adhere to traditional handwriting structures and approaches, even in cases where physical differences or disabilities made such activities far more challenging. While there were available solutions through accessibility options using iPads or other technologies, these were not being taken up, even when they were suggested by other professionals such as occupational therapists.

As we shared our individual stories from our own observations and experiences, we also recognized a common thread across a number of early years classrooms where we had researched that spoke to our experiences with handwriting challenges for our own children. We realized that our autoethnographic experiences provided powerful representative examples. However, as we continued to dialogue, our conversation turned to ethical considerations. Could we include aspects of our own experiences and still maintain confidentiality for our children? Could we write an article that would be powerful *without* any recognition of what we knew through our experiences as parents? And how could we take up both of our own autobiographical experiences in ways that might work alongside what we had gathered as research evidence?

In our time together in the summer heat in Australia, as we watched our children play and we started scratching out some notes, we began to consider using fictional strategies to represent the research data from two projects as well as our autobiographical experiences. Then, as we continued to work after Linda had returned back home—writing across time zones, seasons, and geographies—our paper developed in a dialogic manner, with drafts going back and forth, and examples polished and adapted. We eventually decided to use a *narrative tableau* approach, which provided a way for us to curate and weave together the multiple and different observations of handwriting, through such "fictionalized snapshot[s]"—from our lives and our research that addressed concerns for literacy and technology connected to "difference, disability and accessibility":

> Our use of this form is intentional, providing a form of a vignette, a structure that Linda has used elsewhere as a "narrative tableau" structure (Laidlaw, 2005, p. xvi). Within the theatre and in drama education, tableau is a dramatic form where participants freeze into place creating a 'still image' that others might view and interpret, similar to the 'statues' game children sometimes play. The tableau is a complex structure, and can be viewed, 'read' and interpreted in multiple ways, and provides a concrete yet abstract form for resymbolizing layers of meaning. We

use this tableau structure to efficiently bring together multiple layers of meaning, and observations from our data and autobiographical experiences. We present this as a kind of provocation for response, in addition to its interpretive value. (Laidlaw & O'Mara, 2015, p. 59)

In this way, we were able to create a fictionalized compilation, developing characters that brought together our observations of research examples, as well as our own autoethnographic observations as parents, and efficiently "bringing together multiple events across different children, times and locations, into one description" (p. 59). This method provided a way to acknowledge some of our own experiences with difference in relation to our children's handwriting struggles, as well as including relevant research examples. And it also allowed us a way in to effectively address what seemed at the time to be a rather contentious topic, as the decline of handwriting in schools was often in discussion in our graduate classes or in the local media, and teacher participants in our studies were reluctant to have their own critiques voiced when they were sharing what they saw as unpopular perspectives in relation to technology usage.

Following Behar (1996), we understand that the complex "web of stories" (p. 132) that emerges as individual, collective, and our own stories are shared can provide insights into how children and families might experience differences impacting literacy learning, and the ways in which schooling can both include and exclude children. Although our stories are our own, they also belong to others. Thus, for us this second example of our *writing from home* points to the ethical issues that parent-researchers/researcher-parents can often encounter—where our own autobiographical experiences of home are intersected with those of our children and where we had to take particular care about how we shared these stories. We note that, because we also wrote in response to our own dialogues, the lines that might identify any of our own children, or those children and teachers from our research studies, became blurred further, in addition to our use of techniques from fiction.

We noted as we developed this work—initially as a conference presentation—that the small stories and narrative tableaux we developed also created new dialogues with others, who shared both their own observations and sometimes their critiques, which also led to more dialogue and recursive processes and re-thinking, consistent with theories of reader response (Rosenblatt, 1994), where this article and fictional anecdotes within it continued to evoke new thinking. Even now, we continue to understand it differently as our own background understandings of difference, handwriting, and literacy have evolved.

5   Shaping Ideas and Directions: *Questions for a Changing World:*
       Students as Researchers

We provide a final example from our work on a recent chapter collaboration, "Questions for a Changing World: Students as Researchers," we wrote for the book, *Asking Better Questions* (Saxton, Morgan, Laidlaw & O'Mara, 2018). Years ago, we were introduced to each other by Professor Juliana Saxton, who has been an influential mentor to both of us, and who, in many ways, has provided us with a model for working across disciplines (theatre and education) and intertwining threads of professional, artistic, research and personal realms. In late 2017, we jumped at the opportunity to collaborate with Juliana and Carole Miller in the rewriting of Juliana's earlier text, which had been co-authored with Norah Morgan (Morgan & Saxton, 2004). The invitation and our process of writing together was dialogic, building on relationships between ourselves, Norah and Juliana's original text, the work we have done together, and our background worlds from home. This chapter illustrates the ways in which our knowledge from research and home has blended, and in our discussion, we illustrate the dialogic merging of theory and practice.

The focus of *Questions for a Changing World* is how teachers might work with their students positioned as researchers and inquirers. We both have been committed to this ideal throughout our professional teaching and academic lives, and for our contributions we wanted to provide a focus of high interest and relevance across elementary and secondary schooling, and that would resonate across Canada and Australia and acknowledge the land masses and oceans in between. In devising a topic we established a question-based framework: What are the questions that matter to young people? What are their concerns? What are some of the big issues for their generation and succeeding generations? In making a selection we noted that

> Although there are many matters we have observed students acting upon and working with, concerns that are connected with human impacts on the natural environment, such as climate change, species extinction, and resource management, are typically highlighted. (p. 79)

Particularly, there was a moment we reflected on, when Jo's son, then 6, sighed as he stared at a cigarette butt on the footpath and said, "Oh no! That is going to be washed to the sea and pollute the ocean." He had been studying how rubbish ends up in the ocean and started to see it happening around him, even though we were 15 km from the beach. He had followed his interest in this at home, searching for information on the internet, and he was then able to apply this information to the cigarette butt in question. We also remembered engaged conversations across all of our children as they compared systems for dealing with refuse, recycling and composting across their Canadian and Australian homes, observing these when they were together during our various to trips to visit the other for research or conferences. We could see from these examples how immersive the topic might be for young people, and how it had the capacity and breadth for them to develop their own specific inquiries from starting points in school.

We developed a unit of work on the questions raised "through a deep investigation of the materials that we, as individuals and societies, discard: garbage, rubbish, trash" (p. 79). We had a series of disagreements about the actual wording of what to call the discarded objects: Was it trash? Was it rubbish? Was it garbage? Jo did the first draft of the opening and used "rubbish" throughout, which is the Australian term most frequently used, but in Canada, "trash" and "garbage" are more commonly used, and "rubbish" seemed foreign to Linda. Untangling the meanings of these words enabled us to position ourselves with the topic, and think simultaneously about the localised domesticity and universality of the topic, and how the meaning, issues, and values of the words had changed over time, yet how we were at a crisis point with rubbish. As evident in the quote above, we left the terminology unresolved, and used all terms—garbage, rubbish, trash—interchangeably.

In revisiting this work, we have noted how our dialogism is present in the text itself, as is the positioning of "us" and "we" and individually to "Jo" and "Linda" or "at home" "in our families" or roles such as "as mothers," "as teachers," "as academics." For instance:

> In our work with young people, we see how questions lead to the development of theories, to the testing of ideas, and to the increased understanding of worldviews and ways of being in the world. As teachers, we have all experienced the drive and engagement of students pursuing a question that is important to them. As authors, we are forever working and reworking the questions we ask. The processes for asking questions at the university level are surprisingly similar to those of our work with younger students in schools. No matter the level, we support students as they revise, rethink, and rework their questions, revisiting the questions over the duration of the inquiry. Then, finally, at the end of the process, we work with them to consider how their questions have been answered. If there is one thing we have learned from our engagement in supporting students in such processes, it is that a good question and a solid research

investigation often open more questions and that interesting answers typically open doors to further inquiries. Contemporary students have access to a myriad of different resources in their investigative pursuits, as well as access to online, digital, and multimedia sources. For these students, information that addresses their questions is multi-layered and complex, requiring new skills to process and evaluate the "answers" they find. (Saxton et al., 2018, p. 79)

The dialogism with our past (as teachers) and present selves (as mothers and academics) is present in this section of the text, with this paragraph being framed after a series of conversations we had about the nature of inquiry in schools. These conversations were punctuated with us checking the current literature, engaging in online media searches, discussing the ways that our children had been working with inquiry in their respective schools, and how inquiry fit within our respective school curricula. When we discussed the topic with our children, who continued to be concerned about it, even into their high school years, we noted their interest in the build-up of plastic debris in the oceans between us.

6   Research Working Practices and Family Life: Dialogism as a
       Research Practice

While not always presented as such, research is a dialogic process, involving conversation with literatures, with the past, the present and the future, bringing together and conversing with knowledges built over time. We would argue that this is true of all research, even more quantitative work, as what is included and what is not, and specific questions and research decisions never occur entirely in isolation, although the dialogic nature is more evident in the sort of qualitative work with which we engage, where it is present in the process, and also the text itself.

In framing our research questions, and especially in the projects we have shared, we have noted that our children's lives and interests have shaped what we are interested in ourselves, and typically provide deeper connections to what we are seeing more broadly in classrooms and educational contexts. These sorts of interconnected research questions have enabled us to experience our children's changing encounters with digital media and popular culture and to understand the ways in which textual experiences are continuing to change for young people. Additionally, we often ask our children (as well as their friends and young relatives) if we are correct about assumptions we make about different aspects of popular culture and about the literacy technologies they are taking up—home provides a "testing space" for what we have observed more broadly and specifically.

Our own children's experiences of schooling, various parental opportunities to be involved on school-based parent councils, as well as further associations with other parents and our children's out-of-school relationships have become experiences intimately known that have provided us with different perspectives in relation to our own and each other's schooling systems. In dialogue with each other, we have been able to notice and attend to phenomena that are normalized for one of us and yet seem foreign or strange for the other, even though Canada and Australia are similar countries in many respects and we live in similar socioeconomic areas of our respective cities, close to our universities. This has not been confined to examples from home, but observations beginning from home have also stretched to analysis of policies and the different ways our education systems have been approaching and paying for digital technology (see O'Mara, Laidlaw, & Blackmore, 2017).

In writing this chapter, we have realized how our process of writing together has become dialogic in ways that were not entirely visible to us before, as well as how our working relationship and mutual trust has developed over time and our practices of working together have evolved, drawing on new technologies and accommodating our shared understandings and capitalizing on our differences. Our dialogic processes also have taken up some practical strategies. Sometimes we take advantage of the different time zones we live in enabling us to write almost around the clock, with Linda writing until Canadian night hits and Jo taking over, our dialogic conversations continuing over days through facetime calls, margin notes, emails and texts, as we save our chapter into our Dropbox and reopen and view the traces of the other's latest contribution. Our busy teaching periods are quite different, as the university year of Canada and Australia does not align; this enables one or the other to lead the conversation and keep the call and response going as the other works with other responsibilities from university or home. Family life continues on through this, with the unpredictable demands, new phases and grade levels, which bring new considerations to our conversations, as well as the highlights, challenges and gifts offered by our parental roles and responsibilities. The sharing of these experiences is in itself a rich gift, as the opportunities to develop friendship and collegiality through our work, alongside parenthood, is one of the delights academic work provides. Of course, none of this was ever planned in advance—and our dialogues, conversations and research plans have unfolded along the way as a complex and sometimes surprising bricolage (Turkle, 1995) informed by a coffee house culture (Johnson, 2010) form of idea sharing and generation. However, while we both often have coffee in hand while working together, rather than being an elegant café conversation, uninterrupted, our coffee conversation is much more a family kitchen table operation often punctuated with various interruptions where children's faces pop into the video call, voices call for our attention, and our conversations stop and start according to various child-centered requirements. While sometimes our family work may impact our research and writing timelines, we both agree that it provides us with the focal activities and involvements that have been key to gaining new insights and have heightened our own understandings in research and professional teaching practice.

7   Future Research and Ethical Considerations

As we have noted earlier in this chapter, including our family lives and our children in our academic work, while extremely valuable to our insights and growth as researchers working in the digital realm, also has necessitated careful consideration of how to include this work ethically. As researchers, educators, and active members of our children's local school communities, we both traverse complicated pathways across our professional and parental lives and identities. When we go to schools in our parental roles, we are sometimes privy to aspects of school life that we would not be were we on a university visit, and these moments, while not ethically reportable on their own, lead us to develop lines of questioning that we might not have otherwise. We often have engaged in lengthy discussions of how, as parents during "meet the teacher" nights or parent/teacher meetings, our own deep knowledge of the field of education, particular content areas, or grade level expertise (both of us formerly taught in public schools for years prior to pursuing graduate studies), is at times silenced, or creates some unease when our roles as "parent of..." crosses boundaries demarking our professional and academic identities. We have knowledge (of school and pedagogical practices, of education systems and mandates) that other parents might not. This means that often we can be terrific advocates for our children and this knowledge presents advantages at times, but also it can mean our children might be acutely aware of our entangled roles. Our everyday lives as academic parents can at times be fraught, with our children simultaneously imploring, "Mum, DO NOT EMAIL MY ENGLISH TEACHER!" and "Can you tell Mr. Buggerlugs why his assignment is biased?!" Our children, living alongside our discussions and questions around curriculum, pedagogy and schooling generate their own questions about the processes they are sub-jected to and often make "helpful" suggestions to their teachers, such as one six-year-old asking, in the nicest possible way, "Don't you think this activity is a waste of our time?" Thus, in our lives as parents, we often exist in a realm that includes ethical tensions and entanglements, and in our work as autoethno-graphic researchers such tensions become even more evident.

As we have elaborated earlier, we use devices from fiction, such as our nar-rative tableaux vignettes, to blur possible identification of our individual chil-dren in our autoethnographic work. Such examples are fictionalized, but true in the sense that sociologist Laurel Richardson elaborated:

> I think of the chapters as palimpsests—pictures that, although taken in particular times and places, allow traces of the past to poke through and be visible. The chapters reflect the ways in which people make sense of their worlds, finding traces of the already experienced in their new expe-riences. (Richardson, 2016)

The tableaux examples help us, similarly, to make sense of our experiences and observations, and while we both can recognize the traces of our children in such examples, importantly, we craft these so that other readers will not be able to identify specific children. We aim for such examples to be inclusive rather than too particular. Curiously, with our narrative tableaux examples, when we seem to hit on a situation or example that resonates with others, we will sometimes hear from teacher or parent participants in our studies ask if we are writing about other children connected to their own examples and lives.

We use both of our shared experiences, where we have noted similar exam-ples in both of our families' lives, as a method to enhance and maintain the privacy of our children, and we draw upon our research examples through par-ticipant data in our studies so that the students/children we write about are often a compilation. As well, we are both aware of our children's preferences about particular topics and examples, when fictionalized or shared as "histor-ical" examples from their younger years—and that there some stories they do wish to have told, written about, or otherwise publicized—and there are aspects of their lives and identities we do not share (even for demographic pur-poses and even when requested by, for example, chapter or article reviewers!). While our children create focal experiences and memories that we take up in our research and scholarly work, for such purposes our focus remains on our shared insights and learning, and, just as in fiction writing, we, as authors, own the interpretations, as often reflecting more about us than about our children.

In considering our future work, we expect that in our own autoethnographic writing and research as literacy educators, we will continue to be informed by the multiple roles we enact, the multiple narratives we live. As Greene (1995) wrote, "Neither myself, nor my narrative can have a single strand. I stand at the crossing point of too many social and cultural forces; and in any case, I am forever on the way" (p. 1). As academics, we have both at times found that our roles as parents were positioned as outside of our academic identities, yet we are forever on the way. As our children grow older, this work will also shift, and we might invite their participation in new ways (perhaps as co-authors), or follow along as they explore emerging digital worlds and experiences. As our children enter their teenage years, we note shifts in how they wish to have their own identities and digital personas represented and expect that our parental academic writing might be increasingly informed by what we learn from our children about digital practices they used, but less about them, as they navigate their own understandings of private and public identities and forge their own ways and roles.

In our research and teaching work with teachers and schools, we continue to consider how lived experience can inform exploration of new practices. We infuse Bahktin's (1984) dialogic perspectives into this work, using our own home/school autoethnographic examples as focal places to begin important conversations regarding how education might bridge particular divides that often are problematic in relation to children's digital experiences and practices at the same time as we understand these places, relationships and events to be in dialogue with our academic selves. As we have illustrated in the chapter, the dialogic practices we use in the production of our research texts are in conversation with our multiple selves and roles as well as with each other. Yet as Richardson (2016) wrote, "People become who they are by what they do in their everyday lives" (p. 7). In our own work, our everyday lives as parents have indeed shaped our scholarly identities.

References

Bakhtin, M. M. (1984). *Problems of Dostoevsky's poetics* (C. Emerson, Ed.). Minneapolis, MN: University of Minnesota Press.

Barthes, R. (1975). *The pleasure of the text* (R. Miller, Trans.). New York, NY: Hill & Wang.

Behar, R. (1996). *The vulnerable observer: Anthropology that breaks your heart*. Boston, MA: Beacon Press.

Carrington, V. (2017). How we live now: "I don't think there's such a thing as being offline." *Teachers College Record, 119*(12), 1–24.

Clifford, J., & Marcus, G. (Eds.). (1986). *Writing culture: The poetics and politics of ethnography*. Los Angeles, CA: University of California Press.

Dezuanni, M., Dooley, K., Gattenhof, S., & Knight L. (Eds.). (2015). *iPads in the early years: Developing literacy and creativity*. New York, NY: Routledge.

Greene, M. (1995). *Releasing the imagination: Essays on education, the arts and social change*. San Francisco, CA: Jossey Bass.

Heath, S. B., Street, B., & Mills, M. (2008). *Ethnography: Approaches to language and literacy research*. New York, NY: Teachers College Press.

Johnson, S. (2010). *Where good ideas come from: The natural history of innovation*. New York, NY: Riverhead Books.

Laidlaw, L. (2005). *Reinventing curriculum: A complex perspective on literacy and writing.*, Mahwah, NJ: Lawrence Erlbaum Associates.

Laidlaw, L., & O'Mara, J. (2015). Rethinking difference in the iWorld: Possibilities, challenges and 'unexpected consequences' of digital tools in literacy education. *Language and Literacy, 17*(1), 59–74.

Laidlaw, L., O'Mara, J., & Wong, S. (2019). Researching in the iWorld: From home to beyond. In N. Kucirkova, J. Rowsell, & G. Fallon (Eds.), *The Routledge international handbook of learning with technology in early childhood*. New York, NY: Taylor & Francis.

Marsh, J. (2017). The internet of toys: A posthuman and multimodal analysis of connected play. *Teachers College Record, 119*(12), 1–32.

McPake, J., Plowman, L., & Stephen, C. (2013). Pre-school children creating and communicating with digital technologies in the home. *British Journal of Educational Technology, 44*(3), 421–431.

Merchant, G. (2015). Keep taking the tablets: iPads, story apps and early literacy. *Australian Journal of Language & Literacy, 38*(1), 3–11.

Morgan, N., & Saxton, J. (2004). *Asking better questions* (2nd ed.). Markham: Pembroke.

O'Mara, J., & Laidlaw, L. (2011). Living in the iWorld: Two literacy researchers reflect on the changing texts and literacy practices of childhood. *English Teaching: Practice and Critique, 10*(4), 149–159. Retrieved from http://edlinked.soe.waikato.ac.nz/research/journal/view.php?article=true&id=754&p=1

O'Mara, J., & Laidlaw, L. (2004, July). *Two continents, two stories: Drama and writerly texts*. Paper presented at the International Drama Education Association (IDEA) 2004 Congress, Ottawa, ON.

O'Mara, J., Laidlaw, L., & Blackmore, J. (2017). The new digital divide: digital technology policies and provision in Canada and Australia. In C. Burnett, G. Merchant, A. Simpson, & M. Walsh (Eds.), *The case of the iPad: mobile literacies in education* (pp. 87–104). Springer Nature: Singapore. doi:10.1007/978-981-10-4364-2_6

Richardson, L. (1997). *Fields of play: Constructing an academic life*. New Brunswick, NJ: Rutgers University Press.

Richardson, L. (2016). *Seven minutes from home: An American daughter's story*. Rotterdam, The Netherlands: Sense Publishers.

Rosenblatt, L. (1994). *The reader, the text, the poem: The transactional theory of the literary work*. Carbondale, IL: Southern Illinois University Press.

Saxton, J., Miller, C., Laidlaw, L., & O'Mara, J. (2018). *Asking better questions* (3rd ed.). Markham: Pembroke.

Sumara, D. (2002). *Why reading literature in school still matters*. Mahwah, NJ: Lawrence Erlbaum Associates.

Turkle, S. (1995). *Life on the screen*. New York, NY: Touchstone.

CHAPTER 8

A Parent-Researcher's Reanalysis of Adolescent Immigrants' Literacy Experiences: Methodological and Theoretical Insight on Parent-Child Research

Bogum Yoon

Abstract

When conducting parent-child research, it is important that parents as researchers continue to examine and reexamine the findings of their studies to better understand their children's experiences in and beyond the classroom. This chapter discusses a parent-researcher's retrospective examination of her findings using a different theoretical framework. It focuses on her children's literacy experiences as immigrant English language learners in the United States. The parent-researcher's detailed reanalysis process might provide a fuller picture of the adolescent immigrants' complex literacy experiences. This study aims to offer insight into the manner by which reanalysis and reinterpretation of existing data with diverse theoretical frameworks can potentially shed light on improving the parent-child research method as an important form of qualitative inquiry and also deepen understanding of children's learning experiences.

1   Introduction

For this parent-child research study, I position myself as a reflective parent-researcher who engages in a retrospective analysis of my previous study which focused on my two sons' experiences as immigrants in the United States (see Yoon, 2012). This reanalysis is the vehicle that helps me as a parent-researcher to learn more about my own children from my initial study. In this previous longitudinal study, I discussed the two siblings' educational journey by focusing on their academic and social success during their middle and high school years by using the theoretical framework of "positioning" (Harré & van Langenhove, 1999). I approached the earlier study from the broader perspective of immigrants and their educational successes. The siblings' powerful narratives showed how they navigated their positional identities to succeed in the

mainstream context and how they contributed to their peers' learning by acting as cultural assets. The findings challenged the pre-conceived assumption
of immigrant students as problematic.

In a retrospective study of the educational journeys of my sons, who were in
their teens during the study and are now in their mid-20s, I, as a literacy educator, was curious about how their academic and social success might be related
to their literacy experiences—which I paid little attention to in my previous
study because I focused on their positional identities as immigrants. I wondered about how the use of a literacy theory as a new lens would influence the
results of this parent-child study and how this approach would help me as a
parent-researcher better understand my children's literacy experiences. Since
literacies are defined broadly to include reading, writing, viewing, and critiquing, based on "new literacies" concepts (New London Group, 1996), I used this
theoretical framework to re-investigate my two children's literacy experiences.

The purpose of this parent-research study is two-fold: (1) to examine if
and how the use of a different theoretical framework extends or refines the
existing findings; and (2) to discuss the potential challenges of a parent-child
research method when using a different theoretical framework. To address
these questions, I first discuss the background of the study and explain why
the reanalysis of the previous study matters for the parent-research method.
Then, the theoretical framework of new literacies that guided this study will
be discussed. Next, the methodology, with a focus on the reanalysis of the
two siblings' excerpts, will be presented. I use their interview data that were
described in a previous article for the purpose of the reanalysis. Findings and
the discussions about the findings will be presented, followed by theoretical
and methodological implications. These implications are presented with the
intention to advance parent-child research that focuses on immigrant students' literacy development in the mainstream context. Finally, suggestions
for future research and ethical considerations for conducting a parent-child
research study are provided.

2   Background of the Study

The motive of the current study is intended to fill gaps of my previous study
(Yoon, 2012) and to contribute new insights to the field of parent-child research.
Since the publication of that previous study, I have received comments from
readers throughout the world who expressed interest in my research including the method of parent-research. The two siblings and I have been invited
to several different classes to further discuss the article and our experiences

immigrating to the United States. I, as a course instructor in teacher education programs, also invited the two siblings to my classes that focused on second language and literacy learning to share their experiences with my students who are pre- and in-service literacy teachers. The siblings were excited to respond to the teachers' questions and comments on their learning experiences in schools.

In the conversation with the teachers, the siblings shared how they were deeply engaged in literacy learning (i.e., reading, writing, speaking, listening, critiquing) as immigrant English language learners. Through the siblings' responses, I learned that their literacy learning might be an important element of their academic and social success. By using positioning theory as a framework in my previous study, however, I did not take their literacy experiences into consideration as an important component of their success as immigrant students. These experiences and the subsequent realization made me wonder how the use of a theoretical framework of literacy might open spaces for other important findings and deepen our understanding of immigrant students' literacy learning.

3   Why Reanalysis Matters to Parent-Child Research

The reexamination and reuse of qualitative data for a new interpretation is not new in the field of qualitative research (Bishop, 2007; Corti & Thompson, 2004; Heaton, 2004; Silva, 2007). Many established scholars interpret the existing data with a new lens for a different audience and purpose (e.g., Blackburn, 2002, 2003, 2007; Kuby, 2011, 2013; Ladson-Billings, 1995, 1997). However, there are few, if any, studies that discuss a parent-researcher's reanalysis of the data on her children's literacy experiences by using different theoretical frameworks. Despite the important contribution to the field (e.g., Bissex, 1980; Long, 1998, 2004), parent-child research methods have received criticism due to inconsistent evidence and due to a dependency on parents' investigations and narratives as a major source instead of those of their children (Yarrow, 1963). More rigorous reanalysis processes that focus on children's narratives from their interview data is important and necessary.

This study focuses on the adolescents' narratives as a major data source and can provide researchers and educators with a deeper methodological and theoretical insight into adolescent students' learning in the mainstream context. In alignment with the parent-child research theme of this book, this chapter focuses on my two sons' literacy learning experiences by adding my detailed reanalysis process and comparing and contrasting the previous and the current findings. I believe the reexamination and reanalysis of their narratives and excerpts by using a different framework provides new insights and directions for future parent-child research.

4   Theoretical Perspectives

To examine narrative data on two immigrant students' literacy learning, this study used the theory of new literacies (New London Group, 1996) as a guiding lens. This framework was helpful to understand my sons' diverse literacy experiences, which included print and non-print texts. In this chapter, I discuss new literacies by focusing on theoretical background and key principles. (For more detailed discussions on new literacies perspectives, see Alvermann, 2002; Gee, 2007; Kinzer & Leu, 2016; Knobel & Lankshear, 2007.) I also discuss how new literacies connect to critical literacies, as well as implications of new literacies for immigrant student literacies. The following discussion on new literacies and its connection to critical literacies is adapted and expanded from Yoon (2016), which includes an extensive review of the literature on literacy theories.

4.1   *Overview of New Literacies*
The theory of "new literacies" was developed by the New London Group (1996), which consisted of 10 scholars from Australia, the United Kingdom, and the United States. As the term "new" implies, new literacies (plural form) was theorized to challenge the idea of "old" and "mono" literacy (singular form) which tends to view reading as an isolated cognitive skill without considering cultural and social factors.

This view of reading as an isolated cognitive skill has a long history in the field of literacy. Along with the New Criticism movement, (cf. Ransom, 1941; Richards, 1924), old literacy, which is considered as traditional and conventional literacy, has dominated the literacy education field for several decades. Pedagogy influenced by New Criticism paid little attention to external factors that were involved in constructing a text, such as the author's individual backgrounds or intentions. Mainly the words themselves in the text were of great significance to the New Criticism movement, and the analysis of these words, without considering other external factors, was taken as the most important element. New Criticism also paid less attention to diverse forms of representation by focusing on mono-modality: the linguistic form exclusively. This aspect promoted an instructional approach for a "close" reading of the text whereby the individual focused on literary elements such as plot and symbol.

In contrast, the approach by new literacies advocates rejected the "words only" mono-representative concept. In new literacies, the concept of literacies allowed for expansive definitions of meaning making to include multimodal representations, previous experiences, and cultural values. New literacies accommodated students' diverse identities in representing and constructing themselves through multiple forms to make meaning about the world and the text. The approach by new literacies was inclusive and broad in that it considered students' complex identities in cultural, social, and political contexts in constructing and understanding the text. Although scholars in the field of new literacies explored different aspects and forms of literacies (e.g., Gee's, 2003, videogames; Luke's, 2012, literacy pedagogy; Morrell's, 2008, popular culture), the common idea was that literacy learning should provide "access to the evolving language of work, power, and community, and [to foster] critical engagement necessary for [students] to design their social futures and achieve success through fulfilling employment" (New London Group, 1996, p. 60). In this respect, new literacies is grounded in critical theory, which allows diverse interpretations and voices to serve as devices for students to empower themselves as they read and interpret texts and make sense of society and the world around them.

4.2   *Key Principles of New Literacies*
The New London Group's (1996) contribution to the educational field is immense. It provides a new vision of literacy that allows and encourages teachers to pay more attention to individual students' different abilities, identities, and backgrounds. Rather than using monolithic and linear teaching and learning modes, the New London Group stressed that students need to be provided opportunities to create meaning in various ways. As a way to promote multiple meanings, the group suggested six different modes: (1) linguistic mode (e.g., vocabulary and grammar), (2) audio mode (e.g., sound and music), (3) spatial mode (e.g., architectural design), (4) gestural mode (e.g., posture and body language), (5) visual mode (e.g., pictures and colors), and (6) multimode, which includes some integration of the previous five modes. Given that the purpose of revisiting the previous data of my sons' learning experiences is to better understand them through a new lens, this new literacies' six modes were particularly helpful for me as a parent-researcher to see how my children navigated various forms of literacies in and beyond the classroom.

Specifically, these modes suggest that students need more opportunities to express their thoughts, opinions, and voices in various forms, including the use of digital media and technology, in order to fully engage in literacy activities in this digital era (see Alvermann, 2002; Lankshear & Knobel, 2011; Vasquez &

Felderman, 2013). Where diverse modes could offer a plethora of learning experiences, sole focus on the linguistic mode as a means of developing vocabulary for reading comprehension and grammar for improving students' writing skills on paper might limit student potential. According to Knobel and Lankshear (2014), "new literacies aren't some single, generic 'thing.' They vary according to the practice, the people involved in using them, and the 'ways of speaking' that have developed within a practice" (p. 100). Within this broader new literacies frame, reading is no longer limited to engaging with print texts and writing is no longer limited to using pen on lined paper.

This broader perspective of literacies is particularly helpful for this parent-child study to see how my two sons engaged in diverse texts beyond print texts in order to make meaning and to construct their identities as adolescent immigrants in the mainstream context.

4.3   *Relation to Critical Literacies*

The key principles of new literacies are aligned with those of critical literacy in that both support dynamic, flexible, and multi-modes for students' literacy learning. Several scholars who established the ideas of new literacies and who are also active critical literacy scholars, including Allan Luke (2012) and Norman Fairclough (2014), shared alignments between new literacies and critical literacies. Although there are commonalities between these two schools of theories, one of the major differences is in the premise of critical literacies: neither a text nor an educational practice is neutral: both are political. The critical literacy view is that texts have a political agenda that functions to serve particular interest groups while also working to limit minority groups' voices. Promoting critical consciousness about the ways the world operates with power, bias, and stereotype is key in critical literacy practices that enable and prepare students to act as agents.

Promoting students' critical consciousness to liberate themselves and to transform society is a central practice in critical literacy (Freire, 1970, 1998). According to Shor (1992), critical consciousness is "the way we see ourselves in relation to knowledge and power in society, to the way we use and study language, and to the way we act in school and daily life to reproduce or transform our conditions" (p. 128). As shown in Shor's definition, the main purpose of critical literacy practice is to help students develop critical consciousness to better understand the world and to (re)name it with their agency. In this respect, literacy instruction must focus on inviting "readers to move beyond passively accepting the text's message to question, examine, or dispute the power relations that exist between readers and authors" (McLaughlin & DeVoogd, 2004,

p. 14). Helping students to become active readers, instead of passive readers who simply accept authors' messages, is key for critical literacy instruction.

In developing students' critical consciousness, use of various texts is fundamental. As new literacies views texts in a broad manner, which includes printed and non-printed materials, critical literacy also approaches texts from broader social, cultural, and political perspectives. As the core element of new literacies, critical literacy values students' diverse abilities and voices. Rather than viewing students' abilities, backgrounds, and primary languages from the dominant culture's norms as a "deficit" to fix, critical literacy values and leverages what it redefines as "difference" for students' growth as socially and politically conscious human beings. If students' differences are continued to be viewed as a deficit, they might be oppressed by the dominant culture, which might hinder their identity development and, as a result, their literacy learning development. In this regard, all students, including immigrant students, need opportunities to see how texts can be used to marginalize them. Recognizing how texts can serve a dominant cultural mindset may provide a way for students to empower themselves to act as agents (Luke, 2004). Given that texts serve certain groups' interests and agendas, students need to learn how to critique, evaluate, and assess the historical, social, and political texts of the world through the opportunities of engaging in critical literacy practices.

4.4   *Implications of New Literacies and Critical Literacy for Immigrant Students*

Despite the immense contribution by the theories of new literacies and critical literacies to the field of education, the question still remains: What do these theories mean to immigrant students' literacy learning? Although they can be applied to the understanding of all students' literacy learning, the field of immigrant English language learners (ELLs) has paid scant attention to the multi-modes by focusing mainly on the linguistic mode. Immigrant ELLs were often taught by concentrating on linguistic skills with the assimilationist ideological assumption that they need to "master" English to be "mainstreamed" to the dominant culture. To actively engage in literacy learning and to understand the political world and the text, it is important that teachers consider offering immigrant ELLs more opportunities to practice all of the diverse modes, rather than focusing on one single mode, that is, the linguistic mode.

In sum, the theories of new literacies and critical literacy provide teachers with implications regarding opportunities they can offer to improve immigrant ELLs' active literacy learning.

5 Method

5.1 Data Sources

For the purpose of this current study, the article that utilized longitudinal data on my two sons' educational journey (Yoon, 2012) was used as a major data source. Due to the extensive data of the nine-year longitudinal study, I selected the siblings' 12 excerpts in the article for a focused reanalysis of their literacy experiences. These 12 excerpts were mostly based on the interview data.

Since I used their previous interview data for the current parent-child research study, it is important to provide the context of how I collected the data. First, as a parent researcher, I shared with the siblings the purpose of the study on immigrants and the interview plans. Then, I shared with them my role as a parent-researcher and their role as participants, and specific interview procedures. For the interviews, I talked with Junsuk (younger son) and Junhyuck (older son) two times individually. At the first interview, both of them said that the interview process was "awkward" since I treated them more "formally" and "seriously" with the set of questions that I had prepared. As the interviews continued, they appeared more comfortable with my positioning of them as research participants. To ensure their privacy, I took some episodes out from the interview data in the previous study. For this current study, I shared my idea of this reanalysis project with my sons and invited them for interviews. However, their busy schedules did not allow me to conduct interviews and member-checking processes with them.

As noted earlier, in my previous study, the interview data that I presented were analyzed from the standpoint of positioning theory (Harré & van Langenhove, 1999), which is defined as "the study of local moral orders as ever shifting patterns of mutual and contestable rights and obligations of speaking and acting" (p. 1). Using the elements of positioning theory, I specifically analyzed the siblings' data using the concepts of "self-positioning" (i.e., reflexive positioning) and "interactive-positioning" (i.e., positioned by others). With respect to the current study, I reanalyzed the data by using the theoretical framework of new literacies.

The secondary data source includes my journal from the previous study, in which I periodically recorded the siblings' schooling experiences in Grades 4 through 12, as well as my own reflections about them. Among the journal notes, I selected my reflection about the siblings' literacy experiences for the purpose of this study. This reflection was used to reexamine the primary data of the siblings' interviews.

5.2   *Participants' Brief Profiles and English Language Levels*

Currently, Junsuk, 26 years old, is in a doctoral program in the United States and Junhyuck, 28 years old, is in the business field in South Korea. When Junsuk and Junhyuck came to the United States, they were in fourth and fifth grade, respectively, and they had very limited English proficiency. They were placed in the beginning English as a Second Language (ESL) program. After three years, the siblings were able to pass the English proficiency tests and were no longer in the ESL program.

5.3   *Reanalysis Process*

The reanalysis of the data was conducted using the framework of new literacies by focusing on the key principles discussed previously (New London Group, 1996). Given that the article was a major data source, the reanalysis consists of reading the article and pulling out the specific excerpts that are instances of literacy for further examination. To answer the two research questions, the reanalysis was based on multiple procedures. I first read the article as a whole, from the beginning to the end to refresh myself about the article and the context. Because it was written in 2012, this initial process was essential. During my second reading of the article, I focused on the siblings' narratives and wrote my initial thoughts in the margin. In this process, I focused on how their narratives were related to literacy experiences. For the reader's understanding, I provide one example of how I used the quotes for the reanalysis. For instance, Junsuk, the younger sibling, stated:

> I know I am here as an immigrant. That's why I felt like working harder. It seemed I was at a disadvantage in the classroom with other kids because I didn't understand much English and American culture. (Yoon, 2012, p. 983)

In my previous analysis, my interpretation of the data focused on Junsuk's identity awareness as an immigrant in the United States. In comparison to this interpretation, my current reanalysis about this quote is as follows:

> *He viewed that his limited literacy skills in English and American culture are "disadvantages" to him in the mainstream context. To him, being an immigrant is to understand both English and American culture. It seems language and literacy learning is inseparable from understanding American culture to him.*

This interpretation shows that I reanalyzed the same data with a different lens by focusing on the siblings' literacy experiences. After this initial analysis process, the more specific theoretical framework of new literacies was used for further analysis by focusing on the multimodality concepts (i.e., six modes) that were discussed earlier.

This reanalysis process showed that while the use of a new theoretical framework on existing data extends and strengthens the previous findings, it also provides challenges. In the findings below, the interpretation of the data based on the framework of new literacies is provided with specific examples and quotes to illustrate the instances of potential for increased understanding created by reanalysis as well as limiting factors and challenges. This full spectrum needs to be considered in light of this approach to conducting parent-child research.

5.4   Parent-Researcher Profile

As a teacher educator and researcher, I currently teach courses in literacy. I have more than 15 years of experience in higher education, and my research interests include critical global literacies (Yoon, 2016), cultural pluralism, positional identities, and English language learners. My own identity as an immigrant to the United States naturally led me to be interested in those topics. In this study, I positioned myself as a *reflexive* (Hertz, 1997) parent-researcher who actively constructs and reconstructs the meaning of the experiences that I had with my two sons as immigrants in the United States. (Note: I remind the reader to consult Yoon, 2012 for a more detailed profile and context.) Despite my positioning as a reflexive parent-researcher, my bias about my own children and my interactions with them could not be excluded from the reanalysis on their literacy experiences. My interactions with them could provide more contexts to interpret their literacy experiences, but they might also limit my interpretations.

6   Findings and Discussions

The reexamination and reanalysis using a different theoretical framework on the existing data of the adolescents' narratives presented both possibilities and challenges; both yield potential avenues that parent-child researchers should consider to improve the method of reanalysis. In terms of the potential benefits of applying a different theoretical framework, the reanalysis was helpful to extend the existing findings. That is, the different theoretical framework yields new insights when reexamining the data. This new finding will be discussed in comparison with the previous findings to show readers how it extends the previous data and how important the on-going analysis process is for parent-child research. The reanalysis approach using the different theory also presents challenges in conducting parent-child research: the theoretical framework needs to be established along *with* research questions, not *after* the research questions were developed, as was the case with this current study. In the following section, potential benefits will be discussed first and challenges follow.

6.1   *Extension of the Existing Findings*

First, although the different theoretical framework was utilized, the existing findings and the new findings were not in conflict. The use of new literacies (New London Group, 1996) expanded the findings of the previous study, which used positioning theory as the theoretical framework (Harré & van Langenhove, 1999). This result shows that certain incidents and events that the siblings experienced as immigrants can be interpreted from many different theoretical and conceptual points of view. More specifically, let us look at the narratives by Junsuk, the younger sibling, about his view about diversity.

> *Junsuk*: In class, we talked about diversity. The interesting thing was when Whites were shown, they were having parties in luxurious houses or having wedding ceremonies at a church. But when the slides showed Asians and Africans, they all depicted how poor they were by showing construction sites, farms, and unsanitary classrooms. So, I raised my hand and asked the teacher whether there are other slides that can accurately portray current images of Asia. When I said that I felt that everyone looked at me doubtfully.
>
> *Researcher*: What did the teacher say?
>
> *Junsuk*: He said, are there any new things? So I said I have lived in South Korea for more than 8 years, but it was hard to find unsanitary classrooms. I also mentioned that I saw many homeless people in European countries when I traveled. I just wanted to point out that the slides don't picture the diverse image of ethnic groups. (Yoon, 2012, p. 987)

As shown in this quote, Junsuk challenged the text (the visual slides) that the teacher showed to promote his students' understanding about diversity in his world history class. Junsuk attempted to point out that the visual images were problematic since they portray prejudiced meaning about Asian and African cultures. This data could be an excellent example of how Junsuk practiced critical literacies (Yoon, 2016), the key element of new literacies.

However, in my previous interpretation, I provided an example to show the siblings' identity negotiation, "situated identity as an immigrant and self-identity as Korean" (Yoon, 2012, p. 988), and how they attempted to negotiate their identities in the mainstream context. More specifically, based on positioning theory, my previous interpretation was how Junsuk, the younger sibling, positioned himself as an active participant in classroom activities by disclosing his identity as Korean. In revisiting the previous data for this parent-child research, I realized that my interpretation focused on Junsuk's and Junhyuck's (older sibling) identities as Koreans by stating that "[i]nstead of hiding their identity as Korean, they began to exhibit it more explicitly. They actively positioned themselves as contributing members by projecting themselves as Korean in the classroom" (Yoon, 2012, p. 987). This interpretation is clearly guided by self-positioning, an element of positioning theory.

Yet, rethinking the data retrospectively as a parent-researcher, I found that the data can be interpreted in a new way. Not only was Junsuk positioning himself as Korean, but also he questioned the text's bias and stereotypes about other countries. This perspective was possible through his positioning of himself as a knowledge constructor, and not merely as a knowledge consumer who simply absorbs knowledge as it is shown in the text. It clearly showed that his identity, which was shown through his self-positioning, was linked to his learning of literacy in a meaningful way. When we compare these data, the original interpretation does not conflict with the interpretation from the reanalysis. This finding from the reanalysis sheds light on how important it is for the field of parent-research to consider the potential for "rich" interpretation that can result from application of a different framework.

Another example which supports the idea that the previous findings were expanded through the reanalysis is shown in the following quotes. The following narratives by Junsuk were interpreted in the previous analysis in terms of how he attempted to maintain his native Korean language in different contexts by focusing on his identity.

> Sometimes, it's better to express certain nuances in certain languages. For example, when I had a chance to go on a trip to Yucatan for church activities, there were many native Korean-speaking friends. We did some games and it was impossible to do the games by translating them in English. There are ways that you need to speak Korean. (Yoon, 2012, p. 989)

From the perspective of reanalysis, these data could be reinterpreted based on how Junsuk was capable of practicing new literacies through utilizing his abilities as a multi-language learner. Although I originally focused on Junsuk's interaction with his Korean friends as an example of his positioning himself as an active participant in Korean, the reanalysis shows how he chooses his language according to different contexts to better express his meaning—an important element of new literacies. In this instance as well, the use of the different theoretical framework of new literacies is not in conflict with positioning theory. Rather, it complements and strengthens the meaning of the qualitative data, which provides a useful example for researchers in the field of parent-child research to consider in order to strengthen the methodological practice.

The data from Junhyuck, Junsuk's older brother, also showed how the use of new literacies supports and extends the previous findings. For example, Junhyuck's narratives on a project in his social studies class included the following:

> If I were in Korea, I don't think I'd be interested in doing this type of project. The reason that I wanted to do the project on Korea is that sometimes I found the wrong information in the social study textbooks about the Korean War and other historical events. I wanted to challenge the limited ideas that American students might have. They don't seem to know much about other countries and what's going on around the world. Someone in my sixth grade even asked me "What's Korea?" He didn't even know that Korea is a country. (Yoon, 2012, p. 988)

In my previous analysis, I interpreted this interview data by focusing on his Korean identities that motivated him to continue to work on his school project. By focusing on his positioning of himself as Korean, my previous analysis missed the opportunity to look at how Junhyuck also practiced critical literacy. Specifically, he pointed out that the social studies textbooks did not accurately portray Korean historical events based on his experience and knowledge about Korea. The data show that Junhyuck did not consume knowledge as it was shown in the text, but analyzed it critically based on his learning experiences in South Korea. He challenged the limited ideas that his American peers might have about other countries. His critical consciousness was evident in the data through the new theoretical framework.

Along with this quote, another excerpt by Junhyuck also shows his critical perspectives about his situation. The excerpt includes the following:

> I spoke in Korean with my Korean friends, Hyunbin and Changmin, in the classroom because I couldn't express myself in English at all. But Mrs. Anderson was upset because of my use of Korean. She said that I shouldn't speak Korean in her ESL classroom...I am Korean, but not being allowed to speak Korean was frustrating. I had to simply sit in the classroom silently. (Yoon, 2012, p. 985)

In my previous analysis, these data were approached from Junhyuck's identity dilemma as Korean in the mainstream context. However, when revisiting these data, I found that it was a very limited interpretation. This data could still be analyzed based on the use of his native language in the ESL classroom. But, with the new literacies and critical literacy framework, my new analysis could focus on how he was not offered opportunities to use his primary language which might have been used as a bridge for his learning of English as a second language. Based on second language scholars' work (e.g., Brown, 2014), I could argue that students' primary language use is useful to develop their second language learning.

It was clear from the previous study that my voice and frustration were not shown in the interpretation. By focusing on how others' positioning influences self-positioning, I did not discuss the issue in detail regarding how he was disempowered. His disempowerment is shown through his behavior: he chose to remain silent in the classroom. Given that the major component of critical literacy is that students need to be empowered in all processes of learning, the data could be reanalyzed in a way that demonstrates a lack of opportunity for the immigrant adolescent to empower himself.

This new analysis based on new literacies and critical literacy provides a distinct perspective on the siblings' case study and a richer, deeper theoretical insight into what they were experiencing in terms of literacy. This application does not minimize how they talked about their experiences as immigrants and their identity dilemmas. Rather, this new analysis highlights not only the ways they express their identities, but also the complex situations that they encountered in the mainstream classroom and how they resisted the oppressed situation by practicing critical literacy with global perspectives. In sum, these examples show the possibilities that reanalysis with a new lens offers. A richer and deeper theoretical insight could be brought to parent-child research.

6.2   *Challenge of the Use of the Different Framework*

Despite the potential for enhanced insights that can accompany the use of a different theoretical framework, challenges were also encountered in the process of the reanalyzing the existing data—more specifically, as related to the issue of alignment between the theoretical framework and the research question. Compared to the previous study in which the theoretical framework of positioning theory was selected along with the establishment of the research questions about the siblings' identities with relation to their academic success, the new literacies framework was chosen after the research questions that guided the original study. Because of the ways new research questions emerged over time, the selected data from the previous study could not be adequately analyzed based on the key principles and six modes of new literacies. That is, the siblings' narrative excerpts used in the original study were selected based on relevance to identity based on the original research questions. The present focus on new literacies does not align naturally with the original research questions.

More specifically, the quotes that were used to support the analysis of the siblings' identities were not entirely useful to explore the key principles of new literacies. In other words, the reanalysis of the existing data could not show that the siblings had any experience in working with multimodality (or even that they were necessarily denied any such experiences). Although there was one example (i.e., Junhyuck's video project on Korea), it was not sufficient to support any interpretation regarding their new literacies experiences in the classroom. This is not surprising given that all the interview data that I presented in the earlier study were based on the research questions that emphasized their identities—data guided by the theoretical framework of positioning theory. Given that the interview questions were informed by broader research questions, they were all related to the siblings' identities as immigrant adolescents, not necessarily to their literacy experiences with diverse modes. If the research questions were on their new literacy experiences, then the interview questions would have been developed around these topics as well.

The reanalysis does not, then, show whether the two siblings were provided with the opportunities to engage in multimodality in the classroom. Research on adolescent English language learners (e.g., Choudhury & Share, 2012; Danzak, 2011; Hughes & Morrison, 2014) shows that, when students have opportunities to utilize a multimodal literacy approach in the process of learning in the classroom, they are actively engaged in literacy practices. Multimodal approaches with a critical lens help students "challenge the taken-for-granted views about their worlds" (Ajayi, 2009, p. 591). Based on the current reanalysis of the data, however, no claim could be made regarding any multimodal experiences through classroom projects. This outcome shows that if the research questions were established along with the choice of the new literacies framework, findings on the siblings' experiences regarding the presence or absence of the diverse six modes could be obtained. The different six modes of new literacies could be useful if they had been the lens from the beginning.

In sum, the practice of reinterpreting existing data through a new theoretical framework can provide new insights for the field of parent-research, but it can also pose limitations in the process of analyzing specific ideas such as a specific framework of six modes of new literacies. The challenges accompanying the reuse of existing data can continue to be further refined with future parent-research.

7 Discussions and Implications

Evidence of consistency between the existing findings and the new findings from reanalysis is important in any parent-child research. The reanalysis of the previous study shows that it is fundamental to follow the participants and continue to assess the quality of the study. The current study with a new theoretical framework provides fuller evidence of the adolescent immigrants' complex literacy experiences in and beyond the classroom. Although the previous analysis of the adolescent immigrants' case study suggests that their identity dilemmas and identity negotiations were important aspects to succeed in the mainstream context, it did not show how their identities are also closely related to the process of literacy development. This current study provides evidence that immigrant adolescents' self-positioning and interactive positioning is part of their literacy development process. It demonstrates how these students' identity process is also a process of literacy construction. Given that scholars (e.g., Gee, 2007; Ladson-Billings, 1995, 1997; Norton, 2000) note that students' identities are crucial components of their successful literacy learning, it was not known how closely and in what context they were related. The new literacies framework helped me as a parent-researcher better understand my sons' identity development in relation to their literacy practices.

Another noticeable finding through this reanalysis is that the immigrant siblings' academic success was associated with their critical literacy practice in reading the text and the world. Compared to other elements of new literacies, there was robust evidence related to the elements of critical literacies in their narratives as presented, such as challenging the bias and stereotypes about other ethnic groups in the visual slides. The siblings' narratives highlight that they did not simply accept the given text, but practiced critical literacy through "second guessing, reading against the grain, asking hard and harder questions, seeing underneath, behind, and beyond texts, trying to see and 'call' how these texts establish and use power over us, over others, on whose behalf, in whose interests" (Luke, 2004, p. 4). While they were negotiating their immigrant identities in the mainstream context, the two siblings were also in the process of developing their critical consciousness to empower themselves by challenging biased views of their primary culture. This is an important finding that I did not realize until revisiting the data with a new lens.

The findings show that the existing data can be used in new ways with new theoretical perspectives to achieve new insights. I believe this chapter provides fresh contributions to scholarly knowledge and theorizing and has the potential to encourage researchers and educators to reanalyze their existing data for on-going qualitative data analysis on parent-research on their children's literacy experiences. Not only are there implications from the methodological and theoretical findings, but also the new findings provide educators with instructional implications on how to support immigrant students for their meaningful new literacy experiences to work as critically conscious human beings in the complex mainstream context.

8   Future Research and Ethical Considerations

Given that the parent-research method is emerging, it is important to discuss potential benefits and limitations. The findings from reanalysis of my data provide several important implications and suggestions for future research and practice for researchers and educators. Since this study discusses the retrospective analysis of a previous study, my suggestions are from my cumulative experience with both studies.

First, although parent research is an innovative method, diversifying the approach by using multiple theoretical frameworks concurrently would be desirable for future researchers to better understand their children. As shown in the current study, the methodological approach, which used a different theoretical framework and the addition of a specific analytical process, strengthened the quality and trustworthiness of the study. The current study, which used the framework of new literacies, provided different dimensions and elements that, in turn, helped me as a parent researcher to view another side of my children's learning that contributed to their academic and social success. This finding suggests that, through the reanalysis process by using different theoretical frameworks, parents can have a richer and fuller understanding of their children.

Second, for trustworthiness of study findings, a parent-researcher's own bias needs to be more closely examined and explicitly discussed in the study as part of the research method. It is important to balance a dual role as a parent and a researcher. All researchers have their own bias to some degree, and parent-researchers might bring more bias since they have more opportunities to interact with their own children on a daily basis inside and outside of the home context. To address the bias issue, more critical reflection about their roles as parent and researcher is needed.

As noted earlier, my sons' verbal expressions about their learning in different contexts as guest speakers in different venues helped me see different sides of their engagement in learning. Before this experience, I thought my older son was more "quiet" and less engaging in literacy activities than my younger son. However, revisiting the original data with a new lens provided me with an opportunity to reflect on what I had missed. As I learned from my previous study that the observations about my children's home experiences challenged my theoretical assumptions, the reflection allowed me to examine my own bias about them, which prompted me to conduct this current study. The data analysis of the parent-research should be conducted with the parent's critical reflection. In addition, a rigorous member check process with children is vital to avoid bias. In my previous study, I presented my findings to the siblings and they confirmed or disconfirmed my interpretation of the data. I learned that this member check process was crucial to establish trustworthiness of the findings.

Third, although the current study focused on the two siblings' voices through their interview transcripts, the analysis of the parent's voice might be useful to strengthen and interpret the findings. It is important to have both parties, parents and children, for strengthening the trustworthiness of the qualitative method. Immigrant parents and children are co-constructors of the life journey and the parent's voice should receive equal attention to deeply understand the children's literacy learning experiences in the mainstream context.

Fourth, it is important to ensure that parent-researchers keep their children's privacy. Compared to other researchers, parent-researchers might have more personal data about their own children. I know that I have more stories to share as their mother to support my interpretations and arguments. However, as I noted earlier, I took some episodes out to ensure their privacy. I could not disclose the data associated with their relationship with particular teachers and peers when my sons did not want to disclose the stories. Because my sons wanted to use their real names on the published article, I could not share specific examples that might disclose their relationship with the relevant people. Parent-researchers need to consider that no matter how rich and interesting the data are, it is important to take ethical compliance as priority.

Finally, parent-researchers' approach to their children who are minors and who are adults might be different, which might influence the study's findings. In my previous study, I felt the study was more like a study of parent and child together. Because we lived together, the data could be obtained more from informal settings. There were more opportunities for me to triangulate the data in different contexts. In addition, my request for the member check process was accepted by my two sons without any hesitation in my previous studies when they were minors. They were willing to listen to my interpreta-tion of the data and to share their own interpretations. They had opportunities to read my draft and provide comments. However, for this current study, they simply expressed that they were "busy." I respected their decision, but it was a challenge to invite them as my participants to read my retrospective account of their stories, which could strengthen the trustworthiness of this current study. It shows that parent-research about children who are adults might be more challenging in some ways.

In conclusion, the current study provides researchers with possibilities and challenges that accompany the process of reanalyzing qualitative data. Indeed, parent-research is vital since it provides a rich context by adding home observations about their children and transactions with them on a daily basis. However, it also presents limitations that researchers should consider for future research. As the current study shows, it is important to recognize both potentials and limitations about conducting research as a parent. These poten-tials and limitations need to be considered to better understand the learning of children that can support their capacity to engage in meaningful literacy experiences. Reanalysis of my children's learning serves this main purpose and opens possibilities for future parent-child research.

References

Ajayi, L. (2009). English as a second language learners' exploration of multimodal texts in junior high school. *Journal of Adolescent & Adult Literacy, 52*(7), 585–595.

Alvermann, D. E. (Ed.). (2002). *Adolescents and literacies in a digital world.* New York, NY: Peter Lang.

Bishop, L. (2007). A reflexive account of reusing qualitative data: Beyond primary/ secondary dualism. *Sociological Research Online, 12*(3), Retrieved from http://www.socresonline.org.uk/12/3/2.html

Bissex, G. L. (1980). *Gnys at wrk: A child learns to write and read.* Cambridge, MA: Harvard University Press.

Blackburn, M. V. (2002). Disrupting the (hetero) normative: Exploring literacy perfor-mances and identity work with queer youth. *Journal of Adolescent & Adult Literacy, 46*(4), 312–324.

Blackburn, M. V. (2003). Exploring literacy performances and power dynamics at the loft: "Queer youth reading the world and the word." *Research in the Teaching of English, 37*(4), 467–490.

Blackburn, M. V. (2007). The experiencing, negotiation, breaking, and remaking of gen-der rules and regulations by queer youth. *Journal of Gay & Lesbian Issues in Educa-tion, 4*(2), 33–54.

Brown, H. D. (2014). *Principles of language learning and teaching.* New York, NY: Pearson Education.

Choudhury, M., & Share, J. (2012). Critical media literacy: A pedagogy for new literacies and urban youth. *Voices from the Middle, 19*(4), 39–44.

Corti, L., & Thompson, P. (2004). Secondary analysis of archive data. In C. Seale, G. Gobo, J. F. Gubrium, & D. Silverman (Eds.), *Qualitative research practice* (pp. 327–343). Thousand Oaks, CA: Sage.

Danzak, R. (2011). Defining identities through multiliteracies: EL teens narrate their immigration experiences as graphic stories. *Journal of Adolescent & Adult Literacy, 55*(3), 187–196.

Fairclough, N. (2014). *Language and power* (3rd ed.). London: Longman.

Freire, P. (1970). *Pedagogy of the oppressed.* New York, NY: Continuum.

Freire, P. (1998). *Teachers as cultural workers: Letters to those who dare teach.* Boulder, CO: Westview Press.

Gee, J. P. (2003). *What video games have to teach us about learning and literacy.* New York, NY: Palgrave Macmillan.

Gee, J. P. (2007). *Social linguistics and literacies: Ideology in discourses* (3rd ed.). London: Routledge.

Harré, R., & van Langenhove, L. (Eds.). (1999). *Positioning theory.* Malden, MA: Blackwell Publishers.

Heaton, J. (2004). *Reworking qualitative data.* Thousand Oaks, CA: Sage.

Hertz, R. (1997). Introduction: reflexivity and voice. In R. Hertz (Ed.), *Reflexivity and voice* (pp. vii–xviii). Thousand Oaks, CA: Sage.

Hughes, J., & Morrison, L. (2014). The impact of social networking and a multiliteracies pedagogy on English language learners' writer identities. *Writing & Pedagogy, 6*(3), 607–631.

Kinzer, C.K. & Leu, D.J. (2016). new literacies, New Literacies. In M.A. Peters (Ed.), *Encyclopedia of Educational Philosophy and Theory.* SpringerLink. https://doi.org/10.1007/978-981-287-532-7_111-1

Knobel, M., & Lankshear, C. (Eds.). (2007). *A new literacies sampler.* New York, NY: Peter Lang.

Knobel, M., & Lankshear, C. (2014). Studying new literacies. *Journal of Adolescent & Adult Literacy, 58*(2), 97–101.

Kuby, C. R. (2011). Kidwatching with a critical eye: The power of observation and reflexive practice. *Talking Points, 22*(2), 22–28.

Kuby, C. R. (2013). Personal histories and pedagogical decisions: Using autoethnographic methods to unpack ideologies and experiences. *Teaching and Learning: The Journal of Natural Inquiry and Reflective Practice, 26*(1), 3–18.

Ladson-Billings, G. (1995). Toward a theory of culturally relevant pedagogy. *American Educational Research Journal, 32*(3), 465–491.

Ladson-Billings, G. J. (1997). *The dream keepers: Successful teachers of African-American children*. San Francisco, CA: Jossey-Bass.

Lankshear, C., & Knobel, M. (2011). *New literacies: Everyday practices & classroom learning* (3rd ed.). New York, NY: Open University Press and McGraw Hill.

Long, S. (1998). Learning to get along: Language acquisition and literacy development in a new cultural setting. *Research in the Teaching of English, 33,* 8–47.

Long, S. (2004). Passionless text and phonics first: Through a child's eyes. *Language Arts, 81*(5), 417–426.

Luke, A. (2004). Foreword. In M. McLaughlin & G. Devoogd (Eds.), *Critical literacy: Enhancing students' comprehension of text* (pp. 4–5). New York, NY: Scholastic.

Luke, A. (2012). Critical literacy: Foundational notes. *Theory into Practice, 51*(1), 4–11.

McLaughlin, M., & DeVoogd, G. (2004). *Critical literacy: Enhancing students' comprehension of text*. New York, NY: Scholastic.

Morrell, E. (2008). *Critical literacy and urban youth: Pedagogies of access, dissent, and liberation*. New York, NY: Routledge.

New London Group. (1996). A pedagogy of multiliteracies: Designing social futures. *Harvard Educational Review, 66,* 60–92.

Norton, B. (2000). *Identity and language learning: Gender, ethnicity and educational change*. New York, NY: Longman.

Ransom, J. C. (1941). The new criticism. *Norfolk*, CT: New Directions.

Richards, I. A. (1924). *Principles of literary criticism*. London, England: Routledge & Kegan Paul.

Shor, I. (1992). *Empowering education: Critical teaching for social change*. Chicago, IL: University of Chicago Press.

Silva, E. (2007). What's [yet] to be seen? Re-using qualitative data. *Sociological Research Online, 12*(3). Retrieved from http://www.socresonline.org.uk/12/3/4.html

Vasquez, V., & Felderman, C. (2013). *Technology and critical literacy in early childhood*. New York, NY: Routledge.

Yarrow, M. R. (1963). Problems of method of parent-child research. *Child Development, 34*(1), 215–226.

Yoon, B. (2012). Junsuk and Junhyuck: Adolescent immigrants' educational journey to success and identity negotiation. *American Educational Research Journal, 49*(5), 971–1002.

Yoon, B. (2016). *Critical literacies: Global and multicultural perspectives*. Singapore: Springer.

CHAPTER 9

The Last Word: Teen Reflections

Charlotte Abrams, Molly Kurpis and Eric Ness

Abstract

In this final chapter, three adolescents provide a window into their experiences with and perspectives of their roles as co-researchers working with their parent-researcher. Three separately authored vignettes are part of the adolescents having "the last word," reminding readers of the authenticity and empowerment in the critical self-reflection and insightful commentaries the teens share.

1   Our Research and Being an Adolescent Researcher (Charlotte Abrams)

My opinion and understanding of being an adolescent researcher has changed over the course of our journey through researching. At first, it was foreign, strange, and I was unsure of what to do. Ask myself a question? Look inside myself and try to self-reflect? How? Is this a test where we are supposed to just answer with what others want to hear? However, as our research progressed, I began to gather knowledge of how research is done, but also how research is done by me. Specifically, for our autoethnography, I learned that I couldn't just sit down at a computer and answer questions easily. In fact, it would stress me out to the point I would get frustrated and need a break.

I'm still learning how to get to the point where I can tune into myself and answer these questions with more ease, but one thing that I have noticed is that if I hear the question and I let myself think about it throughout the day, it can help me answer better and also more accurately because I pay more attention to my activities or lifestyle/habits that are being inquired about. For instance, if we were asked how our digital activities relate to or are different from our non-digital activities, I might pay more attention when I'm online and when I'm at school. As the years went by, I became less hesitant of what to do and Molly and I even began to make questions that we would come back to a month later and answer. Researching helped me open my mind and expand my horizon of knowledge and the progression of twelve-year-old me, unsure what to do, to the fourteen-year-old I am now that writes her own questions with someone she has become friends with through their collaborative research is amazing. What is also quite interesting is that sometimes I find myself self-reflecting throughout the day even when it's not research related. I've become very in-tune with myself and I have come to the point where I am shocked that my friends can't self-reflect the same way. My expectations for them have grown higher as I expect them to reflect upon their actions the way I do mine, which makes me believe that autoethnography should be part of school curriculums because self-refection can help everyone become more in-tune with themselves, which would help people be kinder, make wiser decisions, and consider others. I'm not saying I'm perfect, because I have many flaws, as I am human, but I definitely think that our research has helped me improve as a human being.

I know that many people probably have concerns about children co-researching with their parents because there is a hierarchy or there is a sense of pressure. Yes, in the beginning there was hierarchy, but we were able to get past that. We have spoken about it and it was important to be honest about how we felt. In the beginning, not only was it unusual to be asked questions, but I still wasn't accustomed to being a researcher and I hadn't fully acknowledged that what I was doing was real. I needed the *parents* to assert themselves a little so that I could figure out my position and my methods. Eventually, Molly and I created our own questions. One thing that I hope we can follow up on, is having the *adult* researchers answer all the questions as well. I think that would balance the researching a little more in the sense that all the researchers are doing and analyzing the same things.

In the beginning of our work, we were all new to the concept of co-researching with our parents/children and I think that since Molly, Eric, and I weren't familiar with research other than for school, we needed the adults to lead. However, this method of research was foreign to the adults as well, so they initiated the research in the way they *were* familiar with and I believe that is why there was the sense of hierarchy. Because the adults were writing the questions, we didn't experience one of the most important parts of autoethnography, which is *wondering*. A really important breakthrough in our research was when Molly and I asked to create our own questions. I believe this helped us begin to understand autoethnography a little more, and also may have helped the adults begin to feel less as our parents and more as our co-researchers. By making our own questions, Molly and I were able to better understand the process of autoethnography. Being an adolescent researcher has opened my eyes to how much more there is to learn and that research is an ongoing process because life is full of changes.

2   Research Overture (Molly Kurpis)

Working with adult researchers on an adolescent project inspires a mature, grown-up attitude. The data we collect and analyze is different from any other source I have ever been used to: in school, for example, we would use the Internet and charts to gather information that has been verified from an outside source. To be an adolescent researcher is to create the data yourself and draw the conclusions, form a hypothesis, and follow the procedures without the backhand of another outside source guiding you. These experiences we reflect on and the work we have mastered differentiate from any other type of research I have ever done. Manipulating this handcrafted data makes me feel matured and important to the entirety of learning as well as finding creative ways to interpret our own personal data. This, in return, formulates data that makes the entire project much easier to understand. We are not robots, and we are not basing our information off of what others have done.

When I was first taught the word research, it meant, "type your question into the Google spacebar, read reliable sources, and don't copy it word for word." Research was gathering variables and data in order to solve something, such as a science experiment or a history paper. However, once I started working on this project, the data we collected was our own data. My coworkers and I would reflect on our activities and write about how we felt while doing them. These answers, as vague and sometimes a bit messy as they can be, became our OWN data. The only way we could plagiarize was off of ourselves. We were the heads of our variables and it was up to us to manipulate and understand them. I could no longer type into google "how do I feel about homework?" because the research we were doing had no definite answers. People tend to associate the word "research" with exploring the internet until they find the best answer. This project expanded my field of vision on the term: research really has no answer. Research is more of the steps and the variables you collect on the way and the whole understanding at the end of how these variables connect and intertwine. Research is professional, research is personal. Research can have one answer, many answers, or absolutely no answers. Research is not depending on the search bar, but rather depending on how all of the pieces of a project reflect one another and the impact they can create.

I'm one to doubt my variables. I look at the conclusion I formed and think to myself, "Wow. What if I missed the big idea? This could be all wrong, and this project would fall to pieces." The thing about this adolescent research is that there are NO directly wrong answers. I could say, "I don't like watching TV," and then one of my coworkers would respond, "Wrong answer. You messed up everything and you're kicked off." The difference between knowing and not knowing is what made this project so fascinating. Nothing was right, and nothing was wrong. If a piece of data was starting to lead in the wrong direction we would not fret, just simply slice off its inconvenience and grow a new branch of information that related back to our overarching theme. There is a relaxed atmosphere when working with others on our research. If nothing is declared wrong, then none of my work would pull anyone down or cause chaos to the project. Rather, we grow on our differentiating ideas and draw new variables as to why this could be. This alone is inspiring: now I can go out into the world comfortable that my research is never truly right, but can never be declared wrong (unless it's history, but how cool would it be to change the year WWI started?).

Doing this parent-child research is something I would personally love to continue. My mom and I grow off our conclusions and help each other through words and phrases we can not quite understand. She checks my essays for school, and every mistake I have made I learn to correct for next time. We read similar books and have similar thought processes. We got the same exact English score on the PSAT, which was a little strange, but it goes to show how like-minded we are. I love working with her, and going to conferences with her has been a blast. I also love working with my coworkers and formulating new ways to interpret the new things we learn about ourselves and others. These experiences pave a way to fun and original ways of interpreting research instead of boringly scrolling through articles written by old fancy people for hours on the Internet. This data my mom and I create is new, fresh, and exciting. Adolescents and their quick way of thinking makes for a challenging yet interesting study.

3   Child-Parent Research: The Rebel (Eric Ness)

I still play cello and piano, and I take fencing lessons regularly, as well as being on the school varsity fencing team. As what I do digitally and nondigitally, I usually just go onto Google and search up whatever I need to find out, as it only takes a few seconds to get the gist of it, though it may take longer depending on what I need to study. I don't really associate myself with mobile devices as much as other people, though I may need to in the future when considering college and career choices.

In terms of how I see myself resisting or accepting something through play, I feel that any sort of physical experimentation is essential in learning new things, especially in what I personally enjoy doing. While my personal hobbies are admittedly uncommon among my peers, it is my honest opinion that anything, including music, sports, art, and countless other activities, can be learned by anyone with the proper exposure in the proper fashion.

I find that while the development of new technologies is imperative in our advancement, people seem to be getting more and more dependent on the trivial aspects of these new inventions, for lack of a better term. Then comes the question of resistance—that is, how do I view resistance, did it happen to me recently, and in what events did they occur? For me, resistance is not following the party line. It means that you don't have to be pressured by your peers. Just because peers might partake in actions they find enjoyable doesn't mean that I have to do it in order to be happy or satisfied. I have my own personal interests, and I will pursue them on my own accord.

In discussing how I engaged in digital activities last year when compared to this year, nothing greatly has changed. Last year, most of my digital activities came from homework and watching an occasional Youtube video. For example, I took notes on various subjects when researching topics on internet. I also wrote compositions for English, lab reports for Science, and research papers for a plethora of history projects, all of which were on Google Docs. As for the YouTube videos, I watched various clips on topics in my current study. I listened to performances to help me with the music I was playing as well. I sometimes use my parents' phone because it has a metronome and a tuner that I can use when practicing piano and cello, since the apps on the phone are much more portable and practical. I also completed online courses a few years back on various platforms.

With regard to researching things, I love to read, fence, and play my two instruments (piano and cello). The only reason I don't read as much these days is because of my constantly growing pile of schoolwork. Considering that I am already a junior, a whole hour of sitting down to read won't really help with my studies. I love to fence because, well, who doesn't like to poke other people with long metal sticks? As for my instruments, my only explanation is that listening to music is one thing. *Playing* it is another. I don't really have any sort of internet account except for my school email, so the only way (and possible they best way) to interact with people is to talk with them in person. On a device, nobody knows how the other person is feeling except for that person. It's also pretty easy to misinterpret the things people type or text. However, when I talk to someone, it just feels more natural and I feel more comfortable expressing how I feel that way. I would emphasize that digital activities do not play any significant role in my life. I don't really do much in terms of digital activities. Outside of school, the most I do is watch videos, research, and listen to music. Yes, electronics are extremely important in this day and age, but I don't feel like they are weighing down on my productivity and lifestyle as much as other things.

As a sort of return to the core purpose of the project in general, I think the research we did as a group was rather interesting. Prior to the start of the research process, I had already done research myself for projects, both in school and out. Of course, while I was capable of handling myself in independent research, cooperative research (as well as being the research subjects, of course) was a new concept to me. As to be expected, I was the tiniest bit apprehensive as the process itself began, but I quickly was able to draw connections between the research we did here and my previous and current research experience. By connecting my different backgrounds, I now have the best of both worlds when doing any sort of research, and I feel like my various experiences put together create a sort of network that I can now draw from and incorporate into any new endeavor. Another aspect of the research we did together that I found to be very illustrative was the act of looking upon myself as a person. I, like most people, had done this before, as self-reflection is something very useful in making future decisions. What made this experience unique was the act of communicating my views of myself with others. I can say that, with confidence, this project has, above all, developed my ability to accurately communicate my feelings with others in a more emotionally on-point and concise way. It is my hope that this project can show others that while some things we do may only have subtle differences, it is these minutiae that, when interlocked together, produce a form of personal growth achievable in no other way.

Child-Parent Research: Towards an Ethical Process for Avoiding Being PRICED out of Research

Anthony J. Onwuegbuzie

1   Towards an Ethical Process for Avoiding Being PRICED out of Research

Al-Karaouine mosque and university in Fez, Morocco, founded on Islamic tradition in 859 AD by Princess Fatima al-Fihri, the daughter of a wealthy merchant, was the first degree-granting university in the world. Students attending this university were taught grammar, mathematics, astronomy, and medicine (Glenday, 2013). Since the establishment of this university more than 1,100 years ago, tertiary institutions worldwide have been considered to represent the primary source for education in general and expert knowledge and skills in particular, containing intelligent faculty members who generate theory and disseminate research findings pertaining to issues that serve the needs of various stakeholders in their communities and beyond (Dorn, 2017; Geiger, 2015; Gleason, 2018). However, in recent years, the expertise and authority of tertiary education faculty members in general and their knowledge production in particular have been challenged and undermined in a contemporary period that, in social and political discourse in the United States and beyond, is referred to as the *post-truth era*. Consistent with my contention, in 2016, the Oxford Dictionaries selected *post-truth* as its word of the year, which the Oxford Dictionaries publisher defines as an adjective "relating to or denoting circumstances in which objective facts are less influential in shaping public opinion than appeals to emotion and personal belief" (Oxford Dictionaries, 2018, para. 1). In fact, simply Googling the phrase "post-truth" yields numerous books (e.g., d'Ancona, 2017), journal articles (cf. Wolgemuth, Koro-Ljungberg, Marn, Onwuegbuzie, & Dougherty, 2018a), news stories, and Web 2.0 posts (e.g., blog posts, twitter posts, FaceBook posts) that explain how and why we are now operating in a post-truth era, as well as how to address it (e.g., d'Ancona, 2017).

This post-truth era has been distinguished by discourses that are no longer anchored in T/truth. Consequently, it has motivated at least some, if not many, academicians not only to rethink (education) research, methodology, and policy (cf. Wolgemuth et al., 2018a), but also to rethink theory, data, fact, evidence, and validity/legitimation in (educational) policy-making, as well as the onto-ethico-epistemology of (educational) research and evaluation ethics. Moreover, in this ongoing era of post-truth, T/truth has been problematized, amidst continuously shifting and unstable intersections among policy, methodology, and evidence (cf. Wolgemuth, Koro-Ljungberg, Marn, Onwuegbuzie, & Dougherty, 2018a). Further, this era has generated both challenges and opportunities for scholars and researchers to reconsider the purpose, justification, and value of their work, as well as the validity/legitimation of their knowledge claims (Wolgemuth, Koro-Ljungberg, Marn, Onwuegbuzie, & Dougherty, 2018b).

During this process of rethinking and re-evaluation, researchers and evaluators have been encouraged to (re-)consider their roles, disposition, positionality, and, most importantly, humanness in the research process (see, e.g., Frost, 2016). Even the roles, characteristics, and experiences of methodologists have been questioned (cf. Forzani, Abrams, & Onwuegbuzie, in press). However, the assumption underlying virtually all of this discourse is that researchers/evaluators are of *adult* age. And this assumption rules out child-parent research, unless the child is of adult age.

Yet, as argued and demonstrated by Onwuegbuzie, Mallette, and Mallette (2010)—a child-parent-colleague team—research *can* be conducted by children. Indeed, there are several developmental psychological theories that support this contention, including cognitive, constructivist, and socio-cultural theories. Cognitive theories include Piaget's theory of cognitive development (cf. Piaget, 1950, 1952). This theory was based on his interviews of children that represented the form of child-parent research that Abrams, Schaefer, and Ness (Chapter 1) refer to as the *child-as-co-constructor-of-knowledge*. According to this theory (see Table A.1), children who are (approximately) between the ages of 7 and 11 years enter what Piaget called a *concrete operational stage*, which, among other aspects, is characterized by children (a) being able to think logically about concrete events; (b) having thoughts that are becoming more logical and organized; (c) being able to recognize logical relationships among elements in a serial order, and, therefore, perform transitive inferences (e.g., if A is smaller than B, and B is smaller than C, then A must be smaller than C; i.e., *transitivity*); (d) being able to sort objects in an order according to shape, size, or any other characteristic (i.e., *seriation*); (e) being able to name and to identify sets of objects according to shape, size, or other characteristic (i.e., *classification*); (f) beginning to use inductive logic (i.e., reasoning from specific information to a general principle); (g) can take into account multiple aspects of a problem to solve it (i.e., *decentering*); (h) understanding new kinds of logical operations wherein they can mentally reverse actions (i.e., *reversibility*); (i) understanding that number, length, liquid, mass, weight, area, and volume are unrelated to the arrangement or appearance of the object or items (i.e., *conservation*); and (j) can solve problems that apply to actual (i.e., concrete) objects or events, but not abstract concepts or hypothetical tasks. These traits might suggest that children aged 7 to 11 have the ability to conduct qualitative research, which often is characterized by the use of inductive logic—at least to some degree. Also, in terms of quantitative analyses, children aged 7 to 11 also can conduct basic forms of descriptive analyses (e.g., frequency counts, proportions). That is, because of their propensity for transitivity, seriation, classification, decentering, reversibility, and conservation, being at the concrete-operational development stage does not prevent primary or secondary school students engaging in an array of data collection techniques (e.g., interviewing, counting observations) and data analysis strategies (e.g., counting observations, summarizing interview data).

TABLE A.1   Piaget's stages of intellectual development (cognitive-developmental theory)

Stage	Approximate age	Major characteristic
Sensorimotor	Infancy (birth to age 2)	Thought restricted to *action schemes* (children begin to record experiences symbolically); knowledge of the world is limited (but developing) because it is based on physical interactions/experiences; *object permanence* is acquired at approximately 7 months of age (memory); physical development (mobility) allows the child to begin developing new intellectual abilities
Preoperational	Preschool (age 2 to 7)	*Representational thought* (i.e., children can think about objects and people that are not present); thought intuitive but not logical; intelligence demonstrated via symbols; use of language matures, and memory and imagination are developed, but *thinking occurs in a nonlogical, nonreversable manner*; *egocentric thinking predominates*

(cont.)

TABLE A.1   Piaget's stages of intellectual development (cognitive-developmental theory) *(cont.)*

Stage	Approximate age	Major characteristic
Concrete operational	Childhood (age 7 to 11)	*Systematic logical thought* occurs but only with regard to concrete objects; understanding of new kinds of logical operations in which *they can mentally reverse actions*; evidence of seriation (i.e., ability to sort objects in an order according to size, shape, or any other characteristic); *transitivity* (i.e., ability to recognize logical relationships among elements in a serial order, and perform "transitive inferences" [e.g., If A is slower than B, and B is slower than C, then A must be slower than C]); classification (i.e., the ability to name and to identify sets of objects according to appearance, size, or other elements, including the idea that one set of objects can include another); decentering (e.g., child takes into account multiple aspects of a problem to solve it); reversibility (e.g., child understands that numbers or objects can be changed, then returned to their original state); *conservation* (i.e., seven types: number, length, mass, weight, liquid, area, volume; understanding that these attributes of items are unrelated to the arrangement or appearance of the object or items)
Formal operational	Adolescence and adulthood (from age 11)	*Abstract, logical thought* (i.e., intelligence demonstrated via the logical use of symbols related to abstract concepts); *propositional thought* (i.e., "If...then"); hypothetical-deductive reasoning used (i.e., development of hypotheses, and systematic deduction of the best path to follow in solving the problem)

Contrastingly, children who are (approximately) 12 years of age and older enter what Piaget called a *formal operational stage*, which is characterized, among other elements, by children (a) being able to think abstractly and to reason about hypothetical problems; (b) beginning to use hypothetical-deductive logic (i.e., reasoning from a general principle to specific information; applying logical reasoning to hypothetical situations to draw conclusions from the available information); (c) engaging in propositional thought (i.e., "If...then" logic); and (d) beginning to think more about philosophical, social, political, moral, and ethical issues that necessitate theoretical and abstract reasoning. These traits might suggest that children aged 12 and older, in addition to being able to conduct qualitative research, have the ability to conduct quantitative research, which often is characterized by the use of deductive logic. Therefore, Piaget's theory of cognitive development indicates that children can operate as a child-as-researcher who Abrams, Schaefer, and Ness (Chapter 9) refer to as a co-constructor of both knowledge and research—which represents the research relationship that comes closest to reaching equity and that promotes maximum participation by children in the research. Piaget's theory supports my own experiences as a secondary school mathematics teacher, wherein I was able to teach my students, starting from 11 years old, how to conduct research and to write up research findings using the scientific method (cf. Onwuegbuzie, 1986). Moreover, I even started writing a mathematics textbook with my 11-year-old students but, unfortunately, never had the opportunity to complete this project because I left teaching to enter higher education. And just as Piaget believed that children should take an active part in their learning, it makes sense that children should take an active part in the research process.

Selman's (1971) development of social role-taking ability is another theory that can be used to support my argument that research can be conducted by children. According to Selman, a matured role-taking ability allows people better to appreciate how their actions will affect others. Moreover, a failure to develop the ability to role-take will lead a person to judge incorrectly that others are behaving solely due to external factors. Table A.2 provides Selman's (1971) four stages of social role-taking. It can be seen from this table that the self-reflective, role-taking stage (i.e., Stage 2; 8 to 10 years old) marks a period when child-parent research can be fruitful, although the manual role-taking stage (i.e., Stage 3; 10 to 12 years old) lends itself even more to child-parent research. Indeed, because 10- to 12-year old students know that both they and another person can simultaneously consider their own views and those of the other and that they can step outside an interaction with another person and see how a third person would interpret it, students at the beginning of their secondary schooling can begin to interpret the extant literature and their own findings. However, the social and conventional system role-taking stage (i.e., Stage 4; 12 to 15 years old) can be especially productive because children are aware of social conventions.

TABLE A.2   Selman's (1971) stages of social role-taking

Stage	Approximate age	Major characteristic
Stage 0: Egocentric viewpoints	3 to 6 years	Children cannot distinguish between their own thoughts and feelings and those of other children. They do not realize that other people's ideas, thoughts, feelings, intentions, and motivations might differ from their own.
Stage 1: Social-informational role-taking	6 to 8 years	Children realize that others have their own views but believe that those views differ from their own views because they are based on different information. They are unable to judge their own actions from another's viewpoint.
Stage 2: Self-reflective role-taking	8 to 10 years	Children realize that the views of others stem from their own purposes or set of values. They can expect another person's judgment of their own actions. Yet, they still cannot process simultaneously their own views and those of another.
Stage 3: Manual role-taking	10 to 12 years	Children realize that both they and another person can simultaneously consider their own views and those of the other. They are able to step outside an interaction with another person and see how a third person would interpret it.
Stage 4: Social and conventional system role-taking	12 to 15 years and older	Children are aware of the shared points of view of the social system (i.e., social conventions). They realize that mutual awareness of views does not always yield complex understanding.

Vygotsky's (1978) theory of social development provides another support for child-parent research. According to Vygotsky's (1978) theory, social interaction is essential for cognitive development. Vygotsky believed that learning is facilitated by someone with more knowledge. That is, Vygotsky's theory supports children as active learners (i.e., researchers) and parents as facilitators, resulting in a reciprocal learning/research experience. According to Vygotsky (1978), a young child follows a parent's example and gradually develops the ability to undertake certain research tasks without assistance. Subsequently, the role of child-parent research is for parents to provide children with experiences that lie within their *zones of proximal development* (i.e., the difference between what a child can do without help and what he/she can do with help), thereby advancing and maintaining their individual research skills.

Child-parent research also can be supported by Bruner's (1990) Theory of Constructivism. Bruner (1990) developed three stages of representation: *enactive* (i.e., knowledge is largely in the form of motor responses; children might be able to perform a physical task better than describing it, showing that the learner is more in the enactive stage of representation); *iconic* (i.e., knowledge more largely represents visual images; when presented with new information, it can be helpful for children in this stage of representation to be given a visual display); and *symbolic* (i.e., knowledge mostly takes the form of arbitrary words, mathematical symbols, and other symbol systems). Bruner contended that learners go through various stages of development but these stages are not age dependent. Rather, the instruction dictates the stage that learners utilize when constructing interpretations of the concept. According to Bruner (2009), "(w) e begin with the hypothesis that any subject can be taught effectively in some intellectually honest form to any child at any stage of development" (p. 33). Thus, Bruner's theory suggests that, to some degree, child-parent research can be introduced at primary/elementary school.

As a final example, Bandura's (1977) Social Learning Theory, a theory of learning and social behavior, posits that people learn from one another via observation, imitation, and modeling. According to social learning theory, there are four requirements for people to learn and model behavior, specifically, attention, retention (remembering to what attention was being paid, such as symbolic coding, cognitive organization, mental images, symbolic rehearsal, and motor rehearsal), reproduction (ability to reproduce the behavior or image), and motivation (having a good reason to imitate, which includes promised [i.e., imagined incentives] and vicarious [i.e., seeing/recalling the reinforced model] motives). Therefore, this theory suggests that child-parent research can take place under the conditions of attention, retention, reproduction, and motivation.

The theories of Piaget, Selman, Vygotsky, Bruner, and Bandura, represent just five of the many developmental psychological theories that support child-parent research. Therefore, the question should not be *whether* child-parent research should occur. Rather, the six important questions for information collection and problem solving, known as the Six Ws or 5W1H—namely, Why?, Who? Where? When?, What?, and How?—can be used to advance the notion of child-parent research. Each of these questions will be answered respectively in the following sections.

2   *Why* Should Child-Parent Research Be Conducted?

Conducting child-parent research potentially has many benefits. Optimally, in child-parent research, when there is familiarity (Fitzgerald, Graham, Smith, & Taylor, 2010) and a healthy relationship between the child and the adult, children are transformed to "social actors, active citizens, and sentient beings who help bring and create knowledge when participating as researchers and co-researchers" (Abrams, Schaefer, & Ness, Chapter 9). Moreover, when the child-parent research process reflects ethical symmetry wherein the child is treated as a fully fledged researcher (Christensen & Prout, 2002), the child is empowered to make research-based decisions at the various stages of the research process (i.e., research conceptualization, research planning, research implementation, and research utilization)—which is advocated by critical dialectical pluralists (cf. Onwuegbuzie & Frels, 2013). As Charlotte Abrams (Chapter 9) concluded: "Being an adolescent researcher has opened my eyes to how much more there is to learn and that research is an ongoing process because life is full of changes"; as Molly Kurpis (Chapter 9) declared: "These experiences pave a way to fun and original ways of interpreting research instead of boringly scrolling through articles written by old fancy people for hours on the Internet"; and as Eric Ness (Chapter 9) yearned: "It is my hope that this project can show others that while some things we do may only have subtle differences, it is these minutiae that, when interlocked together, produce a form of personal growth achievable in no other way."

Child-parent research also has the potential to enrich the relationship between the parent and child, by adding a *professional* dimension to the relationship—a dimension that otherwise likely would never have occurred. In turn, this dimension could improve the quality of the familial relationship. In Chapter 4, Kathleen Alley documents this enhancement in her relationship with her daughter Cassandra, as follows:

> I believe whole-heartedly that the stance we took as co-inquirers many times throughout Cassandra's teen and emerging adult years supported

our journey as parent and child, helping us to successfully traverse the bumps we met along the way and resulting in the strong adult friendship that is now blossoming between us.

Another benefit of conducting child-parent research is that the research can address the interest or problem belonging to the child, the parent, or a mutual interest or problem. Regardless, this form of research can lead to shared problem-solving and shared responsibility. These elements, in turn, yield a shared understanding of the interest or problem.

Further, by the child-as-researcher serving as a co-constructor of both knowledge and research (Abrams et al., Chapter 1), child-parent research also has the potential to make *thick description* (Ryle, 1949) more likely, allowing both the child and the parents better to understand and to process the context of the underlying experience, behavior, or phenomenon (Ryle, 1971). Also, this rationale for conducting child-parent research is consistent with Denzin's (1989) notion of thick description, which involves doing

> more than record what a person is doing. It goes beyond mere fact and surface appearances. It presents detail, context, emotion, and the webs of social relationships that join persons to one another. Thick description evokes emotionality and self-feelings. It inserts history into experience. It establishes the significance of an experience, or the sequence of events, for the person or persons in question. In thick description, the voices, feelings, actions, and meanings of interacting individuals are heard. (p. 83)

In other words, through this interpretive characteristic of description that emerges from ethical symmetry, data collected, analyzed, and/or interpreted by only the parent (i.e., thin[ner] description) is supplemented by richer and thicker descriptions that emanate from the child's collaboration. More specifically, as a result of this ethical symmetry, the child-parent researchers are more able to portray "a sense of the emotions, thoughts, and perceptions" of research participants (Holloway, 1997, p. 154).

3   *Who* Should Conduct Child-Parent Research?

As the phrase *child-parent research* suggests, this form of research involves one or more children and one or more parent. However, bearing in mind the changes in family structure worldwide in recent decades, it is too limiting to restrict the adult partner of child-parent research only to parents. Rather, all *parental* figures should be included in the definition of child-parent research, including step-parents, grandparents, and uncles and aunts. Interestingly, Guy Merchant's is a grandfather of the child that he studies (Chapter 2). As a personal example, a few years ago, I conducted research with my nephew, Osarobo Omomoh, examining characteristics of article titles used by researchers.

Further, child-parent research should not only have to involve the child and parent(s); it could include one or more *non-parental* co-researchers. Indeed, as a non-parental co-researcher, I have been involved in several child-parent research projects over the years. For example, several years ago, I co-delivered a presentation at the *International Mixed Methods Conference* in Baltimore with a 15-year old high school student, Kasey Mallette, and her mother Marla Mallette (Onwuegbuzie et al., 2010), whereby Kasey presented her two mixed methods research studies, one which she conducted as a middle-grade student at Unity Point School, Carbondale, IL., while she was in the seventh grade (Mallette, 2008), in which she used experimental techniques to investigate how the way in which a stimuli is encoded affects retrieval from long-term memory among seventh- and eighth-grade (n = 118) students; and a follow-up study that she conducted the following year, while she was in the eighth grade (Mallette, 2009), wherein she examined the difference between episodic memory and semantic memory among eighth-grade students as they took a field trip to Springfield, IL, to study Illinois history and government. Deservedly, both of Kasey's applied psychology studies received an outstanding paper award in both the local science fair and the regional science fair. Also, her papers received the highest honor possible at the state of Illinois science fair. And, to my knowledge, at that time, Kasey was the youngest person not only to present at the *International Mixed Methods Conference* but at any international research conference! (Since then Charlotte Abrams—then age 13—has this distinction given that she presented with Molly Kurpis and Eric Ness at the Piaget Society Conference in Amsterdam in 2018!) It was fascinating to observe the interactions between mother and daughter during the whole research process! I recall vividly teaching Kasey virtually (i.e., via GoToMeeting) one Saturday night before the conference how to use SPSS to compute a correlation coefficient and conduct an independent samples t test so that she could use these inferential analyses for the data that she had collected, whose findings she ended up presenting at the conference. It made both Marla and I so proud and so much in awe to watch her presenting t values, p values, correlation coefficients, scatter plots, bar charts, and emergent themes—to name a few elements—at the age of 15!

At the same *International Mixed Methods Conference*, I co-presented a research paper with Rebecca Frels, and her son, Jason (Frels, Frels, &

Onwuegbuzie, 2010), who served as lead presenter. We presented on the topic of geographic information systems (GIS). What was most impressive about this presentation was that Jason did not possess a graduate degree at the time! Jason, who is an expert in GIS, mentored her mother and me through our GIS journey. Once we had obtained a basic knowledge of GIS—for example, by flying from Texas to Georgia to take a 1-day course in GIS, reading books on GIS (e.g., Elwood & Cope, 2009; Steinberg & Steinberg, 2006) and numerous research articles (e.g., Fielding & Cisneros-Puebla, 2009)—we decided to take our knowledge to another level by co-writing an article on it, which was published subsequently in the *International Journal of Multiple Research Approaches* (i.e., Frels, Frels, & Onwuegbuzie, 2011) and have used it to inform several of our subsequent works (e.g., Onwuegbuzie & Frels, 2016).

A few years later, I had the pleasure of co-presenting a qualitative research methodology workshop at the 13th Annual Thinking Qualitatively Workshop Series, Edmonton, Alberta, Canada with three of my doctoral students, Rachel N. Smith, Valerie Tharp Byers, and Eunjin Hwang, as well as Eunjin's daughter, Chaerin Park, who was only 8 years old at the time. She performed many roles during the workshop, including playing the role of an 8-year-old girl being interviewed by me to illustrate to the workshop participants how adults can effectively interview children. An interesting aspect of my relationship with Eunjin and Chaerin is that because Eunjin was a single mother, Chaerin would accompany her mother to my classes. Therefore, over the space of the three semesters before our workshop, Chaerin sat in a quantitative research class, a qualitative research class, and a mixed methods research class that I taught to Eunjin's doctoral cohort. As a result, at only 8 years old, Chaerin was aware about the so-called *paradigm wars* between qualitative research purists and quantitative research purists. She quickly learned the importance of respecting each paradigm. In fact, a funny story emerged during the workshop. Specifically, when Chaerin was asked by one of the participants if she liked qualitative research, she replied that she did, but later told her mother and me that if "this had been a mixed methods research workshop, she would have told this attendee that she liked mixed methods research!"

The research projects that I conducted with Marla and Kasey, Rebecca and Jason, and Eunjin and Chaerin, all involved child-mother research partnerships. Although I have never served as a co-researcher in a child-father research partnership, I did have the pleasure of observing such a partnership involving the late prolific Professor Isadore Newman and one of his sons, David Newman, which led to several published works (e.g., Newman & Newman, 2012).

As can be seen, even though I do not have any children, this has not prevented me from being involved in child-parent research. And what is interesting about participating in these research projects is that I have been able to serve the role as an *active-member researcher* (Adler & Adler, 1987), one who becomes involved with the central activities of the group, sometime even taking on activities that advance the group—without being a full member of the group (i.e., a *complete-member researcher*; Adler & Adler, 1987).

4   *Where* Should Child-Parent Research Be Conducted?

There are two dimensions pertaining to where child-parent research should take place: (a) the location(s) in which the data are collected, analyzed, and interpreted; and (b) the location(s) in which the experience or construct being examined took place. Therefore, for instance, the child-parent data in all seven studies were collected, analyzed, and interpreted at the family's home. In contrast, not all experiences being documented occurred at the family's home. Specifically, in Chapter 4, Kathleen M. Alley co-writes with her daughter, Cassandra R. Skrobot, about the anxiety disorder that Cassandra experienced during college. Also, in Chapter 8, Bogum Yoon re-analyzes data that she collected while her two sons, Junsuk and Junhyuck, were in beginning English-as-a-Second-Language (ESL) programs at their school.

It should be noted that child-parent research can involve data collected and/ or generated via both offline and online spaces. Online spaces include situated communication that arise via modes such as Facebook, Twitter, blogs, forums, wikis, and listservs (cf. Gerber, Abrams, Curwood, & Magnifico, 2016). And in the age of *big data* (cf. Gerber, Lynch, & Onwuegbuzie, in press), the opportunity for collecting virtual data is increasing exponentially. Interestingly, only the study involving Kathleen and Cassandra (Chapter 4) and involving Bogum Yoon and Junsuk and Junhyuck neither involved the use of online spaces to collect or to generate data.

5   *When* Should Child-Parent Research Be Conducted?

As discussed earlier via developmental psychological theories, child-parent research can involve the participation of children at a very early age. And this notion is supported by the set of chapters in this groundbreaking book. In particular, Guy Merchant's grandson was 7 years old (Chapter 2); Sarah Prestridge's son, Cooper, was studied between the ages 8 and 12 (Chapter 3); Roach O'Keefe's son, named "E," was studied between the ages of 2 and 5 (Chapter 5); and one of Joanne O'Mara's and Linda Laidlaw's children was 3 years old and one was 6 years old (Chapter 7). It should be noted that the younger the child in the child-parent relationship, then the more difficult it is for the parent to ensure ethical symmetry in the research study such that the child is simultaneously a co-constructor of knowledge and of research.

6   *What* Should Be the Subject of Child-Parent Research?

Virtually, any research topic can be examined. However, the utility of child-parent research is increased substantially when the underlying research topic reflects the child's interest and gives voice to the child. And, ideally, this utility is optimized when there is mutual interest in the research topic.

7   *How* Should Child-Parent Research Occur?

Child-parent research can be conducted informally and formally. Further, the child-parent research can involve (a) researching the child(ren) exclusively, (b) researching the parental figure(s) exclusively, (c) researching the child(ren) and parental figure(s) exclusively, (d) researching one or more other people, or (e) researching one or more other people, alongside researching the child(ren) and/or parental figure(s). Alternatively stated, using Bronfenbrenner's (1979) ecological systems model, child-parent research can take place at one of four levels, or layers, of environment that impact a child(ren)'s and/or parental figure's development: (a) the microsystem (Level 1): the immediate environment with which the child(ren) and/or parental figure(s) closely interacts (e.g., home, classroom, playground, recreation center, religious institution); (b) the mesosystem (Level 2): the other systems in which the child(ren) and/or parental figure(s) spends time, such as family, school, or work; (c) the exosystem (Level 3): the systems by which the child(ren) and/or parental figure(s) might be influenced but of which he/she/they is/are not directly a member, such as the relationships among school teachers, school administrators, work colleagues, or other close family members of the child(ren) and/or parental figure(s); or (d) the macrosystem (Level 4): the larger cultural world surrounding the child(ren) and/or parental figure(s), such as the society at large that includes societal belief systems, cultural norms, laws, or policies that indirectly influence the child(ren) and/or parental figure(s). Figure A.1 illustrates this mapping of Bronfenbrenner's (1979) ecological systems model onto the child-parent process.

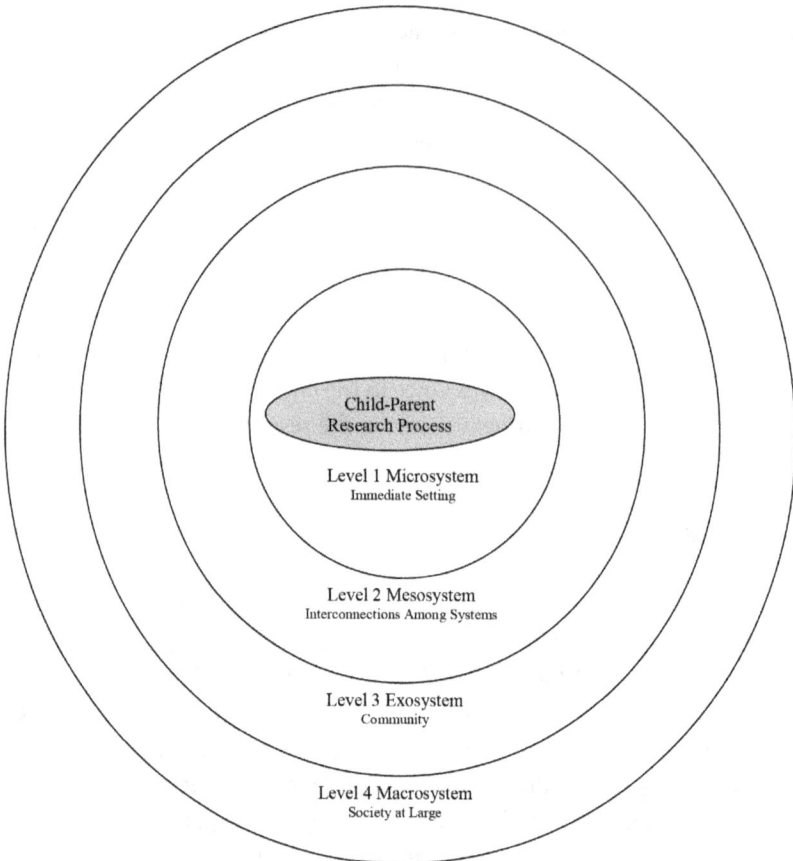

FIGURE A.1   A visual representation of Bronfenbrenner's (1979) ecological systems model
being mapped onto the child-parent process

With respect to research approaches, child-parent research can represent quantitative research approaches, qualitative research approaches, and mixed methods research approaches. In particular, in terms of child-parent research involving the child(ren) and/or the parental figure(s), quantitative research approaches especially can involve use of a descriptive research design or an experimental research design—specifically, a single subjects design; qualitative research approaches can involve, but are not limited to, use of an intrinsic case study design, some form of grounded theory research design, an ethnographic design, some form of phenomenological research design (i.e., a descriptive phenomenological research design or an interpretive phenomenological research design), some form of autoethnography, a narrative research design, oral history, and life history.

However, I recommend that, whenever possible, mixed methods research approaches—which represents "the class of research where the researcher mixes or combines quantitative and qualitative research techniques, methods, approaches, concepts or language into a single study" (Johnson & Onwueg-buzie, 2004, p. 17; see also Johnson, Onwuegbuzie, & Turner, 2007)—be used for child-parent research because (a) it involves the mixing or integration of descriptive precision (e.g., words, images) yielded by qualitative instruments (e.g., interviews) and the empirical precision (i.e., numbers) yielded by a quan-titative measure(s) (e.g., surveys); (b) it can increase the child-parent research-ers' level of creativity (e.g., Onwuegbuzie, 2012) in both meaning making and reporting of the findings; and (c) it can lead to richer, thicker data. Further, using mixed methods research approaches can facilitate the pursuit of mastery over self and the world, understanding through recomposition, complexity reduction, innovation, truthfulness, and meaningfulness (Dzurec & Abraham, 1993). Additionally, as outlined by Greene, Caracelli, and Graham (1989), the use of quantitative and qualitative research approaches can help child-parent researches to fulfill the following goals: *triangulation* (i.e., compare findings from the qualitative data with the quantitative results); *complementarity* (i.e., seek illustration, elaboration, enhancement, and clarification of the results from one analytical strand [e.g., quantitative] with findings from the other analytical strand [e.g., qualitative]); *development* (i.e., use the results from one analytical strand to help inform the other analytical strand); *initiation* (i.e., dis-cover paradoxes and contradictions that emerge when findings from the two analytical strands are compared that might lead to a re-framing of the research question[s]); and *expansion* (i.e., expand breadth and range of a study by using multiple analytical strands for different study phases).

8   Towards an Evaluation of the Chapters in *Child-Parent Research Reimagined*

Because, to date, with few exceptions (e.g., Abrams et al., Chapter 1; Kalantzis & Cope, Foreword to this volume), relatively few works appear to have been published that describe *how* child-parent research has been conducted, evalu-ating these applications has logical appeal. Therefore, my goal for the remain-der of this afterword is to outline how the authors in this innovative book have applied child-parent research.

8.1   *Method of Evaluating Chapters*
All seven outstanding chapters (i.e., Chapters 2–8) were uploaded to QDA Miner Version 5.0.30 (Provalis Research, 2019). Then, this computer-assisted mixed methods data analysis software program was used to conduct a constant comparison analysis (Glaser, 1965) of the seven chapters. Constant comparison

analysis originally was designed as an analytical approach for grounded theory research (Glaser & Strauss, 1967); however, this analysis approach can be utilized outside of grounded theory (Fram, 2013) and with any narrative or textual data (Leech & Onwuegbuzie, 2008). Figure 2 displays a screenshot of the first page of Chapter 6 that was coded via QDA Miner 5.0.30.

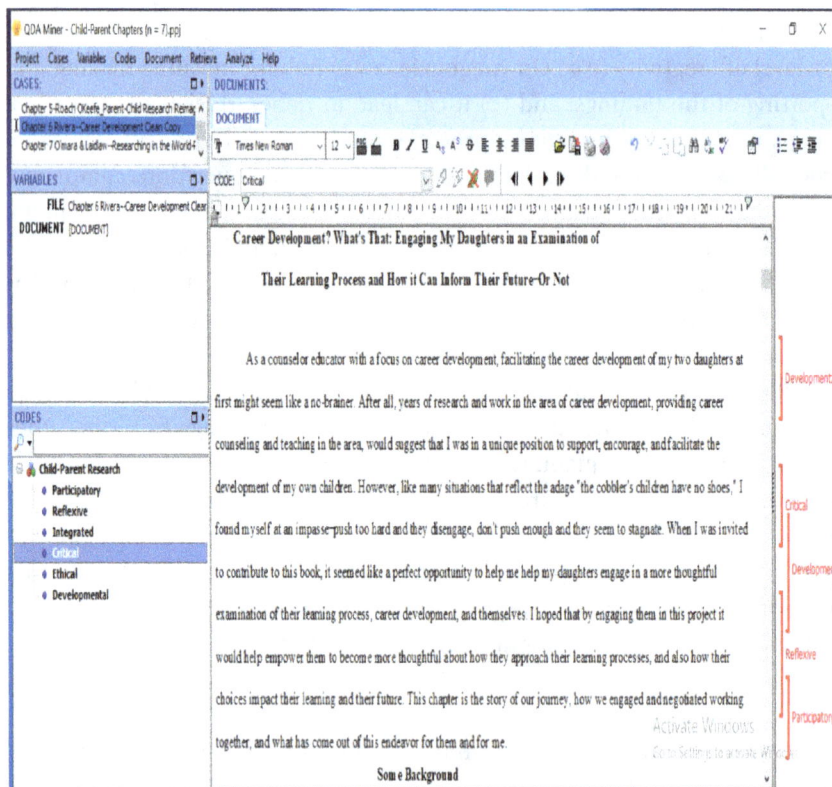

FIGURE A.2　Screenshot of the first page of Chapter 6 coded via QDA Miner 5.0.30

8.2　*Results from Evaluating Chapters*

The constant comparison analysis revealed the following six themes that suggest good practices for conducting child-parent research: (a) *Participatory*, (b) *Reflexive*, (c) *Integrated*, (d) *Critical*, (e) *Ethical*, and (f) *Developmental*. Interestingly, these themes produced the acronym PRICED. Each of these themes is described in the following sections.

8.2.1　Participatory

The *participatory* theme refers to active involvement by the child(ren) and parental figure(s), as well as by any other co-researchers. These co-researchers could be other family members or individuals with important ties to the child(ren) and/or parental figure(s) (e.g., work colleagues, teachers of the child[ren], mentors). At its optimum, participatory approaches involve stakeholders serving as co-researchers alongside the child-parent researchers.

Of the seven chapters, two of them (i.e., Chapters 4 and 6) provide examples of the promotion of participatory approaches within a child-parent framework. Specifically, Chapter 4—a very interesting chapter—reveals that Kathleen M. Alley co-writes, via a collaborative autoethnographic inquiry, with her daughter Cassandra R. Skrobot about the anxiety disorder that Cassandra experienced during college. Although this is extremely noteworthy, the participatory nature of this child-parent project would have been enhanced if, consistent with critical dialectical pluralism (Onwuegbuzie & Frels, 2013), the voice of both Kathleen and Cassandra had permeated the chapter and that the voice of Cassandra had not been filtered through the voice of Kathleen. Indeed, this point is made by Mary Kalantzis and Bill Cope in their excellent foreword: "Kathleen Alley's Cassandra is a co-author, however the voice of the anxious researcher is Kathleen's".

A participatory approach also was promoted in Rivera, Rivera-Larkin, and Rivera-Larkin's excellent Chapter 6, wherein Lourdes M. Rivera, a counselor educator, co-writes jointly with her daughters Nora Rivera-Larkin and Dahlia Rivera-Larkin regarding the process with which they "engage[d] in a more thoughtful examination of their learning process, career development, and themselves." Although the voices of Nora and Dahlia are present in the chapter, it appears that Lourdes made the methodological decisions, especially the analysis, as the following excerpts indicate: "I used an iterative process to review and analyze the responses provided by the girls in order to identify themes" and "As I reviewed their responses again, I identified and labeled themes that seemed to emerge from my reading of both of their responses." However, I applaud Lourdes for requesting feedback from her daughters regarding her initial interpretations: "At this point, I shared the tables with the labeled themes with them and excerpts from their responses that informed the themes and asked them to review them and provide me with their feedback." Yet, the analytical process would have been more participatory in nature if Nora and Dahlia had participated in the analysis (i.e., identification of themes) from the onset.

8.2.2   Reflexivity
As stated by Alvesson and Sköldberg (2009), the theme reflexivity refers to the "complex relationship between process of knowledge production and the various contexts of such processes, as well as the involvement of the knowledge

producer" (p. 8). The importance of reflexivity for critically evaluating the whole mixed methods research process has been extolled by Collins, Onwuegbuzie, Johnson, and Frels (2013). Therefore, reflexivity in child-parent research has much intuitive appeal.

Interestingly, all seven chapters provided evidence of reflexivity, whether it be reflexivity about "the ephemeral, playful, and idiosyncratic production of texts described in the two episodes" (Merchant, Chapter 2); reflexivity about "these accounts with direct speak from Cooper to illustrate what shapes his communication practices" (Prestridge, Chapter 3); reflexivity with her daughter to "tackle issues of positionality and power" (Alley & Skrobot, Chapter 4); reflexivity "to find emergent themes" (O'Keefe, Chapter 5), reflexivity about parent-research; her son's "reflexive discussions about learning, digital technology use, and research" and reflexivity about "how 'E' was learning and growing"; reflexivity by Nora about "what this experience means to her and how it influences her own pursuits" (Rivera et al., Chapter 6), reflexivity about "how their dual roles (i.e., researcher and family member) are playing out in the work itself," and reflexivity about "how one can effectively balance the role of researcher with that of mother/father/grandparent?"; reflexivity about "when Jo's son, then 6, sighed as he stared at a cigarette butt on the footpath" (O'Mara & Laidlaw, Chapter 7); or reflexivity about the periodic recordings of the siblings' schooling experiences in Grades 4 through 12 (Yoon, Chapter 8). I applaud all authors for their reflexivities and I encourage all child-parent researchers to promote reflexivity in their child-parent research.

8.2.3   Integration

Six of the seven child-parent research studies involved the use of qualitative research approaches. Prestridge (Chapter 3) was the only child-parent research that involved the use of a mixed methods research approach. Although I applaud this author for collecting, analyzing, and interpreting both qualitative and quantitative data, these two forms of data were presented separately. Therefore, I encourage child-parent researchers to consider incorporating a higher degree of integration in their studies, for example, by addressing one or more or Greene et al.'s (1989) goals of mixing. Even more integration can be obtained by using the techniques of qualitizing (i.e. transforming quantitative data [e.g., descriptive statistics] into a qualitative form that can be analyzed qualitatively) and quantitizing (i.e. converting qualitative data [e.g., themes] into numerical codes that can be analyzed statistically) (cf. Miles & Huberman, 1994; Onwuegbuzie & Leech, 2019; Onwuegbuzie & Teddlie, 2003; Sandelowski, Voils, & Knafl, 2009; Tashakkori & Teddlie, 1998). Such integration likely would enhance the meaning-making process.

8.2.4   Critical

When conducting child-parent research, it is essential that all parties involved are cognizant of the power hierarchies, differentials, and dynamics that occur at least initially and that (potentially) confront them throughout the research process. And so it is encouraging that all authors, except O'Mara and Laidlaw (Chapter 7), discussed adopting some form of critical stance when conducting child-parent research. For instance, Merchant (Chapter 2) acknowledged the following: "But because the parent-adult-researcher is a hybrid identity it is all the more complex, there are different power dynamics, and consequently different ways of securing co-operation, and withdrawing from co-operation." Similarly, Prestridge (Chapter 3) recognized that "such a power-hierarchical mother-child relationship could also restrict conversation.". O'Keefe (Chapter 5) recognized the potential power that the child has in a child-parent research study: "Moreover, the learning stories presented an ethical, authentic way for E to co-analyze the data, and for him to assert his power in the study." Yoon (Chapter 8) discussed critical literacies and the importance of "Promoting critical consciousness about the ways the world operates with power, bias, and stereotype." However, perhaps one of the most compelling discussion of power dynamics was provided by Rivera et al. (Chapter 6), as follows:

> When I invited my daughters to participate in this project, I provided them with information, described what they could expect and what I believed to be the benefits of having them engage in this project. I gave them time to think about it and eventually they agreed to work with me. But what does their consent really mean in this situation? After all, I am their mother and there is a power differential at play—am I as a parent being seen by my daughters as really giving them a choice? Did they feel a sense of obligation? Did they feel a need to please me when they consented to participate in this project? Although I repeatedly communicated that it was their choice throughout the process (particularly when they were not meeting deadlines), did they truly feel that they could say "no" to me?

Alley and Skrobot (Chapter 4) revealed that "To tackle issues of positionality and power, my daughter and I sought to be aware and reflexive." Moreover, these authors used the framework of Busier et al. (1997) for asking questions when *research intimacy* is involved: (a) "What are the sociocultural power relationships (age, gender, race, class, educational level, professional roles, etc.)?"; (b) "Are researcher and research participant on somewhat equal footing? If not, can inequities be bridged?"; and (c) "Can researcher and research participant engage in critical dialogue about the role of power in their relationships?"

Again, critical dialectical pluralism can play an important role in helping child-parent researchers develop and enhance their critical stances. Indeed, as noted by Onwuegbuzie and Frels (2013),

> critical dialectical pluralism serves as a metaparadigm by promoting the mixing or combining of at least two distinct paradigms in a manner that privileges those paradigms or worldviews (e.g., transformative-eman-cipatory, critical theory, critical race theory, critical ethnography, crit-ical quantitative research, feminist theory) that promote and sustain social justice, but, at the same time, goes beyond the existing social jus-tice-based paradigms (hence the word critical). (p. 16)

8.2.5   Ethical

Authors of all seven chapters discussed the issue of the ethics involved in some aspect of their child-parent research. A particularly compelling comment was that made by Merchant (this volume), as follows:

> I refuse to write about him in such terms. And as a result, I am caught in the horns of an ethical dilemma. No research aims, no design or ethical consent—although in my defense I must say that we regularly talk about what writing about his media play might mean. He likes the idea of see-ing Iron Man, M&M, and all the others in a book, and in fact he's recently started making books of his own with these characters in them. But a chapter in a book about how he makes videos? He doesn't quite get that, but then it's an ongoing conversation. Is that enough? I'm still not sure. Should I stop?

Another compelling statement made by Merchant was as follows: "Foremost of those challenges is how to negotiate the complex ethical terrain, of how to gain consent from children who may not be fully aware of what they are consenting to—to be part of a book that's about their videos and stories." Like Merchant (Chapter 2), Prestridge (Chapter 3), O'Keefe (Chapter 5), Rivera et al. (Chapter 6), O'Mara and Laidlaw (Chapter 7), and Yoon (Chapter 8) had sec-tions/sub-sections devoted to ethical considerations. Alley and Skrobot (Chap-ter 4) provide a useful deconstruction of the concept of ethics in child-parent research by discussing procedural ethics, ethics of practice (i.e., situational ethics), and relational ethics. Throughout their chapters, all the authors raised important ethical concerns that are specific to child-parent research. It is clear that driving their discussion throughout this chapter is the importance of child-parent researchers maximizing non-maleficence (i.e., not causing harm to others) and beneficence (i.e., working for the benefit of others). Adding to their list of ethical concerns, I recommend that child-parent researchers strive for (social) justice (i.e., making decisions based on universal principles and rules, in an impartial and warranted manner in an attempt to guarantee fair and equitable treatment of all people); fidelity (i.e., demonstrating commitment, loyalty, and commitment); professional competence (i.e., recognizing limitations and undertaking tasks within their set of skills and knowledge of the research topic explored and the findings and interpretations reported); integrity (i.e., being fair, honest, and respectful of others people's data and representing their data appropriately); scholarly responsibility (i.e., adhering to best practices via documentation [i.e., leaving an audit trail] and reflecting on the methodological and procedural choices made); social responsibility (i.e., applying awareness of the social dimensions of the underling topic); and respecting rights, dignity, and diversity (i.e., striving to eliminate bias for misrepresenting other people's data and not discriminating research participants based on their exceptionalities) (cf. Onwuegbuzie & Frels, 2016)—the sum of which provide a pathway for child-parent researchers to be meta-ethical, which implies adherence to virtue ethics (i.e., referring to the character and positionality of the researcher as the impetus for ethical behavior, as opposed to focusing on rules) and pragmatic ethics (i.e., using the standards set by communities under the assumption that communities are developing morally and in a manner that is consistent with the progression of scientific knowledge).

8.2.6   Developmental

It appears that virtually all child-parent research that involves studying some aspect of the child(ren) represents a longitudinal study to some degree. As such, a hallmark of child-parent research studies is that they are developmental in nature, at least to some degree. Interestingly, all seven sets of authors recognized this attribute, and discussed either the development of the child(ren) in the child-parent research, the development of the research relationship, and/or the development of the study. For example, Yoon (Chapter 8) discussed the identity development of her sons: "The new literacies framework helped me as a parent-researcher better understand my sons' identity development in relation to their literacy practices." O'Mara and Laidlaw (Chapter 7) revealed that their "paper developed in a dialogic manner" and that

> In writing this chapter, we have realized how our process of writing together has become dialogic in ways that were not entirely visible to

us before, as well as how our working relationship and mutual trust has developed over time and our practices of working together have evolved, drawing on new technologies and accommodating our shared understandings and capitalizing on our differences.

Table A.3 presents the PRICED themes identified in each of the seven chapters. This table indicates that of the five themes, the themes of reflexive, critical, ethical, and developmental were promoted by all seven sets of authors. Interestingly, no chapter promoted all six PRICED themes; however, three chapters promoted five of them, three chapters promoted four of them, and the remaining chapter promoted three of them. Perhaps promoting all six themes should be a goal of future child-parent research studies.

The six (i.e., PRICED) themes suggest the utility of what I call the *PRICED Process for Child-Parent Research*. Figure A.3 displays the PRICED process. This figure shows the active involvement of the child and parental figure(s) in this process. Also presented in this figure are the major phases of the PRICED process—from problem/intervention conceptualization and definition to disseminating findings and meaning. These phases can incorporate an array of research designs that vary with respect to components such as time orientation (i.e., concurrently [i.e., when the different strands occur approximately at the same time and are independent], sequentially [i.e., the strands occur in sequence], or iteratively), emphasis (one or more strands are given more weight in answering the research question[s] than are the other strands), and degree of integration (i.e., the degree to which the strands occur seamlessly) (see, e.g., Leech & Onwuegbuzie, 2009). Interestingly, to a large degree, these six themes echo the statement of Abrams et al. (Chapter 1): "The child-as-researcher continuum also calls attention to the elements we see as inherent in such investigations and discoveries: dialogue, critical reflection, ethics, tension, and participation," thereby providing incremental validity to the PRICED process.

As can be seen from Figure A.3, these phases are not linear; rather, they represent a dynamic, continuous, iterative, interactive, synergistic, integrative, xenophilous, holistic, integral, and developmental process. By *dynamic*, I am implying that each child-parent team should be characterized by energetic and effective action. By *continuous*, I mean that each phase moves directly into the next phase, whether the phase be an earlier or a later phase. By *iterative*, I mean that the phases are recursive (as can be seen by the two-sided arrows in A.3), implying that a later phase might lead to the return of an earlier phase(s). By *interactive*, I mean that each phase is linked to (i.e., dependent on) all the other phases. By *synergistic*, I mean that the PRICED process is consistent with Hall and Howard's (2008) four core principles for synergistic approaches:

TABLE A.3   Themes identified in each of the seven chapters

| Theme | \- | \- | \- | Chapter | \- | \- | \- |
| | 2 | 3 | 4 | 5 | 6 | 7 | 8 |
	Media Transformations: Working with Iron Man	Re-Designing Teaching for Tweens in Times of Streaks, Likes and Gamers	High Anxiety: A Collaborative Auto-ethnographic Inquiry	Remixing Digital Play in the Early Years: A Child-Parent Collaboration	Career Development? What's That: Engaging My Daughters in an Examination of Their Learning Process and How It Can Inform Their Future—Or Not	Researching and Parenting in the iWorld: The Dialogism of Family Life	A Parent-Researcher's Reanalysis of Adolescent Immigrants' Literacy Experiences: Methodological and Theoretical Insight on Parent-Child Research
Participatory					✓		
Reflexive	✓	✓	✓		✓	✓	✓
Integrated		✓	✓	✓	✓		
Critical	✓	✓	✓	✓	✓	✓	✓
Ethical	✓	✓	✓	✓	✓	✓	✓
Developmental	✓	✓	✓	✓	✓		✓

- synthesizing information obtained from the multiple phases of a child-parent research study produces meaning to a greater extent than would have occurred otherwise
- using a dialectical PRICED approach whereby multiple philosophical assumptions and stances of the child(ren)/parental figure(s) are integrated
- treating with equal importance findings and interpretations that stem from all components and phases, and integrating these findings and interpretations into meta-inferences (i.e., inferences stemming from both the qualitative and quantitative findings being combined into a coherent whole; Tashakkori & Teddlie, 1998)
- balancing the multiple roles and responsibilities of the PRICED team

By *integrative*, I mean that the PRICED process facilitates multiple and diverse approaches, yielding a unified and coherent mode of delivery (Onwuegbuzie, 2012). By *xenophilous*, I mean that the PRICED team members have a commitment to keeping pace with the ever-changing world (e.g., the evolution of social media, big data, and artificial intelligence; cf. Gerber et al., in press). By *holistic*, I mean that each PRICED team member should integrate her/his experiences, expertise, lens, and the like into the PRICED process. Finally, by *integral*, I mean that the effectiveness of the integration process depends on the collective willingness of *all* PRICED team members to work collaboratively and cooperatively to address the most important and most complicated and/or complex research questions of interest to the child-parent team.

9   Summary and Conclusions

In this afterword, my goal has been to evaluate how the authors in this innovative book have conducted child-parent research. A constant comparison analysis of these seven chapters revealed the following six themes that suggest optimal practices for conducting child-parent research: *P*articipatory, *R*eflexive, *I*ntegrated, *C*ritical, *E*thical, and *D*evelopmental. These themes, which yield the acronym PRICED, led to the development of the PRICED process for child-parent research. This process promotes ethical symmetry. Simply put, I contend that the PRICED process helps to put the *child* at the forefront in child-parent research!

The six key components of the PRICED process for child-parent research, as informed by the six emergent themes, have generated the following six recommendations:

1.   *P*: Whenever possible, child-parent researchers should promote participatory approaches. At its optimum level, and consistent with the princi-

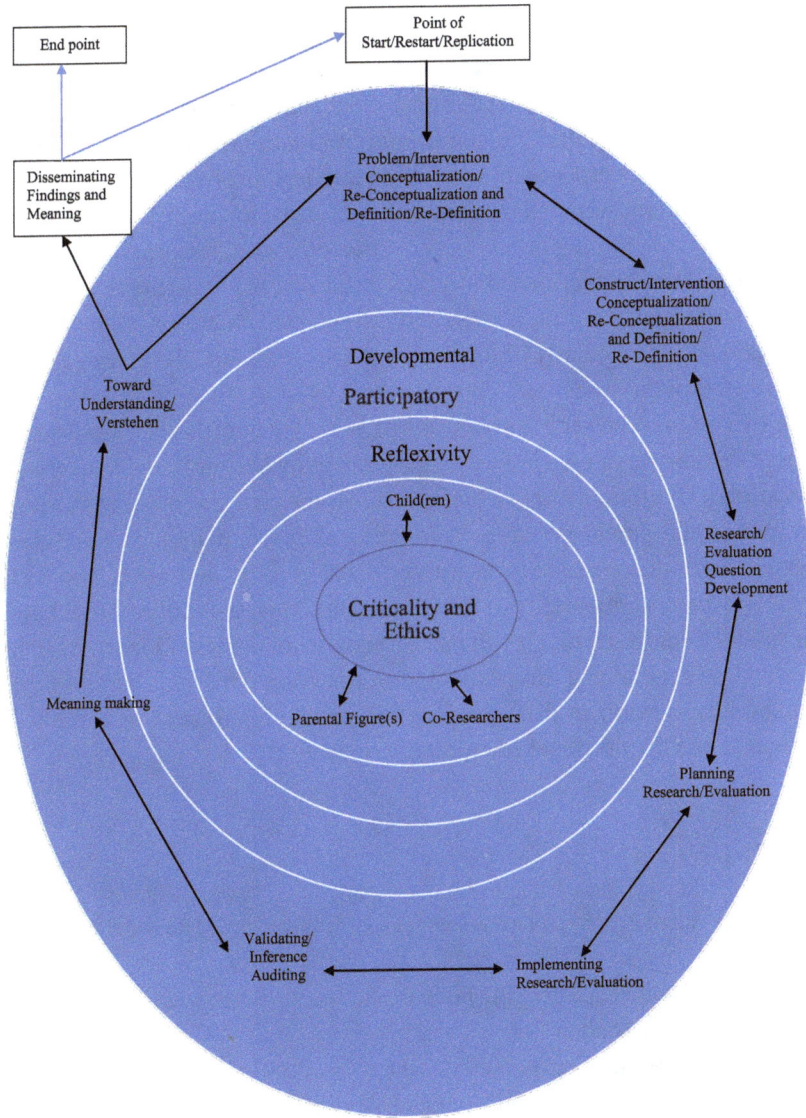

```
End point

Point of
Start/Restart/Replication

Disseminating
Findings and
Meaning

Problem/Intervention
Conceptualization/
Re-Conceptualization and
Definition/Re-Definition

Construct/Intervention
Conceptualization/
Re-Conceptualization
and Definition/
Re-Definition

Developmental

Toward
Understanding/
Verstehen

Participatory

Reflexivity

Child(ren)

Research/
Evaluation
Question
Development

Criticality and
Ethics

Meaning making

Parental Figure(s)    Co-Researchers

Planning
Research/Evaluation

Validating/
Inference
Auditing

Implementing
Research/Evaluation
```

FIGURE A.3   PRICED (*P*articipatory, *R*eflexive, *I*ntegrated, *C*ritical, *E*thical, and *D*evelopmental)
Research and Evaluation Process for Child-Parent Research

ples of critical dialectical pluralism (Onwuegbuzie & Frels, 2013), ethical symmetry should be optimized.

2. *R*: Researchers should exercise maximum reflexivity for critically evaluating the whole child-parent research process (i.e., *meta-reflexivity*).

3. *I*: Whenever possible (e.g., depending on the research question), child-parent researchers should consider incorporating as high a degree

of integration of qualitative and quantitative approaches as possible in their research studies.

4. *C*: In the spirit of critical dialectical pluralism, child-parent researchers should adopt a critical stance towards child-parent researchers, thereby promoting the empowerment of all researchers involved.

5. *E*: Child-parent researchers always should strive to adopt a meta-ethical stance, which implies adherence to virtue ethics and pragmatic ethics.

6. *D*: Consistent with critical dialectical pluralism, in child-parent research, the *process* of research is even more important than the *product* (e.g., findings)—particularly, the process of development of all researchers involved in the study.

I close by commending the authors of this book for writing such innovative chapters that are reader-friendly, thought-provoking, far-reaching, and, above all, inspiring. Indubitably, these authors move forward the conversation on conducting child-parent research. In so doing, they will help make child-parent research more accessible for researchers and stakeholders alike. And with scant child-parent research published to date, this groundbreaking book begins to fill a void such that it will make a significant contribution to the field of research in general and mixed methods research in particular. Without this book and future works in this area, it is likely that child-parent research will continue to be PRICED out of the research community!

References

Adler, P. A., & Adler, P. (1987). *Membership roles in field research.* Thousand Oaks, CA: Sage.

Alvesson, M., & Sköldberg, K. (2009). *Reflexive methodology: New vistas for qualitative research* (2nd ed.). London: Sage.

Bandura, A. (1977). *Social learning theory.* Oxford: Prentice-Hall.

Bronfenbrenner, U. (1979). *The ecology of human development.* Cambridge, MA: Harvard University Press.

Bruner, J. S. (1990). *Acts of meaning: Four lectures on mind and culture* (The Jerusalem-Harvard Lectures). Cambridge, MA: Harvard University Press.

Bruner, J. S. (2009). *The process of education* (Rev. ed.). Cambridge, MA: Harvard University Press.

Busier, H. L., Clark, K. A., Esch, R. A., Glesne, C., Pigeon, Y., & Tarule, J. M. (1997). Intimacy in research. *International Journal of Qualitative Studies in Education, 10,* 165–170. doi:10.1080/095183997237250

Christensen, P., & Prout, A. (2002). Working with ethical symmetry in social research with children. *Childhood, 9,* 477–497. doi:10.1177/0907568202009004007

Collins, K. M. T., Onwuegbuzie, A. J., Johnson, R. B., & Frels, R. K. (2013). Practice note: Using debriefing interviews to promote authenticity and transparency in mixed research. *International Journal of Multiple Research Approaches, 7*, 271–283. doi:10.5172/mra.2013.7.2.271

d'Ancona, M. (2017). *Post-truth: The new war on truth and how to fight back.* London: Ebury Press.

Denzin, N. K. (1989). *Interpretive interactionism.* Newbury Park, CA: Sage.

Dorn, C. (2017). *For the common good: A new history of higher education in America.* Ithaca, NY: Cornell University Press.

Dzurec, L. C., & Abraham, J. L. (1993). The nature of inquiry: Linking quantitative and qualitative research. *Advances in Nursing Science, 16*, 73–79. doi:10.1097/00012272-199309000-00009

Elwood, S., & Cope, M. (Eds.). (2009). *Qualitative GIS: A mixed methods approach.* Los Angeles, CA: Sage.

Fielding, N., & Cisneros-Puebla, C. A. (2009). CAQDAS-GAS convergence: Toward a new integrated mixed method research practice? *Journal of Mixed Methods Research, 3*, 349–370. doi:10.1177/1558689809344973

Fitzgerald, R., Graham, A., Smith, A., & Taylor, N. (2010). Children's participation as a struggle over recognition: Exploring the promise of dialogue. In B. Percy-Smith & N. Thomas (Eds.), *A handbook of children and young people's participation: Perspectives from theory and practice* (pp. 293–305). Abingdon, Oxon: Routledge.

Forzani, E., Abrams, S. S., & Onwuegbuzie, A. J. (Eds.). (in press). Methodologists: Who needs 'em? [Special issue]. *Research in the Schools.*

Fram, S. M. (2013). The constant comparative analysis method outside of grounded theory. *The Qualitative Report, 18*(1), 1–25. Retrieved from http://www.nova.edu/ssss/QR/QR18/fram1.pdf

Frels, J. G., Frels, R. K., & Onwuegbuzie, A. J. (2010, July). *Mixed research and Web 2.0: The role of geographic information systems.* Paper presented at the International Mixed Methods Conference, Baltimore, MD.

Frels, J. G., Frels, R. K., & Onwuegbuzie, A. J. (2011). Geographic information systems: A mixed methods spatial approach in business and management research and beyond. *International Journal of Multiple Research Approaches, 5*, 367–386. doi:10.5172/mra.2011.5.3.367

Frost, N. (2016). *Practising research: Why you're always part of the research process even when you think you're not.* London: Palgrave Macmillan.

Geiger, R. L. (2015). *The history of American higher education: Learning and culture from the founding to World War II.* Princeton, NJ: Princeton University Press.

Gerber, H. R., Abrams, S. S., Curwood, J. S., & Magnifico, A. (2016). *Conducting qualitative research of learning in online spaces.* Thousand Oaks, CA: Sage.

Gerber, H. G., Lynch, T. L., & Onwuegbuzie, A. J. (in press). *Making big data small: Designing integrated digital approaches for social science research.* Thousand Oaks, CA: Sage.

Glaser, B. G. (1965). The constant comparative method of qualitative analysis. *Social Problems, 12*, 436–445. doi:10.1525/sp.1965.12.4.03a00070

Glaser, B. G., & Strauss, A. L. (1967). *The discovery of grounded theory: Strategies for qualitative research.* Chicago, IL: Aldine.

Gleason, N. W. (Ed.). (2018). *Higher education in the era of the fourth industrial revolution.* London: Palgrave Macmillan.

Glenday, C. (Ed.). (2013). *Guinness world records.* London: Jim Pattison Group.

Greene, J. C., Caracelli, V. J., & Graham, W. F. (1989). Toward a conceptual framework for mixed-method evaluation designs. *Educational Evaluation and Policy Analysis, 11*, 255–274. doi:10.3102/01623737011003255

Hall, B., & Howard, K. (2008). A synergistic approach: Conducting mixed methods research with typological and systemic design considerations. *Journal of Mixed Methods Research, 2*, 248–269. doi:10.1177/1558689808314622

Holloway, I. (1997). *Basic concepts for qualitative research.* London: Blackwell Science.

Johnson, R. B., & Onwuegbuzie, A. J. (2004). Mixed methods research: A research paradigm whose time has come. *Educational Researcher, 33*(7), 14–26. doi:10.1177/1558689806298224

Johnson, R. B., Onwuegbuzie, A. J., & Turner, L. A. (2007). Toward a definition of mixed methods research. *Journal of Mixed Methods Research, 1*, 112–133. doi:10.1177/1558689806298224

Leech, N. L., & Onwuegbuzie, A. J. (2008). Qualitative data analysis: A compendium of techniques and a framework for selection for school psychology research and beyond. *School Psychology Quarterly, 23*, 587–604. doi:10.1037/1045-3830.23.4.587

Leech, N. L., & Onwuegbuzie, A. J. (2009). A typology of mixed methods research designs. *Quality & Quantity: International Journal of Methodology, 43*, 265–275. doi:10.1007/s11135-007-9105-3

Mallette, K. M. (2008). *Long term memory: Attention and retrieval.* Unpublished manuscript. Science Fair, Unity Point School, Carbondale, IL.

Mallette, K. M. (2009). *Long term memory: Episodic and semantic.* Unpublished manuscript. Science Fair, Unity Point School, Carbondale, IL.

Miles, M., & Huberman, A. M. (1994). *Qualitative data analysis: An expanded sourcebook* (2nd ed.). Thousand Oaks, CA: Sage.

Newman, D., & Newman, I. (2012). Multilevel modeling: Clarifying issues of concern. *Multiple Linear Regression Viewpoints, 38*(1), 26–33.

Onwuegbuzie, A. J. (1986). *TIME: The Investigational Mathematical Experience: A model for teaching mathematics in secondary schools.* University of London Institute of Education.

Onwuegbuzie, A. J. (2012). Introduction: Putting the mixed back into quantitative and qualitative research in educational research and beyond: Moving towards the radical middle. *International Journal of Multiple Research Approaches, 6*, 192–219. doi:10.5172/mra.2012.6.3.192

Onwuegbuzie, A. J., & Frels, R. K. (2013). Introduction: Toward a new research philosophy for addressing social justice issues: Critical dialectical pluralism 1.0. *International Journal of Multiple Research Approaches, 7*, 9–26. doi:10.5172/mra.2013.7.1.9

Onwuegbuzie, A. J., & Frels, R. K. (2016). *Seven steps to a comprehensive literature review: A multimodal and cultural approach.* London: Sage.

Onwuegbuzie, A. J., & Leech, N. L. (2019). On qualitizing. *International Journal of Multiple Research Approaches, 11*, 98–131. doi:10.29034/ijmra.v11n2editorial2

Onwuegbuzie, A. J., Mallette, M. H., & Mallette, K. (2010, July). *It's never too early to conduct mixed research: A call for the introduction of mixed research in the primary and secondary school years.* Paper presented at the International Mixed Methods Conference, Baltimore, MD.

Onwuegbuzie, A. J., & Teddlie, C. (2003). A framework for analyzing data in mixed methods research. In A. Tashakkori & C. Teddlie (Eds.), *Handbook of mixed methods in social and behavioral research* (pp. 351–383). Thousand Oaks, CA: Sage.

Oxford Dictionaries. (2018). *Post-truth.* Retrieved from https://en.oxforddictionaries.com/definition/post-truth

Piaget, J. (1950). *The psychology of intelligence.* London: Routledge & Kegan Paul.

Piaget, J. (1952). *The origins of intelligence in children* (M. Cook, Trans.). New York, NY: International Universities Press.

Provalis Research. (2019). *QDA miner (Version 5.0.30)* [Computer software]. Montreal, Quebec, Canada: Author.

Ryle, G. (1949). *Concept of the mind.* LondonUK: Hutchinson and Company.

Ryle, G. (1971). *Collected papers. Volume II collected essays, 1929–1968.* London: Hutchinson.

Sandelowski, M., Voils, C. I., & Knafl, G. (2009). On quantitizing. *Journal of Mixed Methods Research, 3*, 208–222. doi:10.1177/1558689809334210

Selman, R. L. (1971). The relation of role taking to the development of moral judgment in children. *Child Development, 42*, 79–91. doi:10.2307/1127066

Steinberg, S. J., & Steinberg, S. L. (2006). *GIS Geographic information systems for the social sciences: Investigating space and place.* Thousand Oaks, CA: Sage.

Tashakkori, A., & Teddlie, C. (1998). *Mixed methodology: Combining qualitative and quantitative approaches* (Applied Social Research Methods Series, Vol. 46). Thousand Oaks, CA: Sage.

Vygotsky, L. S. (1978). *Mind in society.* Cambridge, MA: Harvard University Press.

Wolgemuth, J. R., Koro-Ljungberg, M., Marn, T. M., Onwuegbuzie, A. J., & Dougherty, S. M. (Eds.). (2018a). Rethinking education policy and methodology in a post-truth era [Special issue]. *Education Policy Analysis Archives*.

Wolgemuth, J. R., Koro-Ljungberg, M., Marn, T. M., Onwuegbuzie, A. J., & Dougherty, S. M. (2018b). Start here, or here, no here: Introductions to rethinking education policy and methodology in a post-truth era. *Education Policy Analysis Archives, 26*(145), 1–8.

Index

www.ingramcontent.com/pod-product-compliance
Lightning Source LLC
Chambersburg PA
CBHW070353270326
41926CB00014B/2522